Expanding the Criminological Imagination

Expanding the Criminological Imagination

Critical readings in criminology

Edited by

Alana Barton, Karen Corteen, David Scott and David Whyte

WILLAN
PUBLISHING

Published by

Willan Publishing
Culmcott House
Mill Street, Uffculme
Cullompton, Devon
EX15 3AT, UK
Tel: +44(0)1884 840337
Fax: +44(0)1884 840251
e-mail: info@willanpublishing.co.uk
website: www.willanpublishing.co.uk

Published simultaneously in the USA and Canada by

Willan Publishing
c/o ISBS, 920 NE 58th Ave, Suite 300,
Portland, Oregon 97213-3786, USA
Tel: +001(0)503 287 3093
Fax: +001(0)503 280 8832
e-mail: info@isbs.com
website: www.isbs.com

First published 2007

Hardback
ISBN-13: 978-1-84392-157-8
ISBN-10: 1-84392-157-X

Paperback
ISBN-13: 978-1-84392-156-1
ISBN-10: 1-84392-156-1

British Library Cataloguing-in-Publication Data

A catalogue record for this book is available from the British Library

Project managed by Deer Park Productions, Tavistock, Devon
Typeset by GCS, Leighton Buzzard, Bedfordshire, LU7 1AR
Printed and bound by T.J. International Ltd, Padstow, Cornwall

Contents

List of Contributors

Anette Ballinger is a Lecturer in Criminology at Keele University. Her research interests include gender and capital punishment in the twentieth century. She is the author of the award-winning book, *Dead Woman Walking: Executed Women in England and Wales 1900–1955*, published by Ashgate in 2000. She has also written a number of book chapters on the subject of gender and punishment in modern history. Her current research is concerned with women who were reprieved from the death penalty in England and Wales, as well as women who were sentenced to death in Scotland during the twentieth century.

Alana Barton is a Lecturer in Criminology and Criminal Justice at Edge Hill University. Her main research and teaching interests are histories and theories of punishment, gender and social control, and non-custodial penalties. Her book, *Fragile Moralities and Dangerous Sexualities: Two Centuries of Semi-penal Institutionalisation for Women*, was published by Ashgate in 2005. She is co-founder and co-director of Liverpool Publications. She has published work in journals such as the *Howard Journal of Criminal Justice, British Journal of Community Justice, Liverpool Law Review* and *Drugs: Education, Prevention and Policy.*

Roy Coleman is a Lecturer in Criminology and Sociology at the University of Liverpool. His main research and teaching interests are in the related areas of crime control, social divisions, urban regeneration, partnerships and state formation. His current research explores the experiences of those targeted by surveillance practices in cities, such as homeless people and street traders. Published work appears in journals including the *British Journal of Sociology, Critical Criminology* and *Crime, Media and Culture*. His book, *Reclaiming the Streets: Surveillance, Social Control and the City*, published by Willan, won the Hart Social and Legal Book Prize in 2005.

Mary Corcoran is a Lecturer in Criminology at Keele University. Her research interests are in the areas of gender and crime and punishment, conflict criminology, penal governance and the marketization of the penal system. She has published work on spatial conflict in prisons, research in violent contexts and prison resistance. Her book, *Out of Order: The Political Imprisonment of Women in Northern Ireland, 1972–1998*, was published by Willan in 2006.

Karen Corteen is a Lecturer in Criminology and Criminal Justice at Edge Hill University. Her main research and teaching interests are the construction and management of sexual desires, practices and identities, victimology, and violence and determining contexts. Her PhD thesis is entitled 'The sexual ordering of society: a critical analysis of secondary school sex and relationship education'. She was a researcher on an ESRC Violence Project entitled 'Violence, Sexuality and Space', from which she has numerous publications. Her work has been published in chapters in books, on the internet and in journals such as *Sexualities* and *Sex Education*. She has also recently contributed to an American *Encyclopaedia of Sociology* published in 2006 by Blackwell.

Howard Davis is a Lecturer in Criminology and Criminal Justice at Edge Hill University. His research and teaching interests include the origins, dynamics and consequences of disaster, responses to bereavement and trauma, interagency conflict and the political management of crisis. Having practised as a social worker, trainer and research fellow, he has authored and contributed to edited texts, national and local government research reports and journals such as the *British Journal of Social Work* and the *Journal of Contingencies and Crisis Management*.

Margaret S. Malloch is a Research Fellow in the Department of Applied Social Sciences at the University of Stirling. Her book, *Women, Drugs and Custody*, was published by Waterside Press in 2000, with subsequent journal publications in the *Howard Journal, Women's Studies*

International Forum, Critical Social Policy and the *Probation Journal.* Relevant research has focused on the experiences of women drug users in prison, women's experiences of the criminal justice system and evaluations of recent initiatives in Scotland including the pilot drug courts in Glasgow and Fife and the 218 Centre for women.

David Scott is Course Leader of the MA in Criminology and Criminal Justice at the University of Central Lancashire. His main research and teaching interests are critical approaches to imprisonment, poverty and the sociology of punishment. He is author of *God's Messengers Behind Bars* (CSCSJ: 1997) and he submitted his PhD, entitled 'Ghosts beyond our realm: a neo-abolitionist analysis of prisoner human rights and prison officer occupational culture', in April 2006. He has written a number of articles and book chapters, including contributions to the *Prisons and Punishment Dictionary* and the *Handbook of Prisons,* both forthcoming publications from Willan. He is currently working on a book with Helen Codd, to be published by McGraw-Hill Press, examining the nature and extent of the penal crises, entitled *Controversial Issues in Prisons.*

Elizabeth Stanley is a Lecturer in Criminology at Victoria University of Wellington, New Zealand. She teaches and researches in the areas of state crime, human rights, transitional justice and social justice. She has previously undertaken studies on rights and detention in New Zealand and the UK, and her work in South Africa and Chile has focused on truth commissions and court processes. Her current research project examines the transitional justice experiences of torture survivors in Timor-Leste.

Reece Walters is Professor of Criminology at the Open University. He has taught at universities in the UK, Australia and New Zealand and published in the areas of the sociology of knowledge, crimes of the powerful, crimes against the environment and juvenile justice. He has written and campaigned against the dangers of a 'market-led criminology' and continues to critique the ways in which new modes of governance in contemporary society influence the production of criminological knowledge. He has written three books, including *Deviant Knowledge – Criminology, Policy and Practice*, which critiqued the state and corporate control of critical criminological knowledge and he is completing a fourth book within emerging discourses in 'green criminology', entitled *Crime, Political Economy and Genetically Modified Food.*

David Whyte is a Lecturer in Criminology at the University of Stirling. His main research interests are crimes of the powerful and the regulation of corporate crime. He has recently completed a major study of corporate corruption in occupied Iraq. His work has been published in a wide range of journals, edited collections and websites, including the *British Journal of Criminology, Journal of Law and Society, Critical Criminology, Urban Studies, Crime Law and Social Change* and *Studies in Political Economy*. He is editor (with Steve Tombs) of *Unmasking the Crimes of the Powerful*, published by Peter Lang in 2003.

Acknowledgements

The editors would like to convey their sincere thanks to the authors who have contributed to this text for their hard work, commitment, patience and good humour during, what can be, a long and demanding process. Many thanks to Brian Willan and staff at Willan Publishing for their assistance, encouragement and effort in bringing this book to fruition. Thank you also to David Kershaw for copy-editing the text. Special acknowledgements are due to Paddy Hillyard, Joe Sim and Steve Tombs for their valuable advice and support throughout the editorial process.

For their support and encouragement: Alana Barton and Karen Corteen would like to express their thanks to Helen Finney, Chris Newby and friends and colleagues in the Department of Law and Criminology, Edge Hill University. David Scott would like to thank Gaynor Bramhall, Helen Codd, Barbara Hudson, Munira Patel, Ralph van Clack and Ian Nickson. David Whyte would like to thank friends and colleagues at the University of Stirling.

The process of editing any book can be arduous and difficult, and this text has been no exception. However, the sustained teamwork, collaboration and friendship between the editors has meant that editing this book has been not only intellectually stimulating and challenging but also, sometimes, really good fun. The editors' names appear on the book and on relevant chapters in alphabetical order to reflect the equal contribution made by each.

Chapter 1

Introduction: developing a criminological imagination

Alana Barton, Karen Corteen, David Scott and David Whyte

Future generations of social scientists will look back critically at this period and ask why liberal democracies continued to expand their apparatuses of criminal justice when, at the same time, officially measured and defined rates of 'crime' had been in steady decline. They will question why the UK government's response had been to create more and more criminal offences (over 1,000 since 1997 at the last count), expand the range of 'interventions' in the lives of the young, fill the prisons to bursting point and build a new generation of prisons for profit. They will question how and why some of the fundamental principles of due process, such as the right to trial by jury and habeas corpus, were being eroded. They will question why policing costs were spiralling out of control and why more police officers and new legions of community safety officers were being recruited when they had little impact on reducing reported crime rates or even on reducing the fear of crime (Crawford *et al.* 2003). They will also question how, despite substantial evidence to the contrary, individual or socio-pathological explanations of criminal and anti-social behaviour prevailed and why, subsequently, 'problematic' individuals and their families were subject to greater state surveillance and intervention by Parenting and Anti-Social Behaviour Orders.

Future generations of social scientists will want to know why public resources were being ploughed into the coercive apparatuses of criminal justice while, at the same time, support services for the most vulnerable and facilities that did have a measurable impact upon offending (such as free leisure facilities for young people) were being withdrawn. They will question why social issues, such as drug use, prostitution, 'inadequate' parenting and teenage conceptions, were defined and responded to in a punitive manner with little or no recognition of their structural contexts. If the next generation of researchers ask what criminologists were doing to prevent social and governmental obsessions with crime careering out of control, and to counter the falsehoods and mythical assumptions upon which criminal justice policy is based, they will struggle to find an answer. Criminology's response has largely been to jump upon the bandwagon and greet the expansion of the discipline with open arms, as if the only thing that matters for the enterprise is the enterprise itself. Criminology remains largely a self-referential, self-perpetuating practice that lacks the ability to look outside itself.

The lack of challenge to this social and political obsession with crime is not necessarily down to criminologists' inability to critique: there is no shortage of work within criminology that is critical of the state and of criminal justice agencies. Since the 'radical break' in the 1960s (See Sim *et al.* (1987) for a full discussion of what became known as the 'radical break'), some criminologists have sought to imagine new ways in which the discipline can challenge intellectually and practically the agendas of the powerful. Given the ascendancy and consolidation of a state-driven agenda within and outside criminology, a critical and creative imagination is necessary now more than ever. It is time for criminologists to reflect upon the utility of the discipline in order to reawaken, revive and expand a criminological imagination.

Current developments in mainstream and administrative criminology have presented us with an unimaginative and individualized discourse that has displaced criminal actors from their broader structural, economic and political contexts. However the limitations on what we can and should say about the problem of 'crime' and the contours of possible social policy responses do not have to be reduced to a discourse framed around individual or social pathologies requiring 'solutions' that invariably are exclusionary and punitive.

This chapter will discuss the way in which a more imaginative criminology can help visualize radically alternative visions to those proposed within the current limited framework of mainstream criminological knowledge. Further, through an overview of the chapters that follow, this chapter will expound the contribution that criminology can make to a further expansion of the criminological imagination.

The emergence and consolidation of a criminological imagination

In his classic work, the American postwar radical thinker C. Wright Mills sets out what the *The Sociological Imagination* entails:

> a quality of mind that seems most dramatically to promise an understanding of the intimate realities of ourselves in connection with larger social realities ... [It] enables us to grasp history and biography and the relations between the two within society ... [and] to use it with sensibility is to be capable of tracing such linkages among a great variety of milieux ... [It] enables its possessor to understand the larger historical scene in terms of its meanings for the inner life and the external career of a variety of individuals. It enables him [*sic*] to take into account how individuals, in the welter of their daily experience, often become falsely conscious of their social positions ... [and allows the possessor to] continually work out and revise views of the problems of history, the problems of biography, and the problems of social structure in which biography and history intersect (1959: 15, 6, 11, 5, 225).[1]

The sociological imagination signified a way of thinking about or interpreting the world. It represented a particular way of conceptualizing and approaching social problems, their implications and resolution. It provided a broad-ranging interpretive framework for locating the individual within structural and social contexts, ultimately providing a new way of understanding the social world that makes intimate connections between individual meanings and experiences and wider collective and social realities. The sociological imagination therefore facilitated a form of interpretation that placed understandings of an individual's biography within the sensibilities of wider historical and structural contexts. It demanded that understandings of the present were firmly connected with the ways in which the phenomena under scrutiny had been produced and reproduced. In this sense individual identities and lived experiences could not be considered in isolation, for no meanings could be attributed to a person's actions outside their social, historical and structural contexts. Through this interpretive lens, while the biographical details of individual offenders remain important, their problematic, troublesome or illegal behaviour cannot be detached from their historical and material contexts. To understand the problem of 'crime', therefore, criminologists must use their

3

imagination to provide clear connections between the actor, the event and location of the criminalized incident and the structural, spatial and historical determinants shaping definitions and applications of the label of 'crime', deviance and illegality at that particular time (Becker 1963).

This criminological imagination (as evidenced in Sim *et al.* 1987) provided a new means for conceptualizing 'crime' and its relationship to the social. In this sense it presented an alternative means of interpreting the world. A key influence here were the writings of the Italian Marxist Antonio Gramsci (1971) developed in the work of Stuart Hall *et al.* (1978) and Hall (1988). Hall pointed to the importance of creating an alternative 'counter-hegemonic' discourse, infused with socialist values and principles, that reconceptualized the organization of society. In a similar vein adoption of the criminological imagination challenged existing and dominant individualized ways of thinking about crime and punishment. Connecting individual offenders with their (less visible) historical and structural contexts inevitably provided an opportunity to reinterpret or reimagine the real. This itself, as Gramsci hoped, delivered an opportunity to foster a new form of radical consciousness facilitating alternative means of conceptualizing and dealing with both the personal and the social.

Mills (1959) had made this approach to sociological problems most clear in his discussion of the relationship between 'private troubles' and 'public issues'. A *trouble* is a private matter that occurs within the lived experiences of the individual and affects his or her immediate relationships and social world. An *issue*, on the other hand, is a public matter which should be understood through an analysis of the political and economic structures of a given society. The two are intimately tied as:

> many personal troubles cannot be solved merely as troubles, but must be understood in terms of public issues – and in terms of the problems of history-making. Know that human meaning of public issues must be revealed by relating them to personal troubles – and to the problems of individual life (Mills 1959: 226).

Through the sociological imagination, troubles were translated into issues in terms of presenting the individual with a new and plausible 'bigger picture' of his or her social world, one that offered new orientating values, feelings, motives, understandings and meanings.

What the discussion above draws us towards is an understanding of the importance of fostering and further developing a criminological imagination. That is, the encouragement and enhancement of:

> a kind of criminological imagination that is able and willing to break free of old constraints and look at the problems of crime and punishment with fresh eyes. That kind of criminological imagination has always been a great strength of the movement we loosely call critical criminology (Currie 2002: viii).

As Currie points out, then, the theoretical and political priorities of critical criminology have been the realization of a criminological imagination (Sim *et al.* 1987; Scraton and Chadwick 1991; Scraton 2002). The development of critical criminology since the 1970s has been rooted in a synthesis between the Meadian-inspired symbolic interactionism (Becker 1963), focusing on everyday social relations and the experiential, and social structures, first around class and production by Marxist-inspired criminologists (Taylor *et al.* 1973), but later around 'race' (Hall *et al.* 1978) and gender (Smart 1977). In so doing critical criminology has produced a new vocabulary or critical discourse for understanding lived experiences, and therefore represented a radical departure from the decontextualized analysis found in much criminological, political and media discourses on 'crime'.

Rather than focus upon the individualized or family-centred causes of crime, critical criminologists focused attention on understanding the social, economic and political contexts that produce both crime itself and state responses to crime. Critical analysis has examined the relationship between the individual and the social through emphasizing the boundaries placed upon everyday interactions, choices, meanings and motivations of criminals and deviants through these contexts. Alongside this has been a problematization of the political and ideological construction of 'crime' and deviance and the processes which have led to the naturalizations of these dominant conceptions. This has included a concern not only with the structural processes which have led to the sedimenting of the dominant discourse on what 'crime' is understood as meaning, but also with those social harms which have been excluded from such a definition or under-enforced, for example around gendered and racialized harms, state-sanctioned violence, economic deprivation, poverty, war and crimes of the powerful. Dominant definitions of 'crime' have been understood through an examination of the power–

knowledge axis within social structures arising in a given historical period. This has led to questions concerning power and legitimacy, and as identified above, three structural contexts have been central to their understanding in the criminological imagination: class, 'race' and gender, though concerns around age and sexuality have emerged more recently (Sim 2000; Scraton 2002; Corteen 2003; Wahidin 2004).

Critical criminology has located the problem of 'crime' within the contours of advanced capitalism and the unequal distribution of wealth. Rather than seeing the law as a crude instrument of capitalist oppressors, critical criminologists have pointed to the contradictory nature of the law in capitalist societies. While the law and its enforcement can, and do, protect the general population and while many 'crimes' that are recorded in the official figures tend disproportionately to victimize vulnerable and/or impoverished individuals, the criminal justice system at the same time plays a decisive role in maintaining structural divisions in society. 'Crime' and law enforcement cannot be understood outside this context. Consequently, a central concern within critical criminology has been to connect processes of criminalization, class conflict, poverty and other forms of 'social exclusion'. The almost exclusive focus by law enforcement agencies on the criminality and subsequent punishment of what have been described variously as the 'sub-proletariat' (Hall *et al.* 1978), the non-productive labour force or the un- or underemployed, has reinforced the social marginalization of the most structurally vulnerable.

A further point highlighted in critical analysis has been the statistical over-representation of black people and under-representation of women in the administration of criminal justice and state punishments. This requires explanation. For critical criminologists the continued subjugation of African-Caribbean, Asian, Chinese and other minority ethic groups must be located within the structural context of neocolonialism. Through the combination of xeno-racism and economic, political and social exclusion minority communities are increasingly over-represented in the surplus populations of advanced capitalist societies (Sivanandan 2002). In addition, critical criminology in the last 30 years has started to recognize how law and regulation are intimately connected with reproduction; that the lived experiences of men and women cannot be detached from gendered hierarchies of power (Bosworth 1999; Ballinger 2000; Malloch 2000; Corteen 2003; Barton 2005; Corcoran 2006). Problematizing the masculinist basis of 'criminological knowledge', the marginalization and exclusion of women and the consolidation of heteronormativity, critical criminology has highlighted the complexity of the existing relationship between 'justice' and the exploitation and subjugation of marginalized groups. Concerns around patriarchy and masculinist hegemony reverberate in many current critical imaginaries.

Much recent critical and post-structural literature has correctly highlighted the dangers of reducing complex social phenomena to simplified essentialisms, pointing rather to the hybridity of social factors in shaping human experiences and identities. The relationship between class, 'race', gender, age, sexuality and (dis)ability is complex. Ann Smith (1998: 26) provides an excellent summary of the intertwined nature of social divisions when she states that:

> [c]apitalist formations shape and are shaped in turn by non-class based forms of oppression. We are never actually confronted with nothing but capitalism; similarly, sexism, racism and homophobia never appear in isolated form. We experience, instead, contextually-specific hybrid formations that emerge out of the combination of these forces.

Importantly Smith does not advocate abandoning the notion of structure but stresses the importance of developing an analysis of social structures, especially for developing effective collective resistance, and conceptualizing a basis around which alternative criminological imagery can be formulated. These post-structural insights should leave the critical criminologist with a keen awareness of the dangers of slipping into an exclusionary political discourse which wrongly homogenizes individual and group experiences. Further, theoretically critical criminology must also allow for the interrogation of its own assumptions, imaginaries and alternatives.

Critical criminology is not merely concerned with reflecting some vaguely ascribed 'view from below', but has emphasized the importance of comprehending the relationship between processes of marginalization and criminalization. Central to this task has been the development of work that seeks to explain the aetiology of crimes of the powerful and develop ways of making more visible those forms of offending (for example Pearce and Tombs 1998; Tombs and Whyte 2003; Green and Ward 2004; Walters 2004).

For critical criminologists the power to criminalize is a political process which is, in advanced capitalist societies, always related to the maintenance of a particular order of power relations. Just as critical criminology must explain how the process of criminalization regulates, disciplines and contains subordinate groups, so critical criminology also has to explain how under particular conditions superordinate groups are also exposed to criminalization (for example Davis, Chapter 7, this volume).

Beyond these merely interpretative functions lies a further role, a 'legislative' one (Bauman 1987). Through critical analysis, critical criminology has facilitated the provision of ideas about how society and the criminal justice system can be alternatively organized and structured. The responsibility to provide a plausible alternative interpretive framework around crime and punishment cannot be neglected (Gramsci 1971; Hall *et al.* 1978; Hall 1988; Derrida 1994; Sim 2000). An understanding of the definition of 'crime' and the process of criminalization as political constructs, producing and reproducing broader social contexts open to political contestation, is one key strand in the criminological imagination. But there also must be an acknowledgement that the arguments regarding the connections between biography, history and structure provide opportunities to reconstruct and go beyond mere critique. Following Gramsci (1971) and Hall *et al.* (1978), the arena of crime and punishment is a battle for people's hearts and minds. To engage in this battle requires a realistic assessment of the conditions in which 'crime', social conflict and other problematic and troublesome behaviours occur. It means plausibly rethinking or reimagining safety, security and harm in broader social contexts. It also means continuing to contrast the 'criminalization of social policy' with inadequate policy responses to 'social exclusion', poverty, racism, sexism, homophobia, disability and the range of social harms that remain relatively deprioritized (Hillyard *et al.* 2004).

A genuinely imaginative criminology must provide a means for shaping political consciousness and instilling debates on crime and punishment with a new and more inclusionary 'common sense'. Such a discourse must be self-interrogatory and provide inclusionary visions connected to debates in human rights, democratic accountability, the rule of law and social justice. More than this it must be able to provide a plausible account that taps into people's lived realities and facilitates a new interpretative framework regarding social problems (Hall 1988). Further, it must enable policy interventions that are informed by structural contexts.

Expanding the criminological imagination requires the development of an analysis which recognizes and addresses the realities and complexities regarding the production and application of criminological knowledge and criminal justice policies. Moreover, it requires an analysis of an awareness of harms and social injustices, and their relation to the permeation of crimes of the powerful, the heterogeneity and homogeneity of these powerful actors, an analysis of explicit atrocities and less overt, mundane human rights violations, together with an understanding and realization of the global context within which such events take place (Barak 2001; Cohen 2001; Hillyard *et al.* 2004).[1]

In the following chapter, Reece Walters reflects on the intensification of the authoritarian state – from Thatcherism to Blairism – and its impact on the funding, production, content and influence of criminological knowledge. He examines and critiques the appropriation of academic expertise and knowledges by the state, in a political and economic context which marginalizes and criminalizes some of the most vulnerable and dislocated people in society. Walters questions the role of criminologists in current political and economic climates wherein administrative and technocist criminologies, which maintain and support oppressive state policies and practices, have been in the ascendancy. He documents the lack of critical imagination in contemporary administrative criminology, embodied in 'crime science', drawing attention to the ill-founded and short-term actuarial responses to social problems. Walters also strives to forward an optimistic agenda through, where possible, a resistance to seeking and engaging in Home Office research and private corporate consultancies, at least until a time wherein human rights violations and civil rights abuses are a real and genuine component of these agendas. In so doing he calls on critical criminologists to participate in the production of 'deviant knowledge' through a diversity of narratives and knowledges with the aim of highlighting and challenging oppressive state practices and social injustices. He concludes by arguing that critical criminologists must make visible what the state does not reveal regarding crime and criminality.

In Chapter 3, Roy Coleman critically examines the discourses mobilized to legitimate crime prevention techniques paying specific attention to the proliferation of camera surveillance in cities. He moves beyond questions regarding the 'effectiveness' of crime reduction technologies, and instead explores the exercise of power at the micro and macro levels and how this facilitates the social ordering of urban spaces. Coleman highlights the reinforcement

---

1 This book presents seven case studies which demonstrate how criminologists have utilised and developed their imagination to break free of, and challenge, the oppressive liberal conceptual framework which dominates the criminological arena.

of social relations through these new technologies and questions the implications of these developments in relation to social justice. He asserts that contemporary official rhetoric concerned with '"participation", "partnership" and "social inclusion"' is a fallacy and should be challenged on the grounds that it 'mask[s] inequality and spatial (in)justice'. He argues that in order to deconstruct and move beyond official discourses of crime prevention criminologists require an 'imaginative intelligence' and this requires transcending the boundaries of the discipline altogether.

In Chapter 4, Anette Ballinger presents a critical analysis of five double murder trials that took place between 1900 and 1953. In each of these trials a female and male defendant stood accused of the same crime but in three of the cases it was the female defendants alone who were found guilty and executed while their co-accused left the courtroom free men. Rather than focusing on criminological debates around discrimination or inequity with regard to 'leniency' or 'severity' of punishment for men and women, Ballinger instead engages and applies feminist theory in order to deconstruct law's claims to unprejudiced 'truth'. She argues that it is only by expanding the criminological imagination to encompass a feminist epistemology, that the law's ability to 'produce and reproduce the gendered subject as well as its role in constructing and reconstructing masculinity and femininity' can be exposed and explicated. Ballinger's chapter demonstrates the importance of a retrospective application of critical analysis to past events for the purpose of uncovering connections between structural and historical determinants and in order to contest the androcentric foundations of the law and criminal justice system. It is through this process, she concludes, that academics and advocates can become more empowered to challenge and resist dominant knowledges and thus attempt to prevent such miscarriages of justice in the future.

In Chapter 5, Mary Corcoran presents a critical examination of prison conflict and resistance in relation to women political prisoners in Northern Ireland. She begins by discussing the inherent difficulties in locating a conceptual framework within which the resistance of female political prisoners can be articulated and analysed. She argues that criminological and feminist frameworks are inadequate given the ambiguous position that female political prisoners occupy in political and penal rhetoric and in criminological and sociological analysis. By drawing on a series of personal interviews from her own research, Corcoran examines the dynamics between state power, penal punishment and prisoner resistance during three distinct phases, namely 'reactive containment' (1969–76), 'criminalization' (1976–81) and 'normalization' (1981 onwards). Her research highlights the need for a more creative criminological imagination to address the limitations of existing criminological and feminist paradigms. Only then can an understanding of the 'punitive dynamics which created the "political calculations and contexts" in which women political prisoners resisted' be developed.

In Chapter 6, Margaret Malloch critically discusses the current preoccupation in criminal justice policies and practices with drugs, drug use and drug-related crime. Malloch highlights a lack of critical resistance to government discourses of 'what works' and points to how critical criminology can provide an opportunity to produce more imaginative and arguably more effective responses to drug use and drug-related crime. A shift away from traditional approaches which emphasize 'punishment', 'treatment' and 'rehabilitation' is advocated. In its place an alternative approach is developed in order to recognize how individual and interpersonal agency are structured. This way an oppositional agenda can be formulated in order to seek social justice for, rather than the further criminalization of, already marginalized groups. Malloch's chapter illustrates how a critical imagination can be positively employed to develop an agenda that challenges the criminalization of drug users.

In Chapter 7, Howard Davis focuses on the issues of disaster, justice and impunity. He questions why some actions and harms are deemed criminal while others are regarded as 'accidents' and/or 'disasters'. Davis further questions why some victims of some forms of harm are granted victim status and receive justice while others are not. In so doing, he highlights the problem of criminalizing the harms committed by the 'powerful' when those harms are likely to be rendered relatively invisible by 'blurred lines of responsibility, inadequate law and a reluctance to investigate and prosecute'. This is in stark contrast to the punitive way in which perpetrators of street crime are generally dealt with. Davis demonstrates the endemic nature of differential policing, selective law enforcement and disparities in punishment in disasters. He argues that experiences of, and responses to, disasters caused by powerful actors should take into account the unequal and complex structuring of power.

In Chapter 8, Elizabeth Stanley considers how criminologists might begin to analyse multiple human rights violations that cause death and suffering. She argues that the issue of state criminality highlights key questions about the limitations of the criminological imagination. Focusing on Timor Leste (East Timor), Stanley exposes how victims of gross human rights abuses receive little truth or justice in the wake of their experiences. She moves the discussion on from a mere focus on civil and political rights to economic, social and cultural rights. She conceptualizes human rights violations on a continuum which moves from immediate victimization, through the infliction of direct physical pain and suffering, to everyday violations and human insecurities in the long term aftermath of human rights abuses. Thus she problematizes a mainstream human rights approach which is generally confined to acts of interpersonal or direct violence and instead emphasises the importance of enduring economic, social and cultural rights that impact upon the day-to-day existence of victims. With regard to the perpetrators of human rights violations, Stanley maintains that the criminological imagination must disengage from restrictive individualistic models of criminal responsibility. Instead, it should incorporate and address the 'global power networks that underpin violations in all their forms'.

The theme which unites the chapters in this book is the manner in which a critical criminological imagination is utilized, challenged and/ or expanded upon. For some contributors this is achieved within the discipline of criminology; however, for others, this involves expanding the boundaries and parameters of the discipline of criminology, drawing on critical developments in other disciplines and arguably even moving beyond criminology *per se*. Thus the chapters highlight how criminology necessitates an imaginative, multi-disciplinary approach which has the potential to cultivate mutually beneficial interdisciplinary relationships which could enable theorists, activists and practitioners to escape the dominant criminological paradigm that remains rooted in individual and social pathology.

Note

1   As the list of page numbers indicates, this is not a single direct quote from Mills. Rather, it is an edited composite of Mills' account of the sociological imagination.

References

Ballinger, A. (2000) *Dead Woman Walking: Executed Women in England and Wales 1900–1955*. Aldershot: Ashgate.

Barak, G. (2001) 'Crime and crime control in an age of globalisation: a theoretical dissection', *Critical Criminology*, 10: 57–72.

Barton, A. (2005) *Fragile Moralities and Dangerous Sexualities: Two Centuries of Semi-penal Institutionalisation for Women*. Aldershot: Ashgate.

Bauman, Z. (1987) *Legislators* and *Interpretors*. Cambridge: Polity Press.

Bauman, Z. (1989) *Modernity* and *The Holocaust*. Cambridge: Polity Press.

Becker, H. (1963) *Outsiders*. New York, NY: Free Press.

Bosworth, M. (1999) *Engendering Resistance: Agency and Power in Women's Prisons*. Aldershot: Ashgate.

Cohen, S. (2001) *States of Denial: Knowing about Atrocities and Suffering*. Cambridge: Polity Press.

Corcoran, M. (2006) *Out of Order: The Political Imprisonment of Women in Northern Ireland 1972–1998*. Cullompton: Willan Publishing.

Corteen, K. (2003) 'The sexual ordering of society: a critical analysis of secondary school sex and relationship education.' Unpublished PhD thesis, Lancaster University.

Crawford, A., Lister, S. and Wall, D. (2003) *Great expectations: Contracted Community Policing in New Earswick*. York: Joseph Rowntree Foundation.

Currie, E. (2002) 'Preface' in K. Carrington and R. Hogg (eds) *Critical Criminology: Issues, Debates, Challenges*. Cullompton: Willan Publishing.

Derrida, J. (1994) *Spectres of Marx*. London: Routledge.

Gramsci, A. (1971) *Selections from the Prison Notebooks*. London: Lawrence and Wishart.

Green, P. and Ward, T. (2004) *State Crime: Governments, Violence and Corruption*. London: Pluto Press.

Hall, S. (1988) *The Hard Road to Renewal*. London: Verso.

Hall, S., Critcher, C., Jefferson, T., Clarke, J. and Roberts, B. (1978) *Policing the Crisis: Mugging, the State and Law and Order*. London: Macmillan.

Hillyard, P., Sim, J., Tombs, S. and Whyte, D. (2004) 'Leaving a stain upon the silence', *British Journal of Criminology*, 44: 369–99.

Malloch, M. (2000) *Women, Drugs and Custody: The Experiences of Women Drug Users in Prison*. Winchester: Waterside Press.

Mills, C.W. (1959) *The Sociological Imagination*. Oxford: Oxford University Press.

Pearce, F. and Tombs, S. (1998) *Toxic Capitalism: Corporate Crime and the Chemical Industry*. Aldershot: Dartmouth.

Scraton, P. (2002) 'Defining "power" and challenging "knowledge": critical analysis as resistance in the UK' in K. Carrington and R. Hogg (eds) *Critical Criminology: Issues, Debates, Challenges*. Cullompton: Willan Publishing.

Scraton, P. and Chadwick, K. (1991) 'The theoretical and political priorities of critical criminology' in K. Stenson and D. Cowell (eds) *The Politics of Crime Control*. London: Sage.

Sim, J. (2000) 'Against the punitive wind: Stuart Hall, the state and the lessons of the Great Moving Right Show', in P. Gilroy *et al.* (eds) *Without Guarantees: In Honour of Stuart Hall*. London: Verso.

Sim, J., Scraton, P. and Gordon, P. (1987) 'Introduction: crime, the state and critical analysis', in P. Scraton (ed) *Law, Order and the Authoritarian State: Readings in Critical Criminology*. Milton Keynes: Open University Press.

Sivanandan, A. (2002) 'Poverty is the new black' in P. Scraton (ed) *Beyond September 11: An Anthology of Dissent*. London: Pluto.

Smart, C. (1977) *Women, Crime and Criminology*. London: Routledge and Kegan Paul.

Smith, A.M. (1998) *Laclau and Mouffe: The Radical Democratic Imaginary*. London: Routledge.

Taylor, I., Walton, P. and Young, J. (1973) *The New Criminology*. London: Routledge and Kegan Paul.

Tombs, S. and Whyte, D. (2003) 'Unmasking the crimes of the powerful: establishing some rules of engagement' in S. Tombs and D. Whyte (eds) *Unmasking the Crimes of the Powerful: Scrutinising States and Corportations*. New York, NY: Peter Lang.

Wahidin, A. (2004) *Older Women and The Criminal Justice System: Running Out of Time*. London: Jessica Kingsley.

Walters, R. (2004) 'Criminology and genetically modified food', *British Journal of Criminology*, 44: 151–67.

Chapter 2

Critical criminology and the intensification of the authoritarian state

Reece Walters

Introduction

It is almost 20 years since Phil Scraton edited *Law, Order and the Authoritarian State*. This book critiqued Thatcherism and 'self-styled new realist criminologists', and provided a mandate for critical criminology – notably, that interventionist and critical criminology was central in actively confronting and challenging the oppressive and unjust government policies and practices of criminal justice. The arguments within the works of Scraton, Sim, Chadwick, Hillyard (Scraton 1987) and others are more pertinent today than when they were written almost two decades ago. Ironically, nowadays it is not an intolerant governing apparatus under a Conservative regime but instead a more intense authoritarian state under Tony Blair's New Labour.

Since 1997, the Blair government has set about to criminalize some of the most marginalized and traumatized groups in British society, including the homeless, the welfare dependent, the young and those fleeing persecution. As a result, New Labour's infamous slogan 'tough on crime, tough on the causes of crime' has launched various state crackdowns against some of the most vulnerable and dislocated people in contemporary Britain (cf. Muncie and Goldson 2005).

The Blair government's authoritarian approach to social problems is evident in its punitive policies. A question in the House of Commons from the Liberal Democrats in February 2005 revealed that New Labour has introduced 1,018 new crimes since coming to power. Moreover, the UK currently has the highest prison population in western, northern and southern Europe, with 84,000 incarcerated prisoners (Walmesley 2005) – a rise of 15 per cent in the past six years (see Allison and Muir 2005).

The government's assault on civil liberties, 'anti-social behaviour', 'breaking the drop-out culture' and matching 'rights with responsibilities' are the 'unchanging values' of New Labour that are supposed to take 'Britain forward not back' and bring 'prosperity for all' (see Blair 2005: 1). However, such rhetoric cannot be reconciled with the same government's recent 'war on immigration', with human rights abuses including lengthy detention, dispersal, denying benefits and removing rights of appeal (see Mynott 2005). Or with an illegal invasion and occupation of Iraq (see Kramer and Michalowski 2005); or internment without trial and the suspension of the rule of law in Northern Ireland (Rolston and Scraton 2005). Or the sale of weapons to the tune of £1 billion (approved by the Department of Trade and Industry) to African countries, including those with appalling human rights records (Barnett 2005). Nor can a government proudly protest to be taking its people forward when it faces prosecution by the European Commission (the first-ever prosecution of a member state) in the European Court of Justice for alleged failure to adhere to nuclear safety standards at Sellafield where 30 kg of deadly plutonium has been 'lost' and remains unaccounted for (see Brown 2004; Jameson 2005). The list of state crimes committed by the British government could go on.

This shameful hypocrisy has become normalized within an intolerant regime of denial, cover-up and dismissal. Importantly, for my purposes in this chapter, the question remains: what is the role of the critical criminological voice within conservative and intolerant political landscapes? Inspired by the arguments in Scraton's book, particularly Sim, Scraton and Gordon's chapter on 'Crime, the state and critical analysis', this chapter presents an analysis of critical criminology under the intensified authoritarian state. It explores the influence of new modes of conservative governance on the production of critical criminological knowledge. In doing so, it examines the commodification of criminology and the increasing rise of embedded criminological genres and argues that critical criminology must continue to avoid the lure of relevance that is so frequently used to define the only 'legitimate and useful' regime of truth. This analysis promotes a 'criminology of resistance' and provides an optimistic outlook for the critical voice within existing political terrains of intolerance and moral authoritarianism.

The neoliberal university and critical scholarship

In 1979, the French philosopher, Jean-Francois Lyotard, published his influential book, *The Postmodern Condition*. In this text, he forecasts that universities and the knowledges they produce will experience profound ideological shifts as capitalist societies emphasize the market principles of commercialization and commidification. In the 1984 English translation of Lyotard's work, he writes:

> Knowledge is and will be produced in order to be sold, it is and will be consumed in order to be valorized in new production … It is not hard to visualize learning circulating along the same line as money, instead of for its educational value or political importance; the pertinent distinction would no longer be between knowledge and ignorance, but rather, as the case with money, between 'payment knowledge' and 'investment knowledge' – in other words, between units of knowledge exchanged in a daily maintenance framework (the reconstitution of the workforce, 'survival') versus funds of knowledge dedicated to optimizing the performance of a project (pp. 5–6).

Numerous contemporary educationalists and academic scholars have since acknowledged the accuracy of Lyotard's prediction. The political and economic transformation from social democracy to market liberalism has created international concern and debate within higher education over issues such as university governance, academic freedom, funding, market-driven curriculum and the commercialization of research (see Marceau 2000; Hillyard *et al.* 2004). While some of these issues have confronted universities for some time, others are new and provide direct challenges to the traditional values of tertiary education.

First, the subordination of universities to external political control has been profoundly accomplished. Most universities have historically relied upon government for financial security and recent cutbacks in funding within the tertiary sector have ignited a need for universities to 'income generate'. Second, the inculcation of new-managerialist economic principles has provided new structures of operation and governance. Ministers and senior university management, as a necessary transformation within changing economic landscapes, have presented the new business-like culture of universities. As a result, individual disciplines within universities are expected to be profit-making units or alternatively face disestablishment. For many scholars,

17

knowledge must coexist with, or be subservient to, market demand. This growing expectation from university management in many western countries has created 'the income generation of academia.' Indeed, government funding formulas are becoming increasingly linked to a university's capacity to demonstrate 'research activity': a phenomenon that is, in part, calculated by an academic institution's level of external grants and contracts. Or, as Marginson (1997: 247) argues, universities are becoming increasingly entrepreneurial as 'islands of expansionary capitalism.'

There is also a growing expectation that academics sustain an acceptable level of 'research activity.' For example, in the UK, the four higher education funding bodies (Higher Education Funding Council of England, Scottish Higher Education Funding Council, Higher Education Funding Council of Wales and the Department of Education for Northern Ireland) jointly conduct the Research Assessment Exercises (RAEs). The RAE is both a mechanism of accountability and a measurement of research activity. It also has been widely criticized by British academics for inhibiting academic inquiry and commodifying academic scholarship. Broadhead and Howard (1998: 9) argue:

> The RAE represents a new phase in the 'commodification' of academic research ... The RAE has linked commodification directly to the overall goal of making the intellectual community 'competitive' with Departments adding up their member's currency for declining governing funding ... Individual researchers are coming under increasing pressure not to undertake complex and/or radical work which may not be compressed into the Exercise's four-year cycle ... It is more important than ever to be, and to be seen to be, a safe bet.

Within criminology, the RAE has also been strongly criticized for other reasons, including its perpetuation of positivist discourse as well as producing an environment of competition that is deleterious to the production of alternative or critical scholarship. As Scraton (2001: 2) argues:

Academics compete with each other to give keynote papers at prestigious conferences, to have their research published in 'stellar' journals and to win ESRC awards. It is a world of collusion and compromise, of horse-trading and back-scratching, and/or exchanging favors and poaching staff. If you opt out, your central funding dries up; if you opt in, you cannot retain a critical agenda.

The RAE is a feature of the neoliberal university and with it has brought an inculcation of unclear and contradictory corporate business principles into academic environments. The tertiary sector is beginning to reap what the government has sowed – which includes, among other things, the production of 'academic embeddedness' and knowledge for sale.

Embedded criminology[1] and academics for hire[2]

To speak of embedded criminology is somewhat tautological. Criminology's origins reveal that it has been an intellectual enterprise largely dominated by a scientific causation of state defined crime for the purposes of developing a more efficient crime control apparatus. Intellectual contributions that have questioned definitions of crime and social order have comprised marginalized knowledges within a body of criminological work focused on the production of solutions to specific crime problems. Criminological research has, therefore, been dominated by a spirit of pragmatism that has promoted a scientific and administrative criminology to aid the immediate policy needs of government (see Walters 2003: 160; cf. Sim *et al.* 1987; Rock 1997). Historically, therefore, criminology has been an 'embedded' discipline. Of course, the advent of critical criminologies in the late 1960s sparked an intellectual debate of conflict and constituted a radical shift within existing positivist criminological discourses. In doing so, criminology came to be recognized as an important part of the sociology of deviance and mainstream positivist theory was challenged for its political alliance with the state's crime control apparatus (Cohen 1988). And while I would argue that we are witnessing a healthy growth in new critical narratives or knowledges of resistance, we are also observing a rise in new forms of embedded knowledge.

Take for example, the recently edited collection by Smith and Tilley (2005) entitled *Crime Science: New Approaches to Preventing and Detecting Crime*. This Jill Dando Institute production constitutes a new form of right-wing positivist criminology in the form of 'crime science.' Criminological positivism is reclaimed by the crime scientists but not for welfare or liberal democratic analyses to crime problems – but for situational and technological crime prevention purposes premised on conservative and intolerant New Labour ideologies. It is unashamedly embedded within government definitions, discourses and processes of crime policy and prevention. Hence, 'DNA fast-tracking', 'rational choice theory', 'crime pattern analysis' and 'routine activities theory' and other recycled and repacked perspectives (from loyal and trusted Home Office protégés and affiliates) form the foundation of this 'separately identifiable endeavour' (Smith and Tilley 2005: xv). Consider the chapter by Wortley and Summers that proposes situational measures to prevent disorder in Leistershire's Glen Parva Prison. Here, crime science is adopted for an anti-bullying strategy, including initiatives for remote control television: 'many prisoners would fall asleep and leave their television on all night, a practice that caused arguments among the inmates. In February 2003, remote controls were given to prisoners to allow them to turn off their sets without getting out of bed' (p. 90).

Moreover, a crime science approach is adopted for addressing noise from cell windows caused by prisoners shouting. Such prison disorder, they argue, can be prevented with noise monitors and more televisions and DVDs. Finally, to avert staff scalding, Wortley and Summers (2005: 98) state:

> before being locked up at night, prisoners were issued with a can of hot water with which to make tea or coffee while in their cells. When receiving this hot water, some prisoners would throw the water over the officer, causing serious scalding … Thermos flasks were issued to prisoners instead of open cans of water.

As a high-school social studies project, this is passable work. As an academic study, it is cerebral inertia. Yet this menial and uncritical 'research' is a trend within academic institutions that see university resources devoted to consultancy-type productions with little or no academic integrity or imagination. Such work is more suited to the commercial world of corporate research than to academic institutions. Yet the income-generation policies of contemporary university managers and politicians will ensure that the menial and the mundane prevails over the creative and the critical. Moreover, offering slight improvements or administrative gestures to an inhumane system of penal practice serves to legitimate the unnecessary shame and brutality for which British prisons are constantly challenged. Yes, bullying in prisons is a problem; it is an unacceptable feature of contemporary institutions that are premised on degradation. The answers lie in critiquing the systems of justice that place people in such institutions in the first instance.

Sim *et al.* (1987: 8) referred to positivist criminological endeavours as the:

golden fleece of criminology – the causes of crime – suggesting reforms which improve the operational effectiveness of the criminal justice system or supporting policies for reforming particular aspects of local environments which are believed to propel individuals into criminality. Either way, structures of power, domination and control were left under researched or untouched.

The crime scientists do even less. They are concerned with criminal justice tinkering and polishing the existing system. Suggested improvements through the design and manipulation of public space, the surveillance or person and property, advanced technologies for policing and other endeavours centred on rational choice, only serve to detect and prosecute – not to understand and interpret. As a result, concepts of power, politics and patriarchy have no place within a 'crime-solving ethos' that pivots on crime science.

The Smith and Tilley book, of course, represents a further example of forensic-related books and articles used by academics, practitioners and government on both sides of the Atlantic to fight 'the war against crime.' Even plant evidence to reconstruct criminal events or 'forensic botany' is seen as the way forward for science to conquer 'the crime problem' (Coyle 2005). Interestingly, crime science could be used to detect and prevent corporate crime, as is the case in Finland where health and safety injuries and deaths are examined with forensic evidence (see Alvesalo *et al.* 2006 forthcoming), but those who proselytize crime science in the UK lack the imagination, the ideological will or are unwilling to jeopardize lucrative government and private industry contracts to redirect the debate towards crimes of the powerful. Or, as the truly embedded, the crime scientists are converted believers in the criminal justice regimes of government.

Moreover, advocates of crime science assert an empirical superiority. There is a presumption that crime science (notably DNA evidence) is grounded in irrefutable and compelling scientific truths than cannot be challenged. However, as Carole McCartney (2005) convincingly argues, DNA crime science is anything but exact. It is a technological approach or 'belief' riddled with ambiguities and errors that present pressing problems for civil liberties and criminal justice. However, such injustices are not forged on the powerful in society but on the powerless. As a result, this growing industry of crime science and technology continues to target and marginalize some of the most disadvantaged and alienated citizens in contemporary western societies (for example, young people, ethnic minorities, asylum seekers, low-income earners and so on). As such, crime scientists will always find favour with the Blair government. We have now reached the stage where academic criminologists appear in the Queen's Birthday Honours list for 'services to the police' (see http://www.number10. gov.uk/output/Page7634.asp). Clearly, the crime scientist currently has the ear and the bourgeois vanity of the British establishment.

The academic expert and the commercialization of knowledge

As mentioned above, there is an increasing recognition that the commercialization of the tertiary sector within neoliberal political and economic discourses continues to colonize research agendas with critical voices demarcated to an increasingly marginalized periphery. However, for many criminologists, it is not necessarily university management or external political pressures that drive the reasons for undertaking research under contract with a client. Why do academics hire their services to governments or private corporations? First, there is a belief by those who sign contracts or accept fee-paying consultancies that they will have access to information that would otherwise be unattainable. I agree with this. However, the limitations often placed upon dissemination renders the access almost entirely useless as the proceeds of the research are often consumed solely by the fee-paying organization. The research that is published for general public access (if at all) is either very watered down or simply reproduces the sorts of information that are obtainable on the Internet. Second, there is a view that private consultancies, notably with a government agency, will have an impact on policy and practice. This is a desirable academic aspiration – namely, the willingness to influence policy debates. However, as Marjone (1989: 164) points out, 'political actors select their ideas and arguments from the supply that happens to be available at a given time.'

The non-utilization of criminological research, and other forms of social science inquiry, for public policy has promoted scepticism among academic researchers for some time (see Patton 1986). For some, there is little intersection between criminological research and public policy formulation, and that public policy 'is largely driven by media generated stories (including celebrated crime stories) instead of social science research' (Daly 1995: 6). Indeed, Barak (1988) has argued that academic criminologists must not remain 'spectators' to media-generated constructions of crime problems. He argues that criminologists should develop a 'news-making criminology', using the mass media to convey a readily and widely consumed knowledge for maximum impact on the processes of policy development (Barak 1988). Yet this role in influencing public policy has been widely criticized. Chan rhetorically asks: 'what is criminological research all about – producing a defensible and useful knowledge about criminal justice related issues. If so, this process I would argue, is never going to keep pace with the six-o'clock news' (1994: 28).

Criminologists undertaking policy relevant research are subject to the vagaries and machinations of party politics. Tombs (2003) persuasively and authoritatively makes this point. Following her 20-year career at the Scottish Executive (formerly the Scottish Office), Dr Jacqueline Tombs examines 'what counts as evidence in the policy making process.' In other words, how and why are certain forms of knowledge used in the policy-making process over and above others? For Tombs (2003: 5), the uptake of criminological research into the policy decisions of government, or what she refers to as 'practical logic-in-use', is 'mediated by three main factors – the control of information, the need to render the control invisible, and short term policy making.' In this revealing insight into the internal workings of the production of criminal justice policy, Tombs identifies how government strategically produces what she calls 'generative knowledges' to be available for 'the policymaking machine to draw on as it sees fit.' In doing so, criminological knowledge serves various bureaucratic functions that include making political bargains, measuring and assessing the effectiveness of the criminal justice system, as well as 'knowledge as non-evidence' where the findings are 'politically unpalatable' and are systematically neutralized through 'questioning its relevance, its methodology; or its objectivity' (2003: 10). While Jackie Tombs uses the category 'formative knowledge' to refer to criminological research that informs and shapes legislation, it is clear from her experience that the ability for commissioned research to influence the system is as much about timing and political appeal as it is about content. The vast majority of reports, by nature of the research parameters, simply endorse government policy. Reports that challenge the status quo are usually shelved or have specific sections (notably those favourable of government) highlighted in executive summaries.

Third, there is a belief that academic careers will be advanced by 'bringing in money' through contract research. In many instances this is true; however, I also see the damaging effects of contract research. In my experience, university promotion committees grant little significance to government-published research reports in favour of refereed journal articles. Moreover, younger or more junior academics are increasingly exploited by university departments that emphasize 'money-led research.' They are expected, in some instances, to be involved in contract and consulting research to the detriment of their academic development as permanent positions in academia require a profile of refereed publications that will contribute to the RAE.

Finally, private consultancies provide opportunities for academics to 'make money' and, hence, we are witnessing a 'research for profit.' Many academics are entering a growing industry or market where their knowledge and expertise have considerable commercial value. There is growing evidence of some academics leaving academia and opening their own consultancy businesses or alternatively operating their own private research companies while maintaining their academic posts. The primary motivation for engaging in these commercial arrangements is not the production of new knowledges or to influence policy and practice, but to make money.

This increasing amount of criminological research conducted under contract has given rise to what may be termed the production of private or, in some instance, 'secret' criminological knowledge. That is, knowledge that is commissioned by a contractor, either government or non-government, where the dissemination of that knowledge is determined by the fee-paying agency. The distribution, and hence the consumption, of criminological knowledge becomes regulated by authorities who have 'purchased' the research. For example, in the UK there is a growing amount of private work undertaken by academic criminologists for security firms (see Walters 2003). This is insidious in both an ideological and ethical sense as the academic responsibility to develop new knowledges and to act as critic and conscience of society is jettisoned in favour of individual profit where academic credentials give credence to the policies of security firms that aim to maximize margins while (often) adopting a range of strategies that serve to marginalize and regulate the already seriously marginalized groups in society. Furthermore, Burnett and Whyte (2005) identify the ways in which academics assist private military companies and help governments shape discourses about terrorism. They argue how the University of St Andrews Centre for Studies in Terrorism and Political Violence (CSTPV) has institutional ties with the RAND Corporation – a research company set up by the US Army in 1945 that remains an influential conservative think-tank for US business and military strategy. The CSTPV, based in one of Britain's most elite academic institutions, is 'at the epicentre of the academic study of terrorism' where its members, who have ongoing links with RAND, have played major roles in shaping US foreign policy, including the occupation and rebuilding of Iraq.

Critical scholarship and the lure of market competitiveness

If as Chan (1994) suggests, broader political and economic change will 'spell the end' of critical criminological scholarship, it is important to examine what impact new modes of governance are having on notions of critique. Criminologists have in recent years begun to question the extent to which criminology is being 'lured by relevance' at the expense of critical scholarship (Cohen 1994; Hogg 1998; van Swaaningen 1999; Tombs and Whyte 2003). Moreover, Barak (2001) suggests that the word 'critical' has become off-putting to academics and practitioners alike. He identifies that having the word 'critical' in the title of a book is likely to reduce its audience and its sales. In his review essay of Ian Taylor's *Crime in Context*, which was a critical account of the political economy of crime and crime control, a book that won the ASC's 2000 Hindelang Award, Barak (2001: 145) argues:

> At the turn of the 21st century, what does it mean and what does it say about the field of criminology when a book receives its discipline's most prestigious award, presented by the largest organization of criminologists in the world, and relatively few of its members bother to read it?

The lure of relevance and the commercialization of criminological research dilute critical scholarship. A 'critical position' about crime, deviance or criminal justice policy and practice is likely to evoke reaction from governing authorities that have become sensitive to, and threatened by, criticism. The increasing amount of 'jobbing criminology' or 'criminology for profit' through consultancies and short-term contract research fails to provide a critique of power and social order and, thereby, reduces the value of criminology to discussions about relevance and usefulness.

Notions of 'critique' have become wedded or subordinate to the politics of existing governing rationalities. Criminological discourses from the left and administrative discourses from the centre-right have, in many instances, become united under the same banner. As a result, criminologies which transcend traditional disciplinary boundaries must begin to re-examine critical scholarship within frameworks that focus on the politics and rationales of new modes of governance. Pavlich (2000: 103) argues that what is needed is a criminological critique that relinquishes disciplinary loyalties and promotes a 'politics of truth' that involves dismantling a priori governmental assumptions about crime. Pavlich (2000: 166) suggests that what is needed is an 'art of governmental critique' that asserts as its modus operandi 'how not to be governed in a particular way.' He argues for a new language or grammar of critique that allows the criminologist to explore existing regulatory authorities within expanded horizons that are not confined to restrictive and compartmentalized analyses. Existing methods of critique are often rendered impotent by their own disciplinary labels. As a result, the parameters of criminology must move outwards and scrutinize new terrains in governance, in regulatory practices, in risk and so on. Such analyses provide new and proactive ways of interpreting processes of criminalization.

Contemporary markets and the value of knowledge

In contemporary global markets, criminological knowledge, like all forms of knowledge, is seen as an essential part of economic growth. The rise of the services sector in recent years has placed significant commercial value on non-tangible company assets such as ideas, education, experience and intellectual networks (Miles and Boden 2000). This transition of growth has seen a shift away from acquiring and converting raw materials and goods-based production, to a sharp rise in computing, telecommunications and other high-skill knowledge-based technologies (Neef 1998). Global commercial environments are continually seeking added-value or competitive advantages through the development and promotion of knowledge economies. These economies, whether individual, organizational or national, are underpinned by a new economic theory that is driven by a cost-reduction productivity (Drucker 1998). Hence, information and knowledge for new and growing service sectors have become the key to economic growth for contemporary business (Boisot 1998). Included among these sectors are areas that require criminological expertise and knowledge – for example, crime prevention, security, insurance and risk.

Discourses on knowledge economies also identify intellectual capital as the most profitable investment and most valuable asset of corporate entities (Edvinsson and Malone 1997). The intersection between intellectual capital and economics has produced a definition of knowledge based on 'a capacity to act' (Svieby 1997: 37). In other words, knowledge has become a key and practical ingredient for corporate practices. Abell and Oxbrow (2001: 267) define knowledge as: 'The combination of explicit data and information to which is added tacit expert opinion, skills and experience to result in a valuable asset which can be used to make key decisions. The essential factor in adding meaning to information.' As a result, corporate environments utilize the knowledge/power nexus for commercial gain. Hence knowledge must be measured and managed in order to realize a company's true value (Edvinsson and Malone 1997). As mentioned earlier, such economic rationales have underpinned changes to the public sector and university management in recent years. This has occurred in the restructuring and relabelling within institutions as well as the ways that knowledge is managed and valued. Various modes of governance recognize that knowledge is a valuable commodity.

The commodification of knowledge and the inculcation of models of corporate management within universities present new challenges for institutions founded on teaching and research and not profit. Criminological research finds itself drawn into this new managerial vortex where its value is increasingly being measured by application, relevance and its ability to attract external funding. This is consistent with university emphases on business principles of 'customer capital' that include networks and clients that are capable of generating income. This is an institutional response to recent government cutbacks in tertiary funding that are often announced, paradoxically, with political rhetoric about the importance of a knowledge society.

Therefore, scholars who produce research are entering unchartered waters where an emphasis is placed on the commercial value of their knowledge. If knowledge is the key to innovative and productive global markets, then universities, corporate research firms and government research units are seen as 'brokers' of ideas for commercial growth and prosperity. Clearly, universities have bought into this position and actively promote their contributions to these new market opportunities. However, the 'knowledge for sale' ethos does not reroute intellectual endeavours beyond existing modes of governance but instead places them firmly within the control of conservative political rationalities. As a result, the producers of knowledge become key players in their own ongoing and entrenched embeddedness. The growing production of relevant and applied criminological knowledge or what I've termed 'embedded criminology' serves to perpetuate governing rationalities premised on actuarialism, risk and management. As knowledge continues to be defined and recast within concepts of commercial value, those forms of knowledge outside the parameters of market utility will continue to be marginalized. To avoid this, universities should promote their distinctive features where the creation of new and critical knowledge is seen as having value within the commercial world. Moreover, critical criminologists must assert their work in a policy and political world increasingly starved of a critical voice. But how?

Boycott and resistance

Scraton (2001) argues that what is needed is the expansion of 'knowledges of resistance.' Such knowledges, he argues, cannot be generated under contract where they are often silenced or neutralized. They require criminologists to stand outside the often lucrative and profitable domains of commercial criminology and actively assert a position of resistance. As Foucault (1977: 131–2) argues, it is important that scholarship 'detach[es] the power of truth from the forms of hegemony … within which it operates': a position of resistance that identifies knowledge/power complexes within contemporary forms of governance and critiques the injustice of governmental regimes that construct notions of truth for material and political gain. As Tombs and Whyte (2003) argue, political economy is important for understanding the silencing and self-regulation of criminological scholarship: 'in other words, current attempts to silence, discredit and marginalize alternative views of the world are both an element in and a symptom of the political re-configuration of university research.'

The development of theoretically grounded critical scholarship cannot occur through the production of technical reports for governments or consultancy advice to private companies. 'Critical' criminological scholarship is now often viewed as anachronistic or, alternatively, as a 'catch-all' term for all forms of research that raise questions or challenge assumptions. All criminologists can, therefore, legitimately lay claim to a critical status. This is clearly problematic as critique becomes softened or watered down. A vast amount of funding for criminological research is directed to administrative projects that aim to improve existing apparatuses of crime control. This research (as discussed earlier) serves the priorities of contemporary governing technologies. In my view, academics must resist the often lucrative markets of contract research and private consultancies. Academics are not paid from the taxpayers' purse to profit personally by granting legitimacy to corporations driven by profit and shareholder interests. Nor should academics participate in government research agendas that ignore, for example, crimes committed by the most powerful and wealthy in society, while endorsing policies that aim to regulate the already over-regulated in society. As Hillyard *et al.* (2004) have persuasively argued, the Home Office has a research agenda heavily skewed in favour of regulating the poor and powerless in society. Any attempt by a researcher engaged in Home Office research to critique government policy or to challenge the decisions of ministers is usually met with a range of techniques of neutralization that aim to silence and suppress the critical voice.

Moreover, the Home Office will abort research that 'is no longer of interest to ministers or policy colleagues, either the research has been so delayed that the results are no longer of any interest or because ministers or officials have changed their priorities' (see Walters 2003: 57). Academics may spend months or even years planning and implementing research that is funded by the Home Office, only to have the plug pulled because a minister has changed his or her mind. Academics should never operate under such conditions and, until the Home Office develops a research agenda that seriously addresses crimes of the powerful and permits independent scholarship to occur without interference and to be published verbatim, then I say academics must boycott the seeking of, and participation in, Home Office research as well as all research for private security firms where the modus operandi is commercial profit rather than addressing issues of social injustice and exclusion.

The negative experiences of academic criminologists engaged in research with the Home Office is vast and yet the message has not sunken in – the Home Office is only interested in rubber-stamping the political priorities of the government of the day. If it were concerned with understanding and explaining the most violent aspect of contemporary British society (notably the modern corporation), it would fund projects that analyse corporate negligence, commercial disasters and workplace injuries – but it doesn't. If it were concerned with violence and human rights abuses it would fund projects to examine the state's role in Northern Ireland or in Iraq or its policies on asylum – but it doesn't. The Home Office remains silent on all those topics that have the potential to reflect poorly on government. Instead, the Home Office employs psychology, economics and physics graduates in preference to criminology and sociology graduates to perform quantitative and statistical analyses to pressing Westminster concerns (see Walters 2003). To participate in Home Office research is to endorse a biased agenda that omits topics of national and global concern in favour of regulating the poor and the powerless. If all academics boycotted Home Office research and refused to provide such research with the credibility that academic credentials bring – then the Home Office would be forced either to change the existing agenda or to engage solely corporate researchers. If the latter was adopted, not only would Westminster begin to question the lack of 'expertise' informing policy but the Emperor would also be without clothes. The policies and research of the Home Office would be seen for what they are – nothing more than financial transactions to the lowest and most reliable bidder, researched and written as quickly as possible, and with the government's interests at heart in order to secure future deals.

My call for a boycott on Home Office research and private corporate consultancies will undoubtedly be perceived as a position of disengagement or isolationism – nothing could be further from the truth. I mean to promote engagement through diverse narratives that are often regulated, curtailed or prevented by the constraints of government and corporate contracts. Michel Foucault urged that critical voices should be expressed through diverse narratives, and Chomsky has identified the need to seek out audiences or communities of 'collective concern' to identify injustice. Moreover, Stan Cohen cogently demonstrated in his excellent book *States of Denial* (2003) that there exists what he calls an 'intellectual denial' where 'well-functioning minds become closed, and the gaze is averted from the uglier parts of their ideological blueprints and experiments. Or they allow themselves – for tangible rewards or an eagerness to please the powerful – to be duped into pseudo-stupidity. These shameful records of collusion go way back' (2003: 280). If academics are to become nothing more than mere information gatherers for government, and not prepared to critique the role of the state, or challenge new modes of conservative governance, or address questions relating to social and political order in fear of losing contracts, then the academic criminologist is reduced to a co-conspirator in the policing of knowledge.

There is much to be gained through establishing networks of collective concern (with academics, professional bodies, parliamentary committees, political parties, campaign and voluntary groups) that advocate for the promotion of multiple narratives, social justice and for the dissemination of new and critical knowledges (cf. Scraton 1987). The promotion of new critical narratives in cultural and green criminology, patriarchy and power, human rights, transnational justice, as well as state and corporate crime provide important voices of resistance against an emergence of embedded criminology. If criminology is to survive or is to make any sense it must embrace diverse knowledges of resistance – in my view, criminology must be a knowledge of resistance. This calls for a politics of engagement that is often prohibited by the proscriptive and regulated culture of government and corporate-led research which many academics are seduced by in the name of income generation or evidence-based decision-making.

In saying this I am mindful that many junior scholars and research fellows in the UK are currently working on Home Office-funded research. Their very livelihoods depend on short-term government contracts – should they also boycott Home Office research and be out of work? While understanding the plight of young criminological scholars (having served a frustrating and uncertain period on the treadmill of short-term governments contracts), my immediate criticism is with the more senior academic staff who have more choice to bid for research projects beyond Home Office money. It is established academic staff who are well positioned to seek grant-based funding who should boycott all Home Office research. As for young scholars, the key question is: how do short-term contract research positions develop or hinder their careers? For example, PhDs are rarely achieved alongside the work and submission of a government report. The PhD is often delayed or withdrawn. Moreover, researchers who spend too long working as a contract researcher may undermine their possible conversion into a full-time academic post (as they often don't have the refereed publications or teaching experience). Alternatively, the corporate research world will often deem them to have inadequate experience as they have not been juggling the volume and diversity of projects demanded of private enterprise.

So where do they go? In my experience, they become entrenched in university contract research or they seek opportunities in government policy and research positions. I'm not sure that is the best way of developing the future careers of up-and-coming criminology postgraduates. Rather than having young scholars employed *en masse* by Home Office-funded projects that are highly regulated to provide government with information that supports its political priorities, I would prefer to see established criminologists employing research fellows on grant funding or universities providing careers for young scholars to pursue research of their own interest. In doing so, they will provide important contributions to theoretical and critical knowledge.

It should be remembered that some of the most theoretically influential criminological works in the past 30 years have been written by scholars using their academic salaries or small university research grants as the only form of financial sponsorship. For example, *Folk Devils and Moral Panics*; *The New Criminology*; *Sisters in Crime*; *Hooligan: A History of Respectable Fears*; *Power, Crime and Mystification*; *Visions of Social Control; Women's Imprisonment: A Study in Social Control; Crime, Shame and Reintegration; Punishment and Modern Society* and *States of Denial* – just to mention a few – were all written without funding or with small university grants, and such works have significantly shaped discourses in criminology. Of course similar lists could be generated in other disciplines, and I'm sure they would reveal that the most influential texts (theoretically and empirically) have not been funded under government contract or from private corporations. While government contracts and corporate sponsorship may, in some instances, produce valuable research contributions, they have, in the main, a more functional and rudimentary purpose – to provide necessary income generation for resource-starved universities while providing governing bodies with quick-fix answers to pressing political and economic problems.

Concluding comment

This chapter concludes that new modes of governance in contemporary society, which focus on risk management and a politics of responsibilization, have provided new political and economic landscapes for the production of criminological knowledge. Emerging from the demands of the market is a 'criminology for profit': a privatization of knowledge where the academic role of 'critic and conscience of society' is replaced by that of service provider to a fee-paying client and by commercial arrangements with legally binding agreements that often determine the parameters and outputs of research. Consistent with broader political and economic trends, criminologists are becoming entrepreneurial as both public and private sector interests seek their expertise. Moreover, new governing rationalities require specific forms of criminological knowledge that address a range of management questions about broader issues of risk and regulation.

We are witnessing a variety of technical criminologies that provide short-term and actuarial solutions to pressing problems. Furthermore, notions of 'critique' have become wedded or subordinate to the politics of existing governing rationalities. As a result, critical discourses must continue to evolve in ways that capture the changing dynamics of politics, power and neoliberal modes of government rule. I suggest what is needed is an increase and a vocal outpouring of the critical voice or what I call 'deviant knowledge' (that which is critical of contemporary forms of governance and challenges the existing social order). I am strongly opposed to academics (notably to senior academics who have more choice) engaging in contract research or consultancy advice that simply grants legitimacy to the ongoing criminalization and marginalization of some of the poorest and most disadvantaged members of society.

As mentioned earlier, the development and diversity of critical criminological narratives spark optimism. This, combined with the increasingly large and vocal number of social movements, suggests that people are hungry for critical voices. Voices that represent the struggles of everyday lived experiences and that systematically challenge the increasingly untruthful and abusive powers that govern us. The critical voice is constantly under threat and engaging in critical scholarship can be a bruising experience. The list of such experiences is ever increasing.

Perhaps one of the most recent involves the excellent work of Phil Scraton and Linda Moore on the appalling and illegal conditions of young female offenders in Northern Ireland (see Scraton and Moore 2004). Their work brought about their immediate ban on access to all prisons in Northern Ireland. At the same time, the research also brought expert testimony that resulted in a court ruling that a young female prisoner be removed from her cell to a prison hospital (Scraton 2004). Hence, the experience of critical scholarship that challenges powerful elites is bruising but always meaningful and often very rewarding.

In an environment where income generation dominates the academia agenda; where government bodies are purchasing university courses to meet their needs; where corporations are funding academic projects and personnel to maximize their profits; where corporate-style conferences discourage robust and critical dialogue; and where public servants more and more determine and regulate the type and nature of academic scholarship – it is time to be buccaneers and to resist existing trends. Just as C.W. Mills' *The Sociological Imagination* (1959) challenged the 'inhibitions, obscurities and trivialities' of mainstream social science, it is important that critical criminology continues to challenge mainstream discourses on crime and criminal justice in the construction of a criminological imagination. To this effect, there is much to be optimistic about. New critical narratives in human rights, state crime, corporate violence, post-structuralism, culture, anarchism, peace-making, queer theory, green criminology – just to mention a few – provide innovative and critical voices of resistance that challenge governmental power and question social order. Sure, there are risks in adopting a position of resistance – you won't get an OBE! Or you may be isolated from certain sources of funding or from certain places and personnel. On the other hand, you may not. As mentioned earlier, in an era when politicians and policymakers are starved of a critical voice, it may be that it's time for the voices of resistance to be heard. Such voices must be dynamic and are, as Scraton (2005: 23) identifies, 'about bearing witness, gathering testimonies, sharing experiences, garnering the view from below and exposing the politics and discourses of authoritarianism. It moves beyond the resources of theory into praxis.' Or, as Steven Box argued more than 20 years ago:

> For too long too many people have been socialized to see crime and criminals through the eyes of the state. There is nothing left, as Matza points out, but mystification. This is clearly revealed in the brick wall of indignation which flattens any suggestion that the crime problem defined by the state is not the only crime problem, or that criminals are not only those processed by the state. There is more to crime and criminals than the state reveals. But most people cannot see it (1983: 14–15).

The future for critical criminology is to make sure people do see it!

Note

1   Embedded criminology is a term adapted from Burnett and Whyte's 'embedded academics' (see Burnett and Whyte 2005).
2   This section is reworked from an earlier version (see Walters 2006: 309–29).

References

Abell, A. and Oxbrow, N. (2001) *Competing with Knowledge: The Information Professional in the Knowledge Management Age*. London: TFPL Ltd.

Allison, E. and Muir, H. (2005) 'Prisoner total rises 15% in six years', *Guardian*, 27 June: 2.

Alvesalo, A., Tombs, S., Virta, E. and Whyte, D. (2006 forthcoming) 'Re-imagining crime prevention: controlling corporate crime?', *Crime, Law and Social Change*.

Barak, G. (1988) 'Newsmaking criminology: reflections on the media intellectuals and crime', *Justice Quarterly*, 5: 565–87.

Barak, G. (2001) 'Review essay', *Critical Criminology: An International Journal*, 10: 137–45.

Barnett, A. (2005) 'UK arms sales to Africa reach £1 billion mark', *Observer*, 12 June 2005: 2.

Blair, T. (2005) *Britain Forward Not Back. The Labour Party Manifesto 2005.* London: HMSO.

Boisot, M. (1998) *Knowledge Assets: Securing Competitive Advantages in the Information Economy.* Oxford: Oxford University Press.

Box, S. (1983) *Power, Crime and Mystification.* London: Routledge.

Broadhead, L. and Howard, S. (1998) '"The art of punishing": the research assessment exercise and the ritualisation of power in higher education', *Education Policy Analysis*, 8: 1–14.

Brown, P. (2004) 'UK faces court action for nuclear safety failings', *Guardian*, 4 September: 9.

Burnett, J. and Whyte, D. (2005) 'Embedded expertise and the new terrorism', *Journal of Crime, Conflict and the Media*, 1: 1–18.

Chan, J. (1994) 'Crime prevention and the lure of relevance: a response to Adam Sutton', *Australian and New Zealand Journal of Criminology*, 27: 25–9.

Cohen, S. (1988) *Against Criminology.* New Brunswick, NJ: Transaction Books.

Cohen, S. (2003) *States of Denial: Knowing about Atrocities and Suffering.* London: Polity Press.

Coyle, H. (2005) *Forensic Botany – Principles and Applications to Criminal Casework.* Boca Raton, FL: CRC Press.

Daly, K. (1995) 'Celebrated crime cases and the public's imagination: from bad press to bad policy', *Australian and New Zealand Journal of Criminology.* Special Supplementary Issue: 'Crime, criminology and public policy.'

Drucker, P. (1998) 'From capitalism to knowledge society', in D. Neef (ed.) *The Knowledge Economy.* Boston, MA: Butterworth-Heinemann.

Edvinsson, L. and Malone, M. (1997) *Intellectual Capital: Realizing your Company's True Value by Finding its Hidden Brainpower.* New York: HarperCollins.

Foucault, M. (1977) 'Truth and power', in A. Fontana and P. Pasquino (eds) *Microfisica del potere :interventi politici.* Turin: Einaudi. Reprinted in Faubion, J. (ed) (2002) *Power: Essential Works of Foucault 1954–1984.* London: Penguin Books.

Hillyard, P., Sim, J., Tombs, S. and Whyte, D. (2004) 'Leaving a "stain upon the silence": contemporary criminology and the politics of dissent', *British Journal of Criminology*, 44: 369–90.

Hogg, R. (1998) 'Crime, criminology and government', in P. Walton and J. Young (eds) *The New Criminology Revisited.* London: MacMillan.

Jameson, A. (2005) 'Nuclear audit says Sellafield "lost" 30kgs of plutonium', *The Times*, 17 February: 1.

Kelsey, J. (2000) 'Academic freedom – needed now more than ever', in R. Crozier (ed.) *Toubled Times: Academic Freedom in New Zealand*. Palmerston North: Dunmore Press.

Kramer, R. and Michalowski, R. (2005) 'War, aggression and state crime: a criminological analysis of the invasion and occupation of Iraq', *British Journal of Criminology*, 45: 446–69.

Lyotard, J.F. (1984) *The Postmodern Condition* (trans. G. Bennington and B. Masumi). Minneapolis, MN: University of Minnesota Press.

Marceau, J. (2000) 'Australian universities: a contestable future', in T. Coady (ed.) *Why Universities Matter*. St Leonards: Allen & Unwin.

Marginson, S. (1997) *Markets in Education*. Sydney: Allen & Unwin.

Marjone, G. (1989) *Evidence, Argument, and Persuasion in the Policy Process*. New Haven, CT: Yale University Press.

McCartney, C. (2005) 'DNA and miscarriages of justice.' Seminar, Department of Applied Social Science, University of Stirling, 7 September.

Miles, I. and Boden, M. (eds) (2000) *Service and Knowledge-based Economy*. London: Continuum.

Mills, C.W. (1959) *The Sociological Imagination*. Oxford: Oxford University Press.

Muncie, J. and Goldson, B. (2005) 'England and Wales: the new correctionalism', in J. Muncie and B. Goldson (eds) *International Developments in Juvenile Justice*. London: Sage.

Mynott, E. (2005) 'Compromise, collaboration and collective resistance: different strategies in the face of the war on asylum seekers', in I. Ferguson *et al.* (eds) *Globalisation, Global Justice and Social Work*. London: Routledge.

Neef, D. (Ed.) (1998) *The Knowledge Economy*. Boston, MA: Butterworth-Heinemann.

Patton, M. (1986) *Utilization-Focused Evaluation* (2nd edn). Newbury Park, CA: Sage.

Pavlich, G. (2000) *Critique and Radical Discourses on Crime*. London: Ashgate.

Rock, P. (1997) 'Sociological theories of crime', in M. Maguire *et al.* (eds) *The Oxford Handbook of Criminology* (2nd edn). Oxford: Clarendon Press.

Rolston, B. and Scraton, P. (2005) 'In the full glare of English politics: Ireland, inquiries and the British state', *British Journal of Criminology*, 45: 547–64.

Scraton, P. (ed.) (1987) *Law, Order and the Authoritarian State: Readings in Critical Criminology*. Milton Keynes: Open University Press.

Scraton, P. (2001) 'A response to Lynch and Schwendingers', *The Critical Criminologist: Newsletter of the ASC's Division on Critical Criminology*, 11: 1–3.

Scraton, P. (2004) 'Critical scholarship under threat', *Socio-legal Studies Newsletter*, 44: 3–4.

Scraton, P. (2005) The Authoritarian Within: Reflections on Power, Knowledge and Resistance. Inaugural Professional Lecture, Queens University Belfast, 9 June.

Scraton, P. and Moore, L. (2004) *The Hurt Inside: The Imprisonment of Women in Northern Ireland*. Belfast: Northern Ireland Human Rights Commission.

Sim, J., Scraton, P. and Gordon, P. (1987) 'Introduction: crime, the state and critical analysis', in P. Scraton (ed.) *Law, Order and the Authoritarian State: Readings in Critical Criminology*. Milton Keynes: Open University Press.

Smellie, P. (1996) 'Fight to put contract research in public realm – criminologists risk gag for "touching raw nerve of state"', *The Australian*, 7 February: 23.

Smith, M. and Tilley, N. (eds) (2005) *Crime Science: New Approaches to Preventing and Detecting Crime*. Cullompton: Willan Publishing.

Svieby, K. (1997) *The New Organizational Capital: Managing and Measuring Knowledge-based Assets*. San Francisco, CA: Berrett-Koehler.

The Times Higher (2003) 'Research appointments', 11 April: 57.

Tombs, J. (2003) 'Evidence in the policymaking process.' Paper presented at the Department of Criminology, Keele University, 7 May.

Tombs, S. and Whyte, D. (eds) (2003) *Unmasking Crimes of the Powerful: Scrutinizing States and Corporations*. New York, NY: Peter Lang.

van Swaaningen, R. (1999) 'Reclaiming critical criminology: social justice and the European tradition', *Theoretical Criminology*, 3: 5–28.

Walmsley, R. (2005) *World Prison Population List*, (6th edn). London: Kings College London, International Centre for Prison Studies.

Walters, R. (2003) *Deviant Knowledge – Criminology, Politics and Policy*. Cullompton: Willan Publishing.

Walters, R. (2006) 'Embedded Criminology and Knowledges of resistance' in Brannigan, A. and Pavlich, G. (eds) *Critical Studies in Social Control: The Carson Paradigm and Governmentality*. London: Glasshouse Press.

White, R. (2002) 'Criminology for sale: institutional change and intellectual field', *Current Issues in Criminal Justice*, 13: 127–42.

Wortley, R. and Summers, L. (2005) 'Reducing prison disorder through situational prevention: the Glen Parva experience' in Smith, M. and Tilley, N. (eds) *Crime Science: New Approaches to Preventing and Detecting Crime*. Cullompton: Willan Publishing.

Chapter 3

Confronting the 'hegemony of vision':[1] state, space and urban crime prevention

Roy Coleman

If, by the 1950s, social science had developed research 'tendencies towards fragmentary problems' and 'conservatively tuned' itself 'to the use of corporation, army, and state' (Mills 1970: 104), then its position today may be characterized as little more than doxology[2] (Bourdieu 1998: 7). In this scenario what is practicable – and indeed what is practised by many social scientists – translates into a servicing of change, and what counts as progress, within today's 'great [urban] institutions' (Bourdieu 1998: 7). In relation to the criminology of urban crime prevention this servicing role identified by Mills can be gauged through the coupling of crime prevention 'science' with a class-based and moralizing politics to 'reclaim' the streets. In re-envisioning class relations and how class identities are being rethought in the urban context, the clamour for reclamation is situated within a neoliberal policy environment that attempts to redraw the struggles and possibilities contained within the terrain and political language of 'the social'. On a range of fronts criminological work sustains rather than challenges this policy environment and decouples theoretical from political concerns through separating crime prevention from normative questions relating to the social world within which it operates. What is taken as crime prevention is tied to discourses and images of class, albeit in a manner that reworks, reinforces and sometimes masks their significance as concretized social divisions. More often than not crime prevention is understood apart from these processes. A downgrading in the analysis of material and ideological power within the larger social landscape is palpable in the linkages made between the 'evaluators and commissioners' of crime prevention research as they seek to work out 'credible and useful findings' (Tilley 1998: 139–40) to be used for the promotion of 'safer shopping' strategies, drawing up codes for behaviour in public space and the fine-tuning of sophisticated security devices. This kind of criminological endeavour sits at the apex of a discipline that lacks, in Mills' sense, imagination in its unwillingness to stand back and question the ideological pressures and confines of state policy as it is played out across a complex configuration of 'public' and 'private' domains.

In contrast, a credible and useful criminology can be, and is being, constructed through taking a dialectical approach in order to understand how crime prevention techniques work *within* and *for* an imaginary of state power that, in its current capacity, is implicated in reinventing a contradictory and tension-fuelled imaginary of the 'utopia of the visibly purified city' (Cohen 1985: 230). If a criminological imagination is to be cultivated here it must involve the situating of contemporary urban crime prevention in its wider socio-spatial context[3] that would allow a radical understanding of the former, not for its techno-fixing potential, but as sets of practices constituted through inter-related surveillance tactics conversant with a politics of vision and visibility that defines today's urban spatial policy and statecraft.[4] Drawing upon aspects of my own research, this chapter investigates the intersection between crime prevention and powerful urban visions with reference to developments in Liverpool in the UK – a city, like others, that is undergoing profound political, socio-economic and cultural change. This research aims to explore the relations between current drives to regenerate local states and city spaces and, by 'studying up' and scrutinizing the perspectives of state personnel, shed light upon local state-ordering practices and the consequences these are having for the broader direction and meaning of *social* control and order.

From the early 1980s, urban crime prevention has become 'part of an overall strategy of governance' (Gilling 1997: xii). However, a material analysis of this governing facet has rarely been undertaken in a period where 'practicality' has meant criminological servility to governing institutions concerned with image management in regenerating cities. Consequently, urban crime prevention has largely been understood in an abstracted sense, as a technical set of procedures for the reduction of legally defined 'crime' and state-led definitions of 'wrongdoing' or 'anti-social behaviour'. Far from problematizing the aims of crime prevention, abstract approaches have reduced it to a problem of 'this or that' technique, which, if fine-tuned in line with expert knowledge, will have 'this or that' effect on some designated category of criminal behaviour.

A criminological imagination requires moving beyond the narrow lexicon of prevention and its bogus promises of techno-fixing (Hughes 1998). Imagination presupposes a replacement of state-corporate categories of micro-knowledge with an intellectual freedom aimed at 'putting together hitherto isolated items, by finding unsuspected connections' within seemingly disparate areas of social life (Mills 1970: 221). These connections will not be revealed and made self-evident by remaining within orthodox crime prevention thinking. Broadening the criminological imagination is necessary in order to seek out an analytical engagement that transgresses disciplinary boundaries and fragmentary concerns. Thinking outside the inevitable associations made between certain ideas and a particular disciplinary domain means scholars can 'identify with learning rather than disciplines' (Sayer 1999: 5). For some this may call into question the utility and relevance of the discipline called criminology, but such questioning is welcome as it raises political inquiry into the association between the work of criminologists and particular socio-spatial projects, where the 'relevance' of criminological work is ascertained in a field of contestation in which strategies of power and practices of domination are forged. A multidisciplinary approach is warranted in an era in which state-spatial projects are collapsing and reworking (in their own terms) distinctions between social, economic and cultural policy domains. Some of the discourses and practices around the contemporary 'prevention of crime' are closely entwined with regenerative discourses that circumscribe notions of 'quality of life' that themselves privilege particular markets and audiences. Thinking critically about such connections means untying the straitjacket of the discipline in order to take into account the wider forces of social change.

In this sense, the call from Mills for a sociological imagination – an imagination born of independence from the 'great institutions' and orthodox political thinking – is more relevant today for a criminology that is dominated by 'the ascendance of neoliberal thinking' through 'market positivism' (Hayward and Young 2004: 262) and the continuing desire 'to represent the fixation of contemporary criminal justice systems' that produce predictable and narrow understandings of crime and criminals (Tombs and Whyte 2003: 3). The limitations of criminology have become more evident – and a radical politicized imagination become more urgent – in approaches to urban 'crime prevention'. For instance, the latter's wider significance in relation to social control has been overlooked precisely because it threatens to raise awkward (though necessary) questions that relate to the dialectics between preventive practices and socio-spatial justice. Broadening the debate into the arena of social control – and thinking about the social element of this concept – is particularly apt at a time when advanced capitalist social orders are increasingly legitimated by an emphasis on 'governing through crime' (Simon, cited in Hudson 2001: 158) and the disparaging impact of this on the poorest of citizenry (Wacquant 1999; Coleman and Sim 2005).

The forging of analytical connections through the engagement with an imaginative multidisciplinarity aids a deeper understanding of what superficially appear to be merely practical and technical problems in the field of urban crime and urban statecraft. Grasping the consolidation of a 'new penal common sense' (Wacquant 1999) requires a wider appreciation of shifts in social control and the manner in which it is becoming ideologically scaled down into a set of tactics for the censure and pursuit of particular groups of urban inhabitants.[5] While it is true that crime prevention is 'contingent and open to contested interpretations' and resistant forces (Hughes *et al.* 2002: 333), this chapter wishes to focus on a slightly different problem; that is, as long as urban inequalities feature in cityscapes, then the role of crime prevention and its connivance with the elucidation of feared others must be looked at in terms of its intended and unintended consequences for the spatial expression and reproduction of such inequalities. A place for the criminological imagination therefore lies in exploring the connections between crime prevention, spatial production and social justice.

The state, social control and urban crime prevention

Remaining independent of political power, as Mills urged, is a necessary and intellectually credible aspect of social scientific work. Independence, however, is a political problem of much criminology today and its pragmatic-with-power approach to urban crime prevention.[6] There has been a general shying away from questions of power, order and the meaning of social belonging within that order that concerned earlier social scientists including Durkheim, and later Becker, through to radical criminologists associated with the National Deviancy Conference in the 1970s. Indeed, theoretical criminology of late has been influenced by analyses that have diminished the importance of the state as a problematic actor and generator of forms of order as well as social disorder. The analytical problematic of the state has shifted in emphasis to focus instead on the localization of power in what are seen as increasingly fragmentary social orders (for example, see Shearing and Stenning 1985; Shearing 2001). In such narratives the state has been reduced to micro-powers, institutionally disaggregated and ideologically disconnected through the seeming upsurge in semi-autonomous governmental domains characterized by non-determinate mentalities and techniques of control (Rose 1996, 2000). Others have identified a limited sovereign state governed by politically driven punitive rhetoric and practice (Garland 1996) and depoliticized by managerialism (see Feeley and Simon 1994). While a vengeful 'governing through crime' reflects a decline in confidence of states to lead meaningfully on issues of welfare and social inequality (Simon and Feeley 2003), what is often overlooked in criminology is a concern with what the state form *is* and what it is *doing* in terms of its complex and uneven spatial, moral and ideological crafting between and across its institutional settings. In particular, losing sight of the process of state building neglects an important dimension (not least in a material sense) of the contingent organization of political domination that so concerned Mills. This retains the importance of state theory in relation to the constitution of urbanity by exploring the types of institutions created in this process – their rationale for organizing social forces, levels of recourse to legal, moral and/or 'civic' authority, and their authorized relationship to notions of the public interest.

In effect, much of theoretical criminology reinforces (in a refusal to go beyond) what Garland identifies as the 'habits of thought of action' (2000: 366) promoted by public/private partnerships and situated knowledge practitioners that are so central to contemporary urban statecraft (Coleman 2004a). Indeed, if 'criminological expertise' is informed by the 'cultural scripts' of this pragmatic domain (Garland 2000: 369) rather than reasoned debate, then it is ever more crucial to understand the current reorganization of the state terrain and explore how 'the state engenders social relations in space' (Lefebvre 2003: 85). Current state reorganization favours corporate expertise, relatively undisturbed by regulation and political scrutiny. Mirroring the early nineteenth-century city, private interests have been responsibilized in the contemporary city to act as sponsors and guardians of the public interest, and this is evident within current practices of risk management contained in spatial interventions such as crime prevention. Studying urban crime control practices in terms of how they are influenced by risk management discourses only paints a partial picture of 'crime fighting' in the city and loses sight of the 'roll-out of state functions' (Peck 2001) in ways that reconfigure the centrality of private property along with the political processes through which class subordination is reconstituted through moral and coercive tactics.

For the purposes of my own analysis the focus is on the field of state action, understood in terms of the hegemonic relations drawn between its educative, moral and coercive efforts in producing particular spatial-social relations. It is the political and definitional nature of 'risk' drawn by local and national political actors, albeit with a complex relationship to selective 'demands from below' (Stenson 2005: 274), that is of concern here. This means thinking about the organization of the state as both defining and being defined by categories of risk that have the effect of privileging certain kinds of socio-spatial relations and the room for manoeuvre these relations allow for particular groups and individuals. For example, amid New Labour's approach to wealth distribution that has seen an increase in earnings inequality (Hills and Stewart 2005), is its self-prescribed 'success' on 'toughness issues' (Watkins 2004). More generally risks construed in official discourse relay class-based notions of respectability and repellence aimed at working-class vulgarity and incivility (Skeggs 2005). Risky working-class behaviour and its potential to contaminate public sanctity and prevailing moral probity is depicted as harmful to the working class themselves as well as to a respectable citizenry who view the former as 'a body beyond governance' (Skeggs 2005: 965). In this scenario there is a lack of political will to reverse the 'grotesque caricatures' of people living on low or no incomes in the UK (Bamfield 2005: 6) whose behaviour has become the target of a range of responsibilizing and disciplinary state policies – not least through the likes of parenting classes and the use of state benefits as a disciplinary tool (Grower 2005). What is apparent is the readiness to unleash get-tough policies and risk-rhetoric that reinforce monstrous imaginaries of the poor as enemies of the contemporary social. The multi-frontal doxa of risk and its moral enmity are redrawing class divisions along with how such divisions are both represented and responded to.

Thinking about urban crime prevention requires that it be located within this broader context of state discourse and practice. It can be situated within a wider – albeit scaled-down – project of social control. Rethinking this latter concept means retaining something of the earlier liberal and critical approaches to social control that debated the relations (whether coercive, consensual or both) between control, social order and the shifting institutional field of the state. As aspects of urban change, the socio-spatial relations identified here force analytical attention on what Mitchell termed the struggle 'over what sort of order is to be materialised' in the city (2003: 235). In a wide sense, therefore, a range of current urban preventive practices justify, and are justified by, prevailing rationales and practices of urban statecraft. For example, part of my research focuses on camera surveillance in the UK[7] as it intersects with urban spatial production. It is not a question of establishing whether cameras 'work' in reducing crime, but of how they 'work' within a wider field of power and urban spatiality. Little has been written that questions why governing authorities in the UK possess a proclivity towards camera surveillance and in what sense this sustains and relates to other ordering practices that seek to cultivate a particular notion of 'quality of life'. This is particularly relevant given the growing acknowledgement that there 'is little substantive research evidence to suggest that CCTV works' (NACRO 2002: 6) with 'little overall effect on crime levels' (Home Office 2005). If this is the case then it is time to ask how today's surveillance-come-crime-prevention practices do 'work' in respect of their contribution to promoting contemporary visions of the city while communicating a sense of order through sociocultural censuring. Cameras are only one dimension that cannot be isolated from a wider proliferation of surveillance practices, including private security, public warden schemes, legal sanctions, and local councils and businesses, that are developing and funding regulatory and policing networks encouraged through the government's *Respect and Responsibility* document of 2003. It is in this flux of central–local state activity that the broader 'hegemony of vision' needs to be located and understood as an expansive notion that prefigures a way of looking at cities, spaces and what activities go on within them. The hegemony of vision, and the forging of urban leadership that this denotes, can be found in city promotional discourses, urban spectacles and government legislation and guidance documents that, taken together, point to preferred (though by no means uncontested) meanings of urban 'regeneration'. These visions are also moral and display inflexibility in relation to the means put in place to realize socio-spatial order in the urban landscape. What this suggests is that the increasingly shallow and selective preoccupation with the visibility of things, events and people as part of the 'regenerative' mentality of the city, prefigures and contextualizes 'crime prevention' practices.

But it is also in this broader context that notions of social control are being recrafted and reduced to a less ambitious set of processes within the political arena; away from a Durkheimian concern with fostering social cohesion in the face of unregulated market relationships that underpinned the 'external inequalities that are the source of our ills' (Durkheim 1984: 340). Today these 'ills' are located in an individualized instrumentalism buttressed by 'the general climate of consumer driven insecurity' (Hall and Winlow 2005: 47) and, as this chapter argues, compounded by partnership based 'crime preventing' roles designated within spatial regeneration strategies. Earlier liberal and expansive conceptions of social control (as having the potential to heal and overcome the worst aspects of social fracture) have been pushed aside in today's cityscapes to be replaced by a 'desperate dystopia of the "management" of "trouble-spots"' (Sumner 1997: 133). Why, how and with what social consequences is this happening? In different ways administrative criminology, risk theorists and latterly cultural criminologists have under-explored these shifts in their respective analyses with regard to how they are unravelling in distinctive and concrete state morphologies. In particular, they fail adequately to understand and confront the 'habits of thought and action' and the tendentious moral universe of powerful agents at the centre of contemporary statecraft and the degrees of ideological unity and fracture they exhibit. It is here that particular notions of risk-threats are ideologically positioned as destabilizing emergent socio-spatial orders. But it is also important to see how these are played out alongside the generation of risk-harms – through state action and inaction – which impact on those at the margins of order. Using Liverpool as a case study, my own research explores a paradigmatic entrepreneurial city in 'renaissance' in order critically to investigate the visionary power centres of urban change. The agents of such change are not simple risk practitioners asking technical questions of 'what works'. Their work needs to be understood within a normative understanding of state power that recognizes ongoing social divisions and asks 'what works' for *whom*? What follows is an attempt to contextualize contemporary trajectories of social control through which 'crime', 'order' and 'risk' and the notion of 'regenerating' cityspace have been increasingly interrelated in a neo-liberalising urban political policy arena.

Urban spatial politics and official discourses on 'crime' and 'grime'

The strategic importance of the image of Liverpool cannot be over-emphasised. The whole regeneration opportunity and process could be thwarted if people from within and outside Merseyside do not perceive Liverpool as a safe place and market its many qualities actively (Liverpool City Council 1997 cited in Coleman 2004a: 145).

The status of Liverpool as a vibrant city is under threat every single day (editorial, *Liverpool Echo* 14 October 2004).

The calculated visibility of urban phenomena is central to spatial production and increasingly important not only in Liverpool but also within the advanced capitalist reorganization of urban rule. In the context of the UK, regeneration vernacular and practice have, under New Labour (NL), extended a 'market state' (Hall 2003: 20) and aided the development of 'the business-friendly city'; a notion that underpins a reconfiguration of ideas around urban 'quality of life' together with notions of behaviour linked to crime, incivility and risk (Coleman 2004b). State activity in the city promotes a renewed sense of spatial visibility and vitality circumscribed by entrepreneurialized primary definers (marketing specialists, police, property developers, university vice-chancellors and 'experts' on urban sustainability) who, as part of their role in representing the city, render some spaces and activities more strategically visible, even desirable, than others (Coleman 2005). Idealized and selective representations of the city aim to create visually pleasing space and extend a view of space propagated through central government urban regeneration documents that tie 'the look' of the urban fabric to successful regeneration (DETR 2000) along with appropriate behaviour and decorum (Home Office 2003a, 2003b). Moreover, official discourses such as these along with representations in the popular press conflate physical waste, dirt or pollution with ideas of 'human waste' and disposable bodies in the city (Bauman 2004). This is the case with the problematized visibility of homeless persons whose 'nuisance and intimidation' is seen as a 'detriment to the very areas where environmental and social improvements are crucial' (Home Office 2003b: 47).

As part of a politics of vision such pronouncements prioritize the look, 'feel' and ambience of urban space as a prerequisite for 'responsible' regeneration. This notion of regeneration underpins the construction of consumption zones alongside the consumption of places as packaged experiences themselves (Urry 1995). References to poverty and structural indicators of quality of life (particularly with regard to social reproduction) are marginalized within these representational practices or are reworked into 'quality of life' discourses that rally around notions of 'inclusion' and 'participation'. As terms of official discourse, these governing mantras address the poor (and poorer areas) in pathologizing tones: childlike, criminogenic, lacking in skills, resources and motivation. The deployment of terms such as the above also invokes the usually unasked question: participation and inclusion in and for what kinds of practices? The strategies of 'participatory' and 'inclusive' reclamation of the 'social' (or 'neighbourhoods'), particularly in their targeting of unruly bodies and activities, are undertaken primarily through a discourse of crime and disorder. It is pertinent to explore how 'community participation' in governing through crime policy agendas links with the evolution of 'a degenerate policy culture' (Imrie and Raco 2003: 6) that co-ordinates notions of 'respectable' and 'non-respectable' in its attempted legitimation of particular forms of state-spatial activity. In relation to state morphology, participation therefore has become more and not less problematic in terms of how it is organized and the actions it seeks to promote. Representations of the city and associated streams of governance have an increasingly politicized significance in attempting to rework and sometimes hide traces of behavioural staining (including poverty) that, together with the management of local identities and reputations, feeds into strategies for the attraction of desirable resources and people. In this sense 'community' is invoked and rendered synonymous with corporate interests through the promotion of particular images of crime, deviance and victimization against which 'successful' regeneration is measured.

In contrast to the treatment of the unruly, the 'great institutions' now governing urban space are often presented in local media through the 'heroic' status of high-salaried 'city slickers' who articulate the means and meaning of state leadership, 'partnership' and local democracy (Coleman 2004a). As a new rationale for state effectivity, 'partnership' is central to reconstituting cityspaces within a 'synergy of capital investment and cultural meaning' (Zukin 1996b: 45) that attempts to sustain a 'self valorisation of capital in and through regulation' (Jessop 1997: 29).[8] The contemporary city itself 'is once again emerging as a strategic site for understanding major new trends that are reconfiguring the social order' (Sassen 2000: 143). In this scenario, the 'reinvention' of urban social order entails '*not* the rolling back of state intervention, but rather its political, institutional, and geographical reorganization' (Brenner and Theodore 2002: 345, emphasis in original). The morphology of local urban statecraft is central in reflecting and weaving trends in urban social control through, for example, the development of Business Improvement

Districts; bringing businesses, elected officials and developers into the domain of urban crime prevention in terms of funding CCTV systems and establishing specialized relations between police, private security and street wardens (Coleman 2004a).[9] The visions for urban space that underpin such powerful institutional developments have a role in both over- and under-valuing certain kinds of spatial activities and must be explored for a fuller understanding of urban crime prevention.

From such developments, a pervasive notion of visually pleasing space implicates strategies of social control to the extent that it interlinks the latter to aesthetic considerations concerning the moral probity and appropriateness of behaviour in public space. The notion of 'reclaiming the streets' from the 'yobs',[10] litterlouts, binge drinkers, petty thieves, beggars and illicit traders assumes a strategic ideological position within the networks of primary definition and, as already indicated, is buttressed by central government thinking and legislation. For example, the Anti-Social Behaviour Act 2003 is connected to the wider rehabilitation of space through its application within worked-out strategies for regeneration that utilizes a language of 'anti-social' to underpin a cleansing exercise aimed at less prosperous urban inhabitants – or 'usual suspects' (Burney 2004). The wider commitment to 'civilize' cityspace – through the politics of making visually pleasing spaces – implicates techniques in partnership and a rejuvenated moral discourse of street civility epitomized in NL's notion of 'the politics of decency' officially launched by Tony Blair in May 2005. The visible cues of 'decency' purported to be located in the dress sense and behaviour of the young in particular are conjoined by town and shopping-centre managers in their bid to eradicate hoods, caps and loitering as indices of degeneration and disorder.[11] The current 'Hats Off To Beat Crime' campaign in Liverpool buttresses the clamour for order as does the reasoning behind anti-social behaviour 'Czars' in the cities of the UK who, under the 2003 Act, seek to rid the streets of beggars and other 'harassers' and polluters of the public realm ('I will clean the streets of crime', *Merseymart* 2 September 2004).

These discourses and practices of reclamation attempt to fabricate a version of the social and reconstitute 'public' space from within the entrepreneurial policy exchanges between national and local authorities. The emphasis on the look and feel of the urban fabric contains a normative dimension in its attempt to educate and hail a 'new' type of entrepreneurialized urban citizen: 'We are saying to [the people of Liverpool] – "you are not just poor or self pitying".

We have to get across that Liverpool people are not all scallies;[12] they have flash and well-dressed young people who drink cappuccinos' (regeneration manager, abridged from Coleman 2004a: 147).

In this sense, entrepreneurialism (in its instructive visionary capacity) lays down an ideal of performance-enhancing space that is visible, marketable and befitting of cultivated and entitled individuals. Spatial strategies prioritize the performance of consumption and tourism and, increasingly, the performed appreciation of 'culture' and 'art' in the 'risk free' city. Changes in the economy are reflected in local state strategies relating to how the working-class city is re-presented to an idealized audience and how the subjects of this city understand themselves in relation to hegemonic entrepreneurialism.

The 'habits of thought and action' that constitute urban surveillance partnerships exert themselves (and increasingly justify their exertions) with reference to the 'the visual in mind' (Lefebvre 1991: 75) whereby performative spaces become embroiled with moralizing discourses that constitute what spaces are and who they are for. As in Liverpool, networks of primary definers, for example, often deploy the phrases 'family-friendly city', 'people's place' or the 'World In One City' to represent the city centre (Coleman 2004a). Such preferred representations displace class division and rule by channelling them through 'cultural' management strategies and identity-based politics (Skeggs 2004). The reassertion, and at the same time denial, of class can be a starting point for thinking about the creation of groups of urban outsiders in the political and popular imagination who require forms of surveillance that, in focusing on degenerate individuals, further obscure the class-specific nature of the contemporary power to punish.

Techniques of urban 'crime prevention' – including camera surveillance, private security and street wardens – share a concern with the management of spatial mobility and take place alongside 'older' policing practices. For the local Chief Constable, Liverpool's new Capital of Culture status for 2008 provided an opportunity for increased police funding to promote a 'safe culture' because 'there will be a lot more people on the streets and that surely means more policing' ('Capital city plays it safe', *Liverpool Echo* 10 June 2003). It is not just the disorderly binge drinkers, hooded youths and litter louts who will be targeted here. In the case of the single street homeless, the use of the Vagrancy Act, Anti-Social Behaviour Orders and tough public order policing aimed particularly at rough sleeping and begging are effecting a curfew on the homeless presence in Liverpool city centre.[13] Furthermore, police stop and search on the streets continues to be aimed disproportionately at young black people (Coleman 2005) in a manner that points to the enduring proximity between risk, racism and state practices.

Risk and the generation of anti-social states

Oh yes, there is a 'big issue' [laughter]. When people come out of Lime Street Station to do some shopping they've already passed seven or eight *Big Issue* sellers and it really pisses them off. People then think this city is seedy and full of beggars and homeless people; *like something you stand on* (superintendent, Merseyside Police, cited in Coleman 2004a: 177).

People want the barrow boys and flower sellers to stay. We are part of the furniture in the city. Not every one in the city can afford to shop at Marks and Spencer. (street trader in *Liverpool Echo* 20 July 1999 cited in Coleman 2004a: 182).

An imaginative criminology moves beyond the taken-for-granted label of 'criminal' and explores this label as a social censure (Sumner 1994: 223) alongside other forms of ineligibility that have the effect of stigmatizing 'the individual who is disqualified from full social acceptance' (Goffman 1963: Preface). Looking beyond the formal institutions and pronouncements of 'criminal justice' agencies provides a necessary step for understanding how deviant categories emerge and are sanctioned within a complex of public–private institutional activity. In Liverpool, this landscape of ongoing statecraft is generating the risk of socio-spatial exclusion for groups already vulnerable, not only through creating 'criminal' censures but also through processes that sanction urban belonging within 'traditional' policy channels. For example, an Audit Commission inspection report in 2004 demonstrates how exclusion operates through what it called 'financial mismanagement' of Liverpool City Council in relation to its support for the city's poorest groups (Audit Commission 2004). These groups included homeless people, refugees, asylum seekers, young people leaving care, the elderly and women fleeing domestic violence, who were rated in the report as receiving 'poor' service from the council ('City wasted our cash', *Liverpool Echo* 4 November 2004). Services for homeless people were described in the report as 'like the workhouses of the 1900s' (*Liverpool Echo* 4 November 2004). The decline of social control in a Durkheimian sense (as a check on the free-market and rampant individualism) is epitomized here by the deprioritization of state provisions for the poor that constitute risks for this group from social neglect rarely explored by criminologists.[14] It is important to explore the contradictory interplay here between aspects of anti-social state policy and the roll-out of reactive social control practices aimed at governing the seemingly self-imposed anomic character of certain city inhabitants.

The building of consent among city populations for the means and meaning of urban 'regeneration' – and the identification of problematic categories that hinder that regeneration – will have an impact upon the trajectory of urban crime prevention. It is important for a criminological imagination to address how institutions not formally associated with criminal justice are able to construct a vision for entrepreneurial city building that circulates idealized constructions of 'self-governing' subjects as well as constructions of those who fail to live up to this self-governing ideal. Tendentious forms of social control constructed within public–private partnerships are, for example, attempting to 'responsibilize' the homeless and homeless agencies into performing entrepreneurial roles by recruiting *Big Issue* vendors and training them as tourist information guides. Responsibilization also means pressuring working homeless people to smarten their appearance and stand in pre-marked pitches (painted on the floor) at particular times. 'Educating' the public not to give money to homeless people is also a feature of urban responsibilization (*Liverpool Echo* 4 November 2004). Similar efforts have been directed at street traders in terms of their sales techniques, litter control and licensing trading within pitch-marked squares. Again such processes are at work in terms of youth who are formally and informally subject to regulations regarding what activities are permissible in certain spaces (including where to sit, skate and collect money on Guy Faulkes night and what clothing is acceptable to be worn in certain spaces). These 'educative' strategies are backed up with a range of regulatory practices such as use of by-laws, anti-social behaviour legislation, street wardens, CCTV and traditional policing (Coleman 2003).

What this range of surveillance measures have in common is a concern for what is visually acceptable and unacceptable in a regenerating city and the consequences this is deemed to have for inter-city competition, gentrification and attracting investment. 'Safe places to do business' are preoccupied with an aesthetic of 'crime and grime' that reinvigorates the perceived necessity of 'broken windows' theorizing which, if nothing else, begins (and probably ends) with a focus on the superficial *appearances* of crime and disorder. Defiling the city with connotations of a 'bargain-basement economy' (see Coleman 2004a: 141–51), the activities of youth and homeless people, for example, skirt the boundaries between deviance, disorder and criminality. In the entrepreneurial city the habits of thought and action within partnerships inform a moral demarcation of space that targets the poor as eyesores or 'broken windows', which as Mitchell suggests in the US context, are not to be repaired but removed (2001: 83). For example, the excessive surveillance of the lifestyle of the poor is reinforced in the UK by central government making begging an arrestable offence and allowing community support officers (with the police) to detain beggars if they fail to provide specific information or refuse to move on ('New begging powers', *The Big Issue in the North* 16–22 August 2004).

'Crime prevention' practice in these cases is neither justified in a deterrent nor preventative capacity. As long as problematised groups are present surveillance performs a disciplinary function regardless of whether strictly criminal suspicion is present; and, in that sense, the preventive surveillance network contributes to the wider political pressure brought to bear on the poor, adding to the message that their presence is 'unwelcome'. Street trading, like homelessness, although not an illegal 'activity', belongs nevertheless to a category of suspicion defined by normative conceptions of place and their associated categories of 'appropriateness' within an imagined 'social' space. Surveillance as crime prevention is, in this case, mobilized so that it communicates and aids 'the rules of the game' in the regenerating city. The message is communicated thus: 'they know we are watching' (city-centre manager cited in Coleman 2004a: 186).

A focus on the discursive and material location of risk construction and risk generation raises questions of social justice in relation to the vested interests underlying political image making and of the recodification of 'the working-class city' into the desired 'classless' and performative spaces articulated by urban state representatives. Although these processes vary between cities, the powerful regeneration vernacular that accompanies these changes conceals both the class relational character of 'risk' and 'safety' discourses *and* the complex tensions within social control strategies between consent and coercion *across* the emerging state terrain. It is the discursive and material terrain of the social that is being reconfigured through complex multi-levelled spatial interventions. Risks to health, quality of life and mobility are being generated for sections of the population through the withdrawal of social support mechanisms alongside a further generation of risks that emanate *from* the practices of state surveillance, curtailing access and mobility between and within city spaces. Contemporary risk discourses and the targets they construct cannot be taken at face value and must be connected to the spatiality of the city where the materialized strategies of 'social' sovereignty undercut alternative visions of social justice and order.

Conclusion: confronting the hegemony of vision

Do not allow public issues as they are officially formulated, or troubles as they are privately felt, to determine the problems that you take up for study (Mills 1970: 248).

A radical criminological imagination in relation to the study of crime prevention can be directed *neither* by state imaginaries *nor* private troubles. However, the contingencies of, and interrelations between, both these arenas must be understood, confronted (where necessary) and even cultivated (in a progressive manner) by the independence of critical research and reasoning. This chapter has attempted to provide a discussion of crime prevention beyond conventional criminological thinking and move towards a multidisciplinary exploration of the key relations between 'crime prevention', the production of spatial order and state power. Confronting the hegemony of vision over contemporary urban space means looking beyond crime prevention techniques in order to raise questions that destabilize the parameters of 'official social control talk' (Cohen 1983) and 'the bureaucratisation of reason' (Mills 1970: 212) ensconced in the politics of city rule. In turn, this raises questions about the 'social' element of social control and leads us to consider how 'full social acceptance' is qualified, by whom and under what conditions. In this vein, the chapter has sought to draw attention to contemporary hegemonic urban visions and how state forces allied with technicians in the field of crime prevention are propagating a kind of 'illiberal practicality' (Mills 1970: 248) that limits the possibilities of social understanding. This practicality may imagine itself as 'new' and criminologists may talk of fundamental transformations in their depiction of contemporary practicalities as being divorced from moral questions and historical trajectories. However, if we attempt to grasp the spatiality of the city as a whole, then many crime prevention practices today can be understood as reworking a persistent past in relation to the construction of class, gendered and racialized identities and their negative reinforcement through shrinking the meaning of personal and public troubles down to a politico-media doxa on crime and incivility. It is in the process of socio-spatial production in the city that the 'anti-social criminologies of everyday life' (Hughes *et al.* 2002: 325) are rendered practicable.

In a Millsian sense, challenging official versions of the troubles of our time requires an imagination that problematizes prevalent 'quality of life' discourses through exposing the mythical tales told through the language of 'participation', 'partnership' and 'social inclusion' as terms deployed in the arena of crime prevention. More often than not, these linguistic tools of governing mask contemporary patterns of inequality and the desocialization of justice (Coleman 2004c). This points to a need to reignite a debate about what 'reclaiming the streets' could mean beyond its narrow criminogenic referents. Attempts to forge a consensus around the definition and response to contemporary troubles within 'the social' are themselves an important area of research. At present, consent (and to what extent this exists) around governing through limited understandings of crime highlights paucity in how the 'troubles of our times' are represented and solutions to them undertaken. It is not at all clear – and nor can we assume as official spokespersons do – that there is straightforward marriage between what the public attitude and perception is towards anti-social behaviour and that of governing authorities (Future Cities Project 2005). We need an imagination that can invert the language of power here and question, for example, what exactly is 'social' (and what the social effects are) of anti-social behaviour sweeps? Is there any alternative to the generation, by design or by accident, of urban outsiders? Alternatively, we can explore how the interface between the generation of poverty, coupled with corporate deregulation and police excesses, structures the possibilities for participation within the parameters of 'the social'. Furthermore, there is evidence to show how the present restructuring of urban state space is promoting a stabilization of opportunity structures for corporate crimes and harms, while at the same time further exposing the relatively powerless to the punitive gaze of the preventive surveillance capacity discussed in this chapter (Coleman *et al.* 2005). A radical imaginative intellectual challenge 'requires no less than the presentation of conflicting definitions of reality itself' (Mills 1970: 211) in order to raise issues for public debate. Confronting the wider hegemony of vision is a step that can aid exposure of 'the unruly forces of contemporary society itself', together with how these forces are organized through 'techniques of political domination' (Mills 1970: 20) within a contradictory entrepreneurial state.

It is not a question of describing techniques of power, but to challenge the rationalizations of powerful action and inaction that lie behind these techniques and their targeting. Such incursive probing has its roots outside a 'statist political imaginary' that has 'assisted the state in setting limits on theoretical imagination' (Neocleous 2003: 6). The discussion here has explored aspects of this state imaginary that seeks to manage cities through partial constructions of risk that fabricate, in an illiberal sense, personal and public troubles. This has been encouraged with criminology and criminologists increasingly pressured into accepting 'evidenceled policy' political rhetoric and its associated lavish funding regimes based in the Home Office in the UK (see Tombs and Whyte 2003: 26–8). Here the state has been able to close off wider theoretical research questions with a narrow re-emphasis on 'crime reduction'. As one of the leading components in crime prevention, over £250,000,000 of public money has been spent on camera surveillance between 1992 and 2002 (McCahill and Norris 2002: 2). Criminologists would do well to explore the kind of social relations and state institutions that preventive practices are reflecting and reinforcing. A consequence of being dominated by state agendas – whether couched in terms of 'regeneration' or 'crime prevention' – is that the state itself disappears off the radar of critical intellectual scrutiny. Accepting state-generated risk categories will not advance our understanding of *why* and under *what* circumstances behaviours and groups are singled out for censorious attention while other harmful activities go relatively unnoticed. Just raising such political questions furthers the 'classic tradition' of social science; a tradition that has a role in stimulating theoretical discussion and redressing a 'dwindling' sense of what 'the public' is and what it can be in the course of wider democratic debate (Mills 1970: 210–14).

Questions still remain as to the uneven nature of local developments in social control that this chapter has discussed. For example, and in contrast to analyses that have construed the localization of order, we equally need to ask how particular 'issues … transcend … local environments' (Mills 1970: 15). Exploring 'the ways in which various milieux overlap and interpenetrate to form the larger structure of social and historical life' (Mills 1970: 15) remains important in countering the fragmentation of social problems in general and the analytical tendency to localize (through sealing off) trends in urban social control in particular. 'Total' explanations of the city (or for that matter the state form) are not what is being argued for here (nor is a position being forwarded that paints a picture of a seamless web of social control), although case studies can and should contribute to more general political and theoretical debates on the relations between urban statecraft, trajectories of social control and social divisions. Raising issues from such cases and relating these to the inequities of our age may require a rethinking of the 'social' and its relationship to 'control'. As Sumner argues, we need to work out 'a vision of social counter-organization which can fire a new mode of counter-cultural cooperation' (1997: 134). A radicalized imagination can counteract state imaginaries, not merely by describing the world from the viewpoint of 'urban outsiders' but understanding how such groups are both constructed and maligned within specific state processes of social control. Denying state agency in favour of variations of a 'hollowed out' state thesis endorses a 'micro-pragmatism' and leads to a failure to question the social forces and inherited institutional forms that help pattern the meaning and trajectory of contemporary social life. The current technical fixation on urban crime prevention endorses 'the politics of immediate "relevance"' which 'is to give up on the social itself' (Sumner 1997: 134) and further reinforce the visions for city life discussed in this chapter.

Taking a Millsian imagination to 'crime prevention' discloses the latter as more than disinterested practices and instead examines these practices as conversant with a particular kind of urban spatial vision and political hegemony. Failure to question powerful blueprints for the rehabilitation of social space (in terms of *where* such rehabilitation efforts take place and who is qualified to engage in them) and their associated anti-social effects will only consolidate the illiberal practicalities characteristic of a 'post-social' and divisive city. On this understanding criminologists need to find ways of recapturing 'the social' beyond simple nostalgia and radicalise its possibilities in ways that place criminologists not merely as describers of resistant forces, but as active players in movements of resistance in and against the state. Because cities and processes of control are not simply panoptic but contain spaces 'that can agitate thought and change practices' (Amin and Thrift 2002: 130), we may well articulate arguments for the 'socialisation of criminal justice' (Hughes 1998: 156) but also be ready to probe and unearth the countervailing tendencies within prevailing materializations of urban order (Mitchell 2003). After all, what kind of cities do we imagine we want? In preference to cities governed through 'crime' – and the way the particular fixation with this category negates a path to urban habitation – must be a consideration of the possibility of socializing state institutions and spatial production more broadly in a manner that addresses inequality while also leaving spaces in which 'deviations' can be lived with and included as part of social justice debates. As this chapter implies, however, such debates will come up against a corrosive form of state institutional activity that also requires investigation if it is to be challenged. For it is here that a 'vision of a fully commodified form of social life' (Brenner and Theodore 2002: 363) threatens to degrade participation in public life in favour of mere consultocracy (Fairclough 2000). This is where the conundrum of Durkheim's 'healthy city' can be re-posed. Like his view of social control, the healthy city did not just relentlessly pursue and punish the criminal or deviant but it allowed spaces for the transgression of moral and political orthodoxies coupled with the possibilities this gave for progressive social debate and change. In this sense, 'an overgrown state' that encompasses a vision of moral inflexibility and is authoritarian rather than authoritative 'constitutes a veritable sociological monstrosity' (Durkheim 1984: liv) that must be confronted by criminologists who have a concern for 'the social' within social control.

Notes

1 This phrase is taken from the title of an article by Sharon Zukin (1996a).
2 Bourdieu speaks of a social science dominated by 'doxosophers', a term taken from Plato and referring to a form of limited intellectual endeavour that seeks to 'pose the problems of politics in the very same terms in which they are posed by businessmen, politicians and political journalists' (1998: 7). Critical social scientists should oppose doxosophers who peddle commonplaces or political orthodoxy (1998: 8).
3 This point is also made by Hille Koskela (2004) who contends that criminology needs to 'spatialize' its understandings of crime prevention practice by placing the latter in a multidisciplinary analysis of spatial production.
4 The term 'statecraft' denotes the political *processes* of state formation and, like aspects of regime theory, helps to stress the integral role of the corporation and business interests in the state-building process and the impact this has on the production of forms of socio-spatial sovereignty and the limits of democratic accountability (see Stoker 1995). Thus statecraft refers to an ongoing process of local rule that, although it cannot be understood at this spatial scale alone, signifies and articulates the political ascendancy of a set of new urban primary definers who ideologically rework and articulate the meanings and strategies for achieving 'regeneration' and a 'safer city' (Coleman 2004a).

5   In merely evaluating whether crime prevention 'works' criminology has produced a limited knowledge of the mentality and behaviour of 'the criminal' as somebody to be rationally controlled-in-space or displaced from space. This knowledge feeds the state-sponsored surveillance industry and has played a part in building a criminology led by a policy-orientated agenda, concerned with trying to find improvements in, and legitimate yet more funding of, community wardens, street camera surveillance, anti-social behaviour schemes and the like. Administrative criminologists have a mindset of 'researchers-cum-policy-entrepreneurs' (Hope 2002: 54) imbuing the criminal justice arena with a managerialist ethos that apparently heralds a break with previous thinking and takes criminological analysis into a post-state, post-ideology and post-censuring world of criminal justice practice.

6   Working within state-spatial projects and evidence-based policymaking may often mean that 'scientific discourse and method falls victim to policy pressures and values' (Hope 2004: 288). Contemporary exceptions to this pragmatic trap include the cultural criminological work exemplified in the volume edited by Ferrell *et al.* (2004). Although much of this work explicitly rejects technical approaches to crime and criminological thinking about urban space and the 'urban experience' it will still need to maintain and develop analyses of the material and political dynamics of criminalization located in the state form.

7   The market growth of camera surveillance in the UK is the largest of its kind in the world and has extended under New Labour (NL) and is now said to be worth £1.1 billion per annum. With one camera for every 14 people and the proliferation of cameras out of city centres and into the estates (not to mention schools, hospital, taxis and buses), the population of Britain are intensely watched, categorized and judged according to normative criteria that accord the prevailing politics of urban public space. Surveillance networks are being developed at a time when advanced capitalist states have masked their political agency in (de)regulating markets while at the same time extending the public visibility of state action against undesirable street activity and forms of crime. Between 1997 and March 2003 NL created 661 new criminal offences overwhelmingly focused on the street ('Turning right to wrong', *Observer* 1 August 2004). To enforce much of this legislation are street wardens working with police and businesses. The British Security Industry Association produced figures charting the growth in street warden schemes that were estimated to be worth, from business revenues alone, £267 million in 2003 (from a value of £17 million in 2001) ('Fearful middle classes turning home security into big business', *Independent* 4 December, 2004). Street cameras therefore take their place alongside other surveillance practices and the interrelationship between these domains and their impact on spatial justice are discussed later. These practices are accompanied by a complex politics of fear that

has an uneven relationship to public concerns and perceptions about crime (Hancock 2004) but nonetheless continues to legitimize crime prevention and surveillance growth and the political and financial returns to government and the security industry.

8   The position of universities in these processes of regeneration cannot be overlooked not least in their role as sponsors of city projects. The status of the university as a recognized ideological player and component in local growth coalitions is illustrated by senior university involvement in Liverpool's Capital of Culture strategy for 2008 along with academics acting as research evaluators in the implementation of regeneration and/or policing initiatives in the city. These wider symbiotic relations provide an example of the political environment in which research takes place and which can serve to bring pressure to bear upon critical work (Coleman 2003).

9   Business Improvement Districts (BIDs) were established under the Local Government and Finance Act 2003 and as the brochure of Liverpool's BID makes clear, BIDs can be 'established where businesses want them'. The self-proclaimed 'culture of cleanliness' (*ibid.*) is derivative of the Liverpool BID that includes the policing of begging, busking and other street activity, thus extending the politics of vision discussed in this chapter.

10 'Yobs' (or 'neds' as they are known in Scotland) is a governmental and media-favoured term in the UK and is used to deride young working-class males. The label comes from the nineteenth-century bourgeois 'respectable' fear of working-class boys ('yob' is back slang for 'boy') in and around the spaces of the city.

11 Operation Cordial, launched in Liverpool in May 2005, picks up on the decency-in-the-street agenda. Merseyside Police, along with a local nun and Christian brother, began street patrols to talk to, advise and arrest – if necessary – young people at risk from, or engaged in, binge drinking, firework misuse, rowdy gatherings, graffiti and littering ('Nun's war on teen drinkers', *Liverpool Echo* 26 April 2005). How developments such as this, with their evangelical underpinning, square with Tony Blair's complaint that 'we are fighting 21st century crime … with 19th century methods' is unclear (Blair cited in 'New powers to tackle drunken troublemakers', *Guardian*,30 September 2005).

12 'Scallies' here refers to working-class youths and is used by moral entrepreneurs and those concerned with order in the city to denote an individual's association with criminality, immorality and/or engagement in activity outside normal economic production. 'Chav' and 'spiv' (the latter being applied in the 1950s) are other denigrating labels used by the middle classes to attack the cultural aspiration of young working-class people.

13 My current research, conducted with Paul Jones, into policing the homeless in Liverpool (including *Big Issue* vendors and rough sleepers)

indicates that homeless people view regeneration and policing as operating hand-in-glove and replete with the message that they are not welcome in the city.

14 In Liverpool the Capital of Culture is purported to be worth £2 billion in investment in the run-up to 2008, with 14,000 new jobs created in the service industries to manage the expected growth in tourism (*City* March 2003). Key signifiers of regeneration such as gentrification and rising property values are, as Shelter point out, leading to actual increases in local homelessness ('Kids suffer in housing boom', *Liverpool Echo* December 21 2004) thus generating risk *within* the regeneration process for already vulnerable groups.

References

Amin, A. and Thrift, N. (2002) *Cities: Reimagining the Urban*. Oxford: Polity Press.

Audit Commission (2004) *Supporting People Programme: Liverpool City Council.* London: Audit Commission.

Bamfield, L. (2005) 'Making the public case for tackling poverty and inequality' in *Poverty: Journal of the Child Poverty Action Group*, 121: 5–8.

Bauman, Z. (2004) *Wasted Lives: Modernity and its Outcasts*. Cambridge: Polity Press.

Bourdieu, P. (1998) *Acts of Resistance: Against the New Myths of Our Time*. Cambridge: Polity Press.

Brenner, N. and Theodore, N. (2002) 'Cities and geographies of "actually existing neoliberalism"', *Antipode*, 24: 349–79.

Burney, E. (2004) 'Nuisance or crime? The changing uses of anti-social behaviour control', *Criminal Justice Matters*, 57: 4–5.

Cohen, S. (1983) 'Social-control talk: telling stories about correctional change', in D. Garland and P. Young (eds) *The Power to Punish: Contemporary Penality and Social Analysis*. London: Heinemann Educational.

Cohen, S. (1985) *Visions of Social Control*. Cambridge: Polity Press.

Coleman, R. (2003) 'Images from a neoliberal city: the state, surveillance and social control', in *Critical Criminology: An International Journal*, 12: 21–42.

Coleman, R. (2004a) *Reclaiming the Streets: Surveillance, Social Control and the City*. Cullompton: Willan Publishing.

Coleman, R. (2004b) 'Watching the degenerate: street camera surveillance and urban regeneration', *Local Economy*, 19: 199–211.

Coleman, R. (2004c) 'Reclaiming the streets: closed circuit television, neoliberalism and the mystification of social divisions', *Surveillance and Society*, 2 (available online at http://www.surveillance-and-society.org/).

Coleman, R. (2005) 'Surveillance in the city: primary definition and urban spatial order', *Crime, Media and Culture: An International Journal*, 1: 131–48.

Coleman, R and Sim, J. (2005) 'Contemporary statecraft and the punitive obsession: a critique of the new penology thesis', in J. Pratt *et al.* (eds) *The New Punitiveness: Current Trends, Theories and Perspectives.* Cullompton: Willan Publishing.

Coleman, R., Tombs, S. and Whyte, D. (2005) 'Capital, crime control and statecraft in the entrepreneurial city', *Urban Studies,* 42: 2511–30.

DETR (Department of the Environment, Transport and the Regions) (2000) *By Design – Urban Design in the Planning System: Towards a Better Place.* London: HMSO.

Durkheim, E. (1984) *The Division of Labour in Society.* London: Macmillan.

Fairclough, N. (2000) *New Labour, New Language?* London: Karia Press.

Feeley, M. and Simon, J. (1994) 'Actuarial justice: the emerging criminal law' in D. Nelken (ed.) *The Futures of Criminology.* London: Sage.

Ferrell, J. (2001) *Tearing Down the Streets: Adventures in Urban Anarchy.* New York, NY: Palgrave.

Ferrell, J., Hayward, K., Morrison, W. and Presdee, M. (2004) 'Fragments of a manifesto: introducing cultural criminology unleashed', in J. Ferrell *et al.* (eds) *Cultural Criminology Unleashed.* London: Glasshouse Press.

Future Cities Project (2005) *Binging on Anti-social Behaviour: The Questionable Logic of City Clean-up Campaigns.* (available online at www.futurecities. org).

Garland, D. (1996) 'The limits of the sovereign state: strategies of crime control in contemporary society', *British Journal of Criminology,* 36: 445–71.

Garland, D. (2000) 'The culture of high crime societies: some preconditions of recent law and order policies', *British Journal of Criminology,* 40: 347–75.

Gilling, D. (1997) *Crime Prevention: Theory, Policy and Practice.* London: UCL Press.

Goffman, E. (1963) *Stigma: Notes on the Management of Spoiled Identity.* Englewood Cliffs, NJ: Prentice Hall.

Grower, C. (2005) 'Inequality and crime', in M. Peelo and K. Soothill (eds) *Questioning Crime and Criminology.* Cullompton: Willan Publishing.

Hall, S. (2003) 'New Labour's double shuffle', *Soundings,* 24, Summer.

Hall, S. and Winlow, S. (2005) 'Anti-nirvana: crime, culture and instrumentalism in the age of insecurity', *Crime, Media, Culture: An International Journal,* 1, No. 1: 31–48.

Hancock, L. (2004) 'Criminal justice, public opinion, fear and popular politics', in J. Muncie and D. Wilson (eds) *Student Handbook of Criminal Justice and Criminology.* London: Cavendish.

Hayward, K. (2004) *City Limits: Crime, Consumer Culture and Urban Experience.* London: Glasshouse Press.

Hayward, K. and Young, J. (2004) 'Cultural criminology: some notes on the script', *Theoretical Criminology*, 8: 259–73.

Hills, J. and Stewart, K. (2005) *A More Equal Society? New Labour, Poverty and Exclusion*. Bristol: Policy Press.

Home Office (2003a) *Building Civic Renewal*. London: HMSO.

Home Office (2003b) *Respect and Responsibility: Taking a Stand against anti-social Behaviour* (CM5778). London: HMSO.

Home Office (2005) *The Impact of CCTV: Fourteen Case Studies* (online report 15/05).

Hope, T. (2002) 'The road taken: evaluation, replication and crime reduction', in G. Hughes *et al.* (eds) *Crime Prevention and Community Safety: New Directions*. Buckingham: Open University Press.

Hope, T. (2004) 'Pretend it works: evidence and governance in the evaluation of the Reducing Burglary Initiative', *Criminal Justice*, 4: 287–308.

Hudson, B. (2001) 'Punishment, rights and difference: defending justice in the risk society', in K. Stenson and R. Sullivan (eds) *Crime, Risk and Justice*. Cullompton: Willan Publishing.

Hughes, G. (1998) *Understanding Crime Prevention: Social Control, Risk and Late Modernity*. Buckingham: Open University Press.

Hughes, G., McLaughlin, E. and Muncie, J. (2002) 'Teetering on the edge: the futures of crime control and community safety', in G. Hughes *et al.* (eds) *Crime Prevention and Community Safety: New Directions*. London: Sage.

Imrie, R. and Raco, M. (2003) 'Community and changing nature of urban policy', in R. Imrie and M. Raco (eds) *Urban Renaissance? New Labour, Community and Urban Policy*. Bristol: Policy Press.

Jessop, B. (1997) 'The entrepreneurial city: re-imaging localities, redesigning economic governance, or restructuring capital?', in N. Jewson and S. MacGregor (eds) *Transforming Cities: Contested Governance and New Spatial Divisions*. London: Routledge.

Koskela, H. (2004) 'Urban exclusion and criminological thought: spatialising criminology'. Paper presented to the European Group for the Study of Deviance and Social Control, Bristol, September.

Lefebvre, H. (1991) *The Production of Space*. London: Blackwell.

Lefebvre, H. (2003) 'Space and the state' in N. Brenner *et al.* (eds) *State/Space: A Reader*. Oxford: Blackwell.

McCahill, M. and Norris, C. (2002) *CCTV in Britain. Working Paper 3: Urban Eye* (available online at www.urbaneye.net/results/eu_wp3.pdf).

Mills, C.W. (1970) *The Sociological Imagination*. Harmondsworth: Penguin Books.

Mitchell, D. (2001) 'Postmodern geographical praxis? Postmodern impulse and the war against homeless people in the "postjustice" city', in C. Minca (ed.) *Postmodern Geography: Theory and Praxis*. Oxford: Blackwell.

Mitchell, D. (2003) *The Right to the City: Social Justice and the Fight for Public Space*. New York, NY: Guilford Press.

NACRO (2002) *To CCTV or not to CCTV? Current Review of Research into the Effectiveness of CCTV Systems in Reducing Crime.* London: NACRO.

Neocleous, M. (2003) *Imagining the State.* Buckingham: Open University Press.

Peck, J. (2001) 'Neoliberalizing states: thin policies/hard outcomes', *Progress in Human Geography,* 25: 445–55.

Rose, N. (1996) 'Governing "advanced" liberal democracies', in A. Barry *et al.* (eds) *Foucault and Political Reason: Liberalism, Neo-liberalism and Rationalities of Government.* London: UCL Press.

Rose, N. (2000) 'Government and control', *British Journal of Criminology,* 40: 321–39.

Sassen, S. (2000) 'New frontiers facing urban sociology at the millennium', *British Journal of Sociology,* 51: 143–59.

Sayer, A. (1999) *Long Live Postdisciplinary Studies! Sociology and the Curse of Parochialism/Imperialism.* Department of Sociology, Lancaster University (available online at: http://www.comp.lancs.ac.uk/sociology/papers/Sayer-Long-Live-Postdiciplinary-Studies.pdf).

Shearing, C.D. (2001) 'Punishment and the changing face of governance', *Punishment and Society,* 3: 203–20.

Shearing, C.D. and Stenning, P.C. (1985) 'Private security: implications for social control', *Social Problems,* 30: 493–506.

Simon, J. and Feeley, M. (2003) 'The form and limits of the new penology', in T. Blomberg and S. Cohen (eds) *Punishment and Social Control* (2nd edn). New York, NY: Aldine De Gruyter.

Skeggs, B. (2004) *Class, Self, Culture.* London: Routledge.

Skeggs, B. (2005) 'The making of class and gender through visualizing moral subject formation', *Sociology,* 39: 965–82.

Stenson, K. (2005) 'Sovereignty, biopolitics and the local government of crime in Britain', *Theoretical Criminology,* 9: 265–86.

Stoker, G. (1995) 'Regime theory and urban politics', in D. Judge *et al.* (eds) *Theories of Urban Politics.* London: Sage.

Sumner, C. (1994) *The Sociology of Deviance: An Obituary.* Buckingham: Open University Press.

Sumner, C. (1997) 'The decline of social control and the rise of vocabularies of struggle', in R. Bergalli and C. Sumner (eds) *Social Control and Political Order: European Perspectives at the End of the Century.* London: Sage.

Tilley, N. (1998) 'Evaluating the effectiveness of CCTV schemes', in C. Norris *et al.* (eds) *Surveillance, Closed Circuit Television and Social Control.* Aldershot: Ashgate.

Tombs, S. and Whyte, D. (2003) 'Scrutinising the powerful? Crime, contemporary political economy and critical social research', in S. Tombs and D. Whyte (eds) *Researching the Crimes of the Powerful: Scrutinising States and Corporations.* New York, NY: Peter Lang.

Urry, J. (1995) *Consuming Places.* London: Routledge.

Wacquant, L. (1999) 'How penal common sense comes to Europeans: notes on the transatlantic diffusion of the neo-liberal doxa', *European Societies*, 1: 319–52.

Watkins, S. (2004) 'A weightless hegemony', *New Left Review*, 25: 5–33.

Zukin, S. (1996a) 'Cultural strategies of economic development and the hegemony of vision,' in A. Merrifield and E. Syngedouw (eds) *The Urbanization of Injustice*. London: Lawrence & Winshart.

Zukin, S. (1996b) 'Space and symbols in an age of decline', in A.D. King (ed) *Re-presenting the City: Ethnicity, Capital and Culture in the 21st Century Metropolis*. London: Macmillan.

Chapter 4

The 'worse' of two evils?[1] Double murder trials and gender in England and Wales, 1900–53

Anette Ballinger

> It is the work of feminism to deconstruct the naturalistic, genderblind discourse of law by constantly revealing the context in which it has been constituted and drawing parallels with other areas of social life. Law is not a free-floating entity, it is grounded in patriarchy (Smart 1989: 88).

During the twentieth century, 15 women were executed in England and Wales. Seven of them stood trial with an accomplice. In one case both defendants were women, and both were executed. The remaining five women stood trial with their male partners. Two of these double trials also led to double executions. However, in the remaining three cases, the men left court as free individuals, leaving their partners to face the scaffold alone.

In analysing such disparities in trial outcomes this chapter argues that explanations focusing on proof beyond reasonable doubt, due process and the rule of law are fundamentally inadequate because such legalistic terms ignore the social construction of femininity and masculinity which had a crucial impact on the final outcomes of these cases. This case-study approach is therefore not intended to be a contribution to the 'leniency *v.* harshness' debate regarding women's punishment compared with men's, because it is not simply a matter of law working in the interests of men, while oppressing women. Rather the issue is law's ability to produce and reproduce the gendered subject as well as its role in constructing and reconstructing masculinity and femininity (Smart 1995: 79). Thus, this chapter offers a critical analysis and deconstruction of law's truth-claims as well as evidence of the very real and deadly impact such claims had on the final outcome of double trials. More specifically, the analytical tools employed will be those of feminist theory and epistemology developed over recent decades, which will be applied retrospectively to these cases in order to gain a full understanding of the trial outcomes. As such, the chapter provides an example of the impact feminism has had on the 'new criminological imagination' which consequently has had to expand its parameters to include this subjugated knowledge generated from 'below'. The significance of this impact stretches far beyond mere academic exercising, for once uncovered, this knowledge can provide a new site from which critical criminology generally, and feminist analysis in particular, can challenge traditional criminological theory as well as the policies which flow from such theory, as I shall indicate in the conclusion to this chapter.

Law, truth and the social construction of femininity and masculinity

For nearly three decades feminist theorists have contributed to the 'criminological imagination' by challenging the truth-claims of traditional criminology – for example, by exposing and discrediting the biologically determined nature of its theories and instead emphasizing the social construction of the 'natural' woman so often referred to in traditional criminological theory (Sydie 1987; Smart 1995: 83). It has also developed a substantial body of work which challenges law's truth-claims – the idea that law always 'gives rise to a correct interpretation or even a direct access to the truth which avoids the problems of human interpretation' and is thus infallible when it comes to discovering and establishing *the* truth about events (Smart 1989: 10; 1995: 74). At an epistemological level, Smart (1989, 1995) has demonstrated that law's claim to neutrality, objectivity and fairness has been arrived at by aligning itself with the Enlightenment discourses of science, rationality and reason which are phallocentric in nature and hence reflect male interests and values. Law's as well as traditional criminology's alignment with these scientific principles means that their claims to speak the 'truth' are favoured over non-scientific truth-claims such as the defendant's commonsense knowledge and biographical and experiential truths which 'are easily undermined by experts' versions of events' (Ballinger 2003: 221; see also Smart 1995). Moreover, law's and traditional criminological theories' support for the construction of women as inherently irrational and illogical – their minds unscientific in nature – helps to ensure that the evidence of female defendants will not be heard through the discourses of authority and scientific 'truth': 'The dominant discourses associated with authority ensure women's exclusion from it by silencing "those forms of expression linked metaphorically and symbolically to 'female' speech'", especially those around "emotive connectedness or compassion"' (Jones 1988: 120 cited in Ballinger 2000: 60).

In contrast, 'knowledge which can claim to be [scientifically] true ... occupies a place high up in the hierarchy of knowledges. The claim to truth is therefore a claim to deploy power' – for example, by disqualifying subjugated knowledges (Smart 1989: 72). Such knowledge becomes 'muted', while the power of law increases. If members of muted groups wish to be 'heard' within the courtroom, they must communicate through 'the dominant modes of expression' (Worrall 1990: 11). That is to say, the defendant must mediate her account into one that is acceptable to the court:

> Everyday experiences must be translated into another form in order to become 'legal' issues and before they can be processed through the legal system ... So legal process translates everyday experience into legal relevances, it excludes a great deal that might be relevant to the parties ... [who] are not always silenced, but ... how they are allowed to speak and how their experience is turned into something that law can digest and process is a demonstration of the power of law to disqualify alternative accounts (Smart 1989: 11).

However, it is not only the defendant's verbal account which must be tailored to the requirements of 'dominant modes of expression', but also her character and conduct. Hence, at a theoretical level, several writers have documented the centrality of women's conduct within our culture and how those who transgress patriarchal definitions of acceptable and appropriate feminine behaviour become regarded as 'dangerous' and 'unruly' – a threat to patriarchal hegemony (Carlen 1985; Heidensohn 1986; Jones 1991). In particular, discourses around motherhood, domesticity, respectability and sexuality have been shown to play a crucial role in the social construction of femininity and hence in defining the 'good' woman – someone who is firmly located within the family and who *by nature* is maternal, caring, gentle, modest, unselfish and passive. While such discourses affect all women, female law-breakers in particular will automatically be identified as failures in terms of fulfilling gender role expectations. Furthermore, if her criminality is overlaid by a lack of conformity to acceptable moral standards within these discourses, the woman defendant becomes 'doubly deviant' which in turn may result in her being judged by 'double standards' (Smart and Smart 1978: 3). Law, and indeed the wider criminal justice system in which it is situated, can therefore be understood as being deeply implicated in both producing and re-producing what may be termed 'idealized femininity'[2] by constructing those who fall outside ideal womanhood as unruly, threatening and dangerous and punishing them accordingly.

Using the concepts of double deviance and double standards as starting-points of their analysis, feminist theorists have consistently challenged traditional criminology's and law's truth-claims by demonstrating that they are neither scientific nor objective; instead, they both take a great deal of notice of what 'type' of woman the defendant is (Worrall 1981; Carlen 1983; Morris 1987; Naffine 1990; Smart 1995).

Overall, therefore, feminist writers have over the past three decades contributed to the 'criminological imagination' by documenting how female defendants are constructed as doubly deviant because they are not only judged according to their crimes, but also according to how they have conducted themselves as women – especially in the areas of motherhood, respectability, sexuality and domesticity:

> The majority of women who go to prison are sentenced not according to the seriousness of their crimes but primarily according to the courts' assessment of them as wives, mothers and daughters (Carlen 1988: 10).

Thus, several writers (Heidensohn 1986; Morris 1987; Naffine 1990) have argued that 'a woman's conduct may come under closer scrutiny than her criminality, and in turn play an important part in determining the severity of her sentence' (Ballinger 2000: 53). In short, such women are likely to find themselves at the receiving end of 'judicial misogyny' (Carlen 1985: 10).

The impact of judicial misogyny and the consequences of breaking the rules governing idealized femininity on the verdicts of all 15 women executed in England and Wales during the twentieth century have been documented elsewhere (Ballinger 2000). Applying contemporary feminist theory to historical data, this chapter develops that analysis, and hence expands the criminological imagination, by arguing that the impact of idealized femininity – especially in relation to the focus on the woman's character and reputation – becomes particularly noticeable in cases of double trials involving a male and female defendant. That is to say, these double trials provide obvious examples of 'doubly deviant' women being judged, sentenced and executed as a result of 'double standards' – rather than according to legal evidence and the rule of law. As such it may be argued they were 'doubly disqualified', as speakers (and actors) compared with their male co-defendants who did not *stand apart from, but formed a part of*, the phallocentric courtroom. Yet, commonsensical notions of what it means to be a 'good' and 'natural' woman – reinforced by the authority of law which places such notions within legal-'scientific' discourses – were so dominant that disparities in verdicts involving the difference between life and death caused barely a ruffle within either the criminal justice system or the public consciousness.

Meanwhile, as a result of the social construction of masculinity, the men who stood trial with their partners in the cases examined below were only ever 'partially' deviant and – unlike their women – never without redeeming features. This is because, unlike femininity and criminality, masculinity and criminality are not in direct conflict with each other – rather, criminality may be understood as an extension or exaggeration of masculinity. Anger, uncontrollable urges and desires, loss of self-control, violent aggression, the right to respond to provocation are all intrinsic components of *normal* masculinity; when such behaviours spill into criminal behaviour, no one expresses outrage, disbelief or even surprise. Quite the reverse in fact, for, as Collier has noted: 'it has been primarily from *within a discourse of crime - and not the family* – that men have been understood to be constituted as masculine in the first place' (1998: 76, emphasis in original).

In other words, the social construction of masculinity has ensured that men's *capacity* for crime in general and violence in particular is never questioned because such behaviour is not in conflict with 'normal' masculine behaviour. As Collier observed, even cases of extreme violence against children carried out on a massive scale such as the Dunblane massacre which involved Thomas Hamilton murdering sixteen 5- and 6-year-old children as well as their teacher, can be rationalized and explained by referring to 'the failed man' – that is, once 'notions of masculine failure' are raised, we understand 'what made him do it' (Collier 1998: 113). The idea that men's damaged egos may potentially give rise to extreme violence – even mass murder – thus appears to be both accepted and normalized. Meanwhile, as a result of the construction of femininity being inextricably connected to women's caring role within the family, the crimes of women such as Myra Hindley cannot be rationalized through her failure as a woman. Hindley's 'failure' as a woman *was* her crime, not the events beforehand.

In terms of the two remaining discourses discussed above in relation to femininity – respectability and sexuality – such is the contrast between the construction of femininity and masculinity within our culture that our language does not contain terms in which we can express loss of male respectability as a result of sexual promiscuity or flirtatious behaviour. On the contrary, a male who appears to be lacking in prowess and sexual virility poses a bigger threat to the construction of masculinity than the over-enthusiastic male who lavishes unwanted attention on his female 'prey' (Smart 1989: 42). Moreover, it is women who are held responsible for men's uncontrollable urges and told to be careful not to inflame 'the desires of men' (Smart 1995: 80), whereas negative descriptions of male promiscuity are noted mainly for their absence (Lees 1993: 28).

The impact of such discourses around masculinity and femininity does not disappear when men stand on opposite sides of the bench in the courtroom. In the trials analysed below the criminal justice system was overwhelmingly represented by men; in some cases exclusively so. In such cases the woman's co-accused shared the characteristics of dominant constructions of masculinity with the criminal justice personnel within the courtroom; in that sense – despite the obvious differences in social class – the male accused and his accusers stood on the same terrain of masculinity, and as such had more in common with each other than the two defendants had.

Yet, as stated above, explanations which focus on law operating in the interests of men, while oppressing women, are too simplistic. This is because an acceptance of the 'male-as-yardstick' is implicit to this explanation, which hides the taken-for-granted assumption that *men* always receive justice, and that we can somehow 'measure' how women are different. Instead the case studies below will demonstrate that law's truth-claims are androcentric in their very premise (Cain 1990: 2), something which becomes particularly visible when both genders are constructed against *each other*.

'Judicial misogyny': five case studies of executed women

The case of Ada and William Williams

The first case to be examined is that of Ada and William Williams, a married couple who stood trial in 1900 for the murder of Selina Jones, a toddler they had obtained through their baby-farming activities. Baby-farmers were despised and stigmatized because their 'existence emphasised the contradictions between dominant images of idealized motherhood, and its reality for those women whose circumstances did not fit this image' such as mothers of illegitimate children who found it a financial impossibility to support their child (Ballinger 2000: 65). Moreover, the baby-farmer herself had transgressed the social construction of motherhood as an innate quality performed by instinct, because taking money for what should be given 'for free in the name of love' is unfeminine and unruly (Smart 1995: 227). Meanwhile, as argued by Cameron (1996: 26–27), the construction of masculinity does not contain similar or equivalent discourses around fatherhood; hence, men's involvement in baby-farming could not be heard through discourses of 'deviant fatherhood'.

The consequences of such constructions of masculinity and femininity became evident, first, when the jury found only Ada guilty of murder and second, in the extensive communications taking place among Home Office personnel after the verdict, whose responsibility it was to decide whether she should be reprieved or hanged. Thus, while they recognized William 'might even have played the dominant part', Ada's role in the crime 'was nevertheless constructed as "worse" since she had also committed transgressions against the "natural" woman and her maternal instinct' (Ballinger 2003: 234). Not only had she entered the despicable trade of baby-farming, but there was also evidence that other children within the Williams household had been abused and neglected – indeed one of them had died (HO144/280XC17335). Yet, the children had been in the care of both the Williamses, but unlike William whose parental skills remained unexplored, 'Ada was on trial not only for murder, but also as a mother' (Ballinger 2003: 234).

Furthermore, despite being half William's age, and uneducated, Ada was constructed as the dominant and manipulative partner in the marriage despite William's status as an ex-Cambridge scholar:

'Mrs Williams was one of those women who exercise great influence over men, and who are thoroughly alive to the extent of their power ... she ... ruled her husband through the medium of this same influence' (Adam 1911: 199–200).

Ada had in fact been forced to seek paid work due to William's hearing disability, yet her acquisition of the masculinist status of 'bread-winner' ensured she was constructed as having transgressed a second discourse of femininity – that of the submissive wife recognizing her husband's authority. Thus, Ada displayed all the symptoms of an unruly wife who did 'not show appropriate deference to her husband' and as such 'disrupted the ideal image of passive and self-effacing femininity' and instead came to represent 'a threat to patriarchal hegemony' within the phallocentric courtroom (Ballinger 2000: 69). In short, while Ada was portrayed as a dangerous mother-figure, and a bad-tempered 'battleaxe' who ruled her 'hen-pecked' husband, William increasingly gained the status as another of Ada's victims. Taken together with his disability and subsequent failure to work, his 'meek' demeanour and 'dog-like devotion' to Ada (Adam 1911: 201), William came to be understood through the discourse of 'the failed man' – a sympathetic figure whose downfall was the result of Ada's domineering and manipulative behaviour.

Yet, the actual evidence suggested the exact opposite. The couple's baby-farming activities were only discovered as a result of a letter written by Ada and sent to the police, proclaiming their innocence. In particular, it exonerated William:

> I must tell you that my husband is not to blame in any way whatever, he has always looked upon the whole matter from the first with the greatest abhorrence but only gave way to me because he was, through illness, not of employment, he never, however, once touched any of the money I made by these means [baby-farming] (CRIM 1/59/4).

The significance of this letter was noted by Home Office personnel who were deliberating whether Ada deserved a reprieve:

> The letter read as if it were the composition of *her husband* an educated man rather than hers. There is not a little evidence to show by whose hand the child met its death whether by the man or woman (HO144/280/A61654).

Indeed, all the evidence against both defendants was purely circumstantial, and not a single piece suggested that one – rather than the other – had been the main perpetrator in this crime. Hence, judgements about Ada's role in the murder were not reached as a result of evidence tested in court, but based on what was known about her character:

> From what H.O. has heard from outside sources … it would appear that the woman is hot-tempered, violent and hysterical; the man meek and small, and so the *probabilities* are in favour of the murder having been committed by the woman, while the tying up knots &c. were *probably* done by the man (HO144/280/A61654, emphasis added).

Probabilities are, of course, not evidence, and the Permanent Under-Secretary Sir Kenelm Digby indicated that the *actual evidence* was indeed inconclusive:

> It is difficult to believe that this was done by the prisoner unaided and alone. Taken in connection with their previous history it appears to me that here is a very grave case of suspicion … *that the husband as well as the wife was concerned in this wicked work. There is evidence connecting him with the murder* … On the whole … *there seems very little to distinguish between the two cases.* The jury might in my opinion have nearly as much justification for drawing an unfavourable view in his case as in his wife's (HO144/280/A61654, emphasis added).

Other state servants also indicated their unease at the prospect of executing Ada while releasing William:

> Can it be fairly said that it is more than a *probability* that this is the true explanation; and would it be safe to hang the woman when *we are absolutely in the dark* as to whether it was her hand that actually committed murder, and when possibly at the last minute the husband might come forward and say 'I did it', and it would be impossible to prove that he was not speaking the truth (HO144/280/A61654, emphasis added).

One Home Office staff member went so far as to suggest that is was William – not Ada – who had committed the murder:

> I am in doubt … whether the hands were those of the husband or of the wife, and I confess it seems to me the more closely I examine the exhibits before me as I write, *that the work is more probably that of the man than of the woman* (HO144/280/A61654, emphasis added).

It is not surprising that Home Office personnel expressed such concerns, because in view of William's education and age compared with Ada's – together with the contents of the letter supposedly written by Ada – it is difficult to discern her motive in writing a letter which drew attention to her baby-farming activities while exonerating him, but of course easy to understand William's motivation. In other words, the *evidence* suggested it was *William* who was manipulating Ada, rather than the reverse. Yet, so powerful were the discourses mobilized around Ada as a deviant mother and unruly wife that even though state servants acknowledged that evidence, they were also prepared to take responsibility for Ada's execution and William's release. That such a conclusion could be reached is a testimony to law's ability to reproduce and preserve the construction of idealized femininity as well as its willingness to utilize judicial misogyny in its most extreme form towards women who challenge that construction. That is to say, this double trial has illustrated 'how Ada was treated *differentially*, not as a result of different evidence, but as a result of different gender expectations'; hence this differentiation was not based on legal evidence, 'but on how she was perceived as a woman … a wife and a mother' (Ballinger 2000: 78). Meanwhile, the fact that William 'had led a wild and roving life' (HO144/280/A61654), that he was a 'failed' man in terms of his work and business ventures,[3] that he had failed to discipline his unruly and 'uppity' wife, that Home Office staff suspected he had manipulated Ada into writing the letter which ultimately led to her execution and his freedom, and that – crucially – his role in the crime might have been equal or dominant to Ada's role, did nothing to disturb the discourses around appropriate masculinity. Rather, William's deviation from dominant masculinity *increased* sympathy for him, as when attention was drawn to his participation in childcare responsibilities: '[he] did his best to care for the foster children … He saw that they were fed and washed and no father could have been kinder' (HO144/280/A61654).

William's portrayal as a caring, devoted father 'doing his best' emphasized Ada's failure to conform to appropriate femininity and increased the ideological gulf between them – apart from having to contend with Ada's unruliness he was even making up for her failures by carrying out her duties and responsibilities. Furthermore, William himself emphasized the shared terrain of masculinity on which he and courtroom personnel stood, and from which Ada was excluded and constructed, against, when he wrote to the Home Secretary that he 'ought to have exercised a more wholesome influence over her moral nature' (HO144/280/A61654).

In sum, a feminist analysis of the Williams case presents a strong challenge to law's claim to neutrality, objectivity and fairness and its consequent claim to establishing 'the truth'. Instead this case has demonstrated that legal knowledge and 'truth' are socially constructed, much like any other type of knowledge. Thus, the final verdict was not reached after establishing conclusive evidence tested within an impartial courtroom. Instead discourses around femininity and masculinity were competing with circumstantial evidence in a battle to establish what was to become the dominant truth about this case generally, and about Ada as a woman in particular. The fact that the criminal justice personnel involved in the final decision about the couple's punishment acknowledged the evidence could not distinguish between the roles that each had played in the crime, while *simultaneously* accepting and permitting Ada's execution and William's release, is a stark reminder of the power such discourses carry.

The case of Dorothea Waddingham and Joe Sullivan

The second case to be examined involves Dorothea Waddingham and Joe Sullivan who stood trial in Nottingham in 1936 for the murder of Ada Baguley, a 50-year-old disabled resident in the nursing home the couple ran. Ada had entered the home with her 87-year-old mother Louisa in January 1935. In May, Louisa signed a will stipulating that Dorothea and Joe were to inherit the Baguley estate after the women's deaths in exchange for their care (ASSI13/66XC6872). Louisa died five days after signing the will, and within four months Ada too was dead. As in the previous case study, suspicion was aroused by a letter, in this case handed to the Coroner by Joe, supposedly from Ada: 'I desire to be cremated at my death for health's sake. It is my wish to remain with nurse and my last wish is that my relatives shall not know of my death' (ASSI13/66XC6872).

The letter had originally ended after the word 'nurse', and the following line – referring to Ada's 'last wish' – had been squeezed between the original letter and Ada's supposed signature; however, it was clearly in Joe's handwriting. Other circumstantial evidence against Joe included, first, he contacted a solicitor and arranged for the will to be written (ASSI13/66XC6872). Second, he admitted writing the above letter, but claimed it had been at Ada's request. Third, he had written to Ada's cousin, again claiming it had been at her request:

> I do not like you saying what you did about Joe as he is kindness itself to me and my mother [.] He is the only one who has done anything for us, and is kindness itself ... You need not worry about me as everything is all right.

Underneath, Joe had issued a threat on his own behalf:

> I should like to know what you mean about that chap you call Jos Has you all him [sic] if ever you cross my path you will know what that means there is always straight-forwardness carried out here, and mark my word we know what you have been trying to do, but if you are not careful you will regret it, so keep your eyes open in future, and Miss Baguley is quite aware of my writing this (ASSI13/66XC6872; HO144/20185).

Fourth, according to several witnesses Joe had played the leading role in keeping visitors away from the Baguleys which the court interpreted as an attempt to ensure no one had the opportunity to interfere with the will (ASSI13/66XC6872). Fifth, he collected the rent for the Baguleys' properties, and solicitor's clerk J.K. Lane gave further confirmation of Joe's involvement in Ada's financial affairs (ASSI13/66XC6872). Sixth, Joe had accompanied Ada when she withdrew all her money for her bank (ASSI13/66XC6872). Seventh, it was he who called the doctor when Ada was on her deathbed after having spent the entire night with her. He had also been present when Louisa died. Finally, Joe was in charge of all funeral arrangements, and signed the appropriate documentation (ASSI13/66XC6872; *The Times* 6 and 26 February 1936).

Circumstantial evidence pointing towards Joe's involvement in Ada's death was therefore abundant. Yet, before he had given evidence, the judge ordered that charges be dropped against him due to *lack* of evidence:

> The only evidence at present is that Sullivan was in this house, assisting in taking about the patients, raising them in bed,

wheeling them about, and doing household work. There is no evidence that he was interested in the house, no evidence as to the relationship of the prisoner, no evidence except what has been given here that he was in the position of servant ... it could not be said that even if every word of the evidence were accepted it raises a case of more than ... Sullivan ... may have been connected with the matter and not that he must have been (quoted in *Manchester Evening News* 26 February 1936; *The Times* 27 February 1936; see also HO144/20185).

Crucially, however, there was no evidence that Dorothea had ever intended to kill either. As had been the case with the Williamses, not a single piece of forensic or circumstantial evidence proved beyond reasonable doubt that one of the accused rather than the other, had committed or had been the dominant partner in this crime. On the contrary, they had identical motives and opportunity to commit the crime. Indeed, unlike all the evidence against Joe, the only circumstantial evidence against Dorothea was her position as matron, while he – as her 'assistant' – was her subordinate. Even this deduction may be regarded as dubious for, despite the judge's claim that there was 'no evidence as to the relationship of the prisoner', Joe had fathered Dorothea's two youngest children, suggesting that his position went beyond that of 'assistant'.[4]

However, Dorothea's case – unlike Joe's – was heard through the discourses of 'carer' and 'poisoner'. The key point here is the close relationship between the construction of femininity and the assumption that caring for others – children, the weak and the sick – is an innate quality in women. In being accused of killing someone she was paid to care for – and worse still, a frail, helpless invalid (*sic*) woman – Dorothea had transgressed one of the fundamental rules of femininity. Furthermore, her murder method exacerbated her transgression even beyond doubly deviant status, because – despite numerous cases involving male poisoners (Watson 2004) – poisoning has historically been regarded as a 'woman's weapon'. The female poisoner was a particularly threatening figure since not only had she abused her domestic role as the provider of nourishment for her family, but she had also subverted the ideology of women's innate caring nature, resulting in her construction as 'sneaky' and 'lethal' (Adam 1911: 3; Jones 1991: 81–2). Dorothea fitted this image of the duplicitous, hypocritical female precisely because she gave the appearance of a hapless, naive, 'ordinary, capable-looking woman, with a face like an amiable sheep's' (Wilson 1971: 283, 288); yet, according to the prosecution – and in keeping with the androcentric nature of traditional criminological theory at the time – underneath this exterior lurked a dangerous and cunning female who secretly harboured poisonous urges so strong that she was capable of killing a helpless invalid (*sic*).

However, while the discourses around Dorothea as a female poisoner and deviant carer were now firmly in place, actual evidence remained minimal, often based on no more than insinuations by disappointed relatives of the Baguleys who had seen what they considered *their* inheritance slip away. For example, relatives admitted that it was Ada herself – not Dorothea and Joe – who had refused to maintain contact with her relatives, and that conflict between the family and Dorothea and Joe had arisen as a result of concern over losing their future inheritance, not over the quality of care Ada and Louisa received. On the contrary, several witnesses testified that the two women 'were happy and comfortable at Devon Drive' (ASSI13/ 66XC6872; HO144/20185).

Ultimately, the sole piece of evidence which affected Dorothea sprang from her own testimony – namely, that Dr Manfield had given her ten morphia tablets to be administered at her discretion, which he denied. Thus, she did not deny giving medication to Ada, only that she did so with intent to murder. Dorothea claimed the tablets had been administered according to Dr Manfield's instructions which – if proved accurate – could have serious consequences for the doctor's professional credibility.

Conversely, while Dr Manfield's professional status placed him well above Dorothea in the hierarchy of credibility, evidence nevertheless emerged which cast doubt over his professional conduct. First, while he proposed that Dorothea must have poisoned Ada with tablets left over from other patients' prescriptions, he also admitted that she had in fact returned such tablets to him following the deaths of these patients (HO144/20185; *The Times* 13 and 26 February 1936). Second, he admitted that he had made a mistake regarding Ada's dosage of medicine on a previous occasion:

> I suppose doctor, it would be no exaggeration to call that a blunder, would it? – Well, I suppose the best of us make blunders at times, I am not going to commit myself.
> Mr Smith repeated his question, and Dr Manfield exclaimed 'I am not going to answer that question. Why should I?' …
> In view of the fact that you had given medicine 300% weaker in

morphia that day, you left at the same time six morphia tablets?
No, I did not (quoted in *The Times* 12 February 1936).

Third, the doctor had omitted to leave instructions on the prescription, and hence none were given on the bottle (*The Times* 12 February 1936). Fourth, the autopsy revealed 'gross neglect in regard to one of … [Ada's] bed sores', and the pathologist subsequently challenged Dr Manfield's claim that 'proper treatment was given' (quoted in *The Times* 14 February 1936; see also HO144/20185). Finally, he had demonstrated a lack of good judgement when he gave Dorothea's son empty medicine bottles to play with (*The Times* 13 February 1936).

The professional conduct of the police surgeon and his staff who carried out the autopsy was also thrown into disrepute when it was revealed that 'there was no representative of Nurse Waddingham there and no opportunity for anybody on her behalf to check whatever results … [were] arrived at'. The organs of the deceased had subsequently been destroyed without the defence having been offered this opportunity (quoted in *The Times* 26 February 1936; see also HO144/20185). Moreover, procedures had not been followed when handling the organs required for examination; hence, jars had not been covered or even labelled, and various organs had been mixed together resulting in Dr Owen-Taylor admitting: 'I cannot say that the organs I examined and in which I found 3.192 grains of morphia are the organs of Miss Baguley' (quoted in *The Times* 15 February 1936).

Thus, given the lack of direct evidence and the highly problematic nature of the circumstantial evidence against Dorothea, together with the sloppy and unprofessional conduct of the various professionals involved, why was her case not dismissed on similar grounds to Joe's? Why was the evidence against Dorothea considered safe, yet the evidence against Joe unsafe?

As documented above, Joe's role as a carer was as prominent as Dorothea's, yet carried no significance for the judge who unreservedly accepted her access to patients as providing an opportunity for murder, but refused to apply the same reasoning to Joe. Hence, it was not *lack of evidence* but *lack of discourses* through which that evidence could be heard which led to Joe's freedom. For while the case against Dorothea was heard and understood through the discourses of the female poisoner and carer, it is the *absence* of such discourses in Joe's case which is noteworthy. Joe's transgression of the masculine role in terms of working for a woman as a domestic servant – ensuring his status as her subordinate – carried none of the negative connotations associated with female transgression of *their* gender role as seen in the earlier case of Ada Williams – whose economic resourcefulness and bread-winner status collided with dominant images of femininity. Instead, the very opposite process took place – that is, powerful attempts were made to re-establish Joe's masculinity. For example, immediately prior to his case being dismissed, a police detective described him as 'a man of first-class character ... [who had] gained the Military Medal for conspicuous bravery in rescuing a wounded officer' (quoted in *The Times* 27 February 1936; see also HO144/20185). Thus, on the one hand – despite the evidence of his involvement listed above – his position as a subordinate servant who merely 'mended the fires [and] swept the floors' was emphasized to support his innocence (*The Times* 27 February 1936; Huggett and Berry 1956: 119). On the other hand, he was immediately re-masculized according to codes of acceptable masculinity such as those established through the 'war-hero' who is characterized by his bravery and fearlessness, yet also 'gentle with the weak' (Girouard cited in Benyon 2002: 29).

Unlike William Williams, Joe was therefore not understood as 'a failed man' but as a brave hero whose construction against Dorothea emphasized his innocence and her guilt, for as Collier has argued in a different context: 'Far from being the main players in this crimino-familial narrative, it is the men who fade into the background, setting the scene for the women to care, to fail and to be judged' (1998: 97).

Joe's construction *against* Dorothea ensured that just as William was not judged as a father, so Joe was not judged as a carer. Thus, while both men had transgressed dominant modes of masculinity, neither experienced the detrimental consequences of this, in sharp contrast to their partners whose transgression of their gender roles activated the double-standards which emphasized their double-deviance, and which ultimately ensured that these double-trials would conclude *without* double-executions.

The purpose of this analysis is not to suggest that William and Joe should also have been executed, or that Ada and Dorothea played no role in the crimes, but to emphasize 'the specific and unique way' such women come to be understood – through the legal process – 'as a result of gender role expectations' (Ballinger 2000: 177). Thus, Dorothea's positioning within the established discourses of woman-carer and woman-poisoner overrode the legal evidence in establishing the dominant truth about her crime. Conversely, the absence of such discourses in relation to Joe is equally noteworthy, for – as demonstrated above – the evidence against him was as strong – arguably stronger – than that against Dorothea. Yet, as in the Williams case, discourses of judicial misogyny rendered such evidence unproblematic within the phallocentric courtroom – yet another reminder not to underestimate their power.

The case of Louisa and Alfred Merrifield

The final case of a double trial concluding with a single execution concerns that of Louisa and Alfred Merrifield who stood trial in Blackpool in 1953 for the murder of 79-year-old Sarah Ricketts, who had hired the couple as housekeepers. As in the previous case, Sarah had been persuaded to make a will in favour of her carers. Within two weeks of signing the will she was dead of phosphorous poisoning which is associated with Rodine rat poison.

The evidence against the Merrifields was purely circumstantial; indeed, much of it was generated by Louisa's own words, for she bragged incessantly about her inheritance – on one occasion claiming that Sarah had died several weeks before her death had occurred (ASSI52/785). Thus, while circumstantial evidence supported Louisa's involvement in this crime, the question remains as to why Alfred was not found guilty too. This disparity of verdicts becomes particularly significant when compared with the Waddingham/Sullivan case, because several of Louisa's actions prior to the poisoning mirrored Joe's, who was freed due to *lack* of evidence. However, in Louisa's case, these actions were used to demonstrate her guilt. For example, like Joe, Louisa made arrangements for Sarah's will to be written only 11 days after their employment commenced. Also like Joe, it was Louisa who called the doctor as Sarah was dying. Furthermore, she was eager for doctors to declare Sarah mentally fit to sign the will, as 'she wanted to keep herself all right with the relatives' (ASSI52/785). Finally, Louisa repeated Joe's actions when she told the funeral director to carry out a cremation, adding that she did not want Sarah's daughters to be informed of her death or funeral (ASSI52/785).

Thus, almost identical actions and behaviour by Joe Sullivan and Louisa Merrifield in these cases secured *his* freedom but *her* execution. Yet, as had been the case with Joe, circumstantial evidence pointing to Alfred's involvement was heard during the trial. For example, he was identified as the man who had purchased Rodine in a chemist shop

(ASSI52/785). When Sarah asked him to contact her solicitor because she wanted to change her will, he refused. When the doctor visited Sarah as she lay dying, he found access to his patient was blocked by Alfred who had pushed the dining-room table up against the sick-bed where he carried on eating his lunch, apparently unperturbed (ASSI52/785). Moreover, he had the same motive and opportunities as Louisa. Nonetheless, she was soon perceived to be the dominant partner – if not the sole participant in this crime – for unlike Alfred (or Joe), she – like Dorothea 17 years previously – was constructed and understood through the discourses of the evil woman poisoner, a process which also involved her construction *against* Alfred. Thus, while Louisa's thinly disguised plots to ensure she received her inheritance confirmed her status as the archetypal evil, scheming woman poisoner, the very simplicity of these plots – coupled with her incessant bragging and lying – ensured her construction as a 'wicked' and 'vulgar' woman who deserved no sympathy (HO29/229XC2573; Wilson 1971: 298).

In contrast, Alfred who at 70 was 24 years older than Louisa and deaf, was constructed as a 'tragic simpleton' (HO291/230, Trial Transcript, Vol. 11, p. 12; Ballinger 2000: 188). Thus, while his apparent inability to comprehend proceedings in the courtroom and his inappropriate conduct during the trial ensured that he could not be constructed through positive, conventional discourses of masculinity as had been the case with Joe, the alternative construction through which he was now understood – as 'guileless', 'a man wandering' and 'at times rather stupid' – nevertheless benefited Alfred by allowing him to be considered 'incapable of this cunning, desperate and vile murder' (HO291/230, Trial Transcript, Vol. 10, pp. 10, 19, 24; Vol. 11, p. 12). Meanwhile, Louisa's apparent rationality, assertiveness and assumed leadership – for example in organizing the will and calling the doctor – served simultaneously to emphasize her deviant femininity and Alfred's feeble-mindedness. It was a construction which ignored the fact that Louisa was clearly not a criminal 'mastermind' since her behaviour and conduct led directly to the discovery of the murder. It was also a construction which reinforced her 'double deviance' for during the trial it was established that she had failed to live up to idealized femininity in every one of the four areas identified earlier – motherhood, domesticity, sexuality and respectability. With two of her children in care, she had been married three times within 10 months and 'drank excessively and habitually became severely inebriated' (Ballinger 2000: 195). Finally, Louisa made sexual allegations against Sarah Ricketts in court which led the judge to call her 'a vulgar and stupid woman with a very dirty mind' (HO291/230, Trial Transcript, Vol. 11, p. 12).

In an era where women falling short of idealized femininity were greeted with particular anxiety, Louisa's transgressions signalled 'an unregulated and undisciplined "out of control" female in particular and dangerous womanhood generally' (Ballinger 2000: 195).

Alfred had generated his share of troubled domesticity too, having abandoned his previous wife and 10 children, and causing Louisa's son to leave home (HO29/229XC2573). Crucially, however, 'as had been the case with Joe Sullivan, Alfred's military record was assessed as "very good" thus providing us with ... [further evidence] of the gendered nature of "relevant" information' in trials concerning life and death (Ballinger 2000: 195–6, fn. 337). Once again, double standards are evident, for Alfred's domestic 'deviance' simply did not count in the way Louisa's did, since the social construction of masculinity minimizes the opportunities for criminal men to be judged as fathers.

In sum, Louisa was constructed as the dominant partner in this crime, despite the fact that much of the evidence against her was similar or identical to that against Joe Sullivan, whose case was dismissed due to *lack* of evidence. As in the previous two cases, there was not a single piece of evidence which proved that one, rather than the other defendant had committed the murder. Yet, Alfred – like William and Joe before him – left court a free man, while Louisa was executed. As such, the Merrifield case provides further evidence of the existence of judicial misogyny, generated by the discursive power of gender role expectations within the androcentric courtroom.

As stated earlier, the remaining two cases of couples in double trials concluded with double executions. However, in contrast to the cases examined already, the guilt of the male defendants was supported by irrefutable evidence, yet the women defendants were still executed, hence denied the benefit of doubt offered to the three male defendants discussed above. These double executions thus provide yet further evidence of double standards in double trials. Space does not permit a detailed analysis; however, the following discussion will demonstrate the contrast between them and the previous three cases.

The case of Emily Swann and John Gallagher

Emily Swann and her lover, John Gallagher, were found guilty of the murder of William Swann, Emily's husband, in 1903. This followed a long, well-documented history of William's violence against Emily for which he had past convictions. After having endured yet another violent attack Emily showed John her injuries. John responded that he would 'give the b-r something for himself'. Neighbours overheard Emily say: 'I hope he will punch him to death'. Fuelled by alcohol, John beat William twice, uttering: 'I'll murder the b-y swine before morning.' During the second beating Emily was overheard saying: 'Give it to him Johnny … Punch the b-r to death' (HO144/736/113887XC2356).

As William had beaten Emily immediately prior to John's attack on him, her urging John on in this manner is, arguably, understandable. However, in an era where women had neither legal nor formal equality and the term 'domestic violence' had not yet entered discourse, the long history of violence against Emily was considered to be the result of *her* provocative behaviour, as demonstrated in the local police report: 'the wonder is that he has not killed her. He has frequently gone home after leaving work and found his wife drunk in the house and nothing prepared for him in the way of food' (HO144/736/113887XC2356). Superintendent Oust did acknowledge that William too was a heavy drinker, but explained this in terms of his work: 'Glassblowers are a class of men who from the nature of their employment imbibe very freely and the deceased man was no execption' (HO144/736/113887XC2356). Emily, on the other hand, was 'a drunken, immoral woman [who] was much more to blame than her husband was' for their unhappy existence (HO144/736/113887XC2356 Superintendent Oust quoted in Ballinger 2000: 208). Her relationship with John provided further provocation as 'it was his presence there that provoked Swann to strike his wife' (HO144/736/113887XC2356).

The superintendent failed to consider the possibility that Emily may have sought comfort in another relationship as a result of the long-term abuse she had suffered, or that *her* anger may have been the result of provocation, having suffered yet another violent attack immediately before enlisting John's help. The concept of double standards is therefore also relevant in relation to domestic violence since, rather than the male perpetrator being judged on his performance as a husband within a domestic setting, it is the female victim who is considered to have 'provoked her own demise' (Edwards 1987). This is because the social construction of masculinity has ensured the normalization of 'men's murderous anger at "provocative" women' (Howe 2002: 41). Consequently, a man's *right* to feel provoked is a mitigating circumstance to subsequent violent acts committed by him. This stands in sharp contrast to idealized femininity within which 'anything resembling anger is likely to be redescribed as hysteria or rage' (Spelman 1989 cited in Howe 2002: 59; see also Naffine 1997), and which consequently ensures that the expression of such emotions in women is identified as deviant and problematic behaviour.

The superintendent's comments provide yet further evidence of criminal women being judged according to their performance as *women*, as well as their crime, and hence also of 'doubly deviant' women being judged according to double standards in double trials, for Emily's construction as a drunken, sluttish housewife and an immoral and unfaithful wife, against William who 'was a good workman attend[ing] regularly at his work', helped to construct him as a victim long before he was murdered (HO144/736/113887XC2356; Ballinger 2000: 208).

It is as a result of feminism's impact on the criminological imagination that we are able to challenge the dominant, legal truth about Emily as an unfaithful wife who deserved her punishment, because the theoretical tools developed by feminism allows us to retrieve the subjugated, experiential knowledge of a woman coping with domestic violence, 11 children and paid employment. As such it is an example of critical criminology facilitating the translation of 'private troubles into public issues' in order to provide an empowering discourse for understanding lived experience. Through this process we are also able to expose the dominant, legal truth as being socially constructed, rather than 'objective' – and thus render it problematic – for, as Stanko and Scully explain, 'removed from *appropriate femininity, violent women must be explained* by their deviance ... [which] overshadow[s] the part played by the violence women endure at the hands of men' (1996: 63–4).

The case of Edith Thompson and Freddy Bywaters

The second case concluding with a double execution is that of Edith Thompson and her lover Freddy Bywaters who in 1922 stood trial for the murder of Percy Thompson, Edith's husband.[5] The evidence against Freddy was even stronger than in John Gallagher's case for he confessed to the stabbing while exonerating Edith:

I swear she is completely innocent. She never knew that I was going to meet them that night ... She didn't commit murder. I did. She never planned it. She never knew about it. She is innocent, innocent, absolutely innocent (quoted in *Daily Express* 8 January 1923; HO144/2685 PT 2 XC2501).

The prosecution therefore did not claim that Edith had participated in the actual murder. However, like Emily before her, Edith *was* guilty of adultery, and in an era where there was considerable concern about the 'smoking, drinking flapper freed from corsets and sexual repression' (Jones 1991: 256), Edith, who was eight years older than Freddy, quickly became constructed as the 'evil seductress': 'She … had egged him on; he the poor young fellow, was under the influence of this dominating woman, this unfaithful wife, this wanton, this enchantress, this seductive siren' (Broad 1952: 87–8).

Her seniority in age, coupled with her sexual transgression, thus played a key role in her construction as 'worse' than Freddy – an older woman who manipulated the passions of a young man. In contrast, Freddy was constructed in sympathetic terms as an innocent youth 'led astray … [by] a wicked woman' (Browne and Tullett 1987: 291):

As a youth of … previous excellent character, he was exposed for many months to the malign influence of a clever and unscrupulous woman 8 years older … An impressionable youth of that age would need to be of unusual strength of character to resist such solicitations … Bywaters fell victim to her machinations (HO144/2685 PT 2 XC2501).

Apart from her adultery Edith also challenged idealized femininity and the social order more generally by remaining childless after several years of marriage; by using her maiden name at work; by earning more than Percy; and by paying for her half of the house they shared during a decade where women had not yet won the vote. Thus, like Emily Swann 19 years earlier, Edith had transgressed expectations of female conduct in the areas of motherhood, domesticity, sexuality and respectability. These transgressions generated a wave of hostility towards her so powerful that various authors have subsequently argued she was hanged for immorality, not for murder (Broad 1952; Du Cann 1960; Twining 1990; Ballinger 2000). Arguably, she therefore provides the ultimate example of law's ability to 'criminalise female sexuality' (Faith 1994: 58) through double standards which render women doubly deviant in double trials within the androcentric courtroom. This contention is supported by Lustgarten who wrote that the trial consisted of 'four days of prim sententiousness and virtuous moralising' (1960: 28), and by Browne and Tullett who wrote that Edith faced 'ridiculous fits of self-righteousness ... [and a] public, a judge and jury, in its most priggish mood' (cited in Ballinger 2000: 224). For example, the judge interrupted the closing speech on behalf of the defence with these words: 'you should not forget that you are in a Court of Justice trying a vulgar and common crime ... you should think it over in that way' (Young 1923: 119).

The construction of the evidence against Edith can be seen to further reinforce this moralizing against her. Based solely on the prosecution's interpretation of letters written by Edith to Freddy, it consisted almost entirely of 'insinuation, suspicion and speculation' (Ballinger 2000: 225) as has been widely recognized since the time of the trial (Broad 1952; Du Cann 1960; Lustgarten 1960; Twinning 1990). In contrast, there was no shortage of evidence of the *type* of woman Edith was – an adulterous, disloyal, deceitful wife. Thus, she was constructed through the discourses of the immoral, scheming woman who preyed on 'innocent' young men (Ballinger 2000: 244). Such was the power of these discourses that they were allowed to fill the void left by the lack of evidence, as has also been recognized since her trial: 'Had Mrs Thompson by her immoralities placed herself so far beyond the pale that proof could be dispensed with?' (Broad 1952: 216).

Eight years later Du Cann answered 'yes' to Broad's question when he observed 'that the disgust of the trial judge ... for marital infidelity ... hanged this unhappy creature' (1960: 206). These authors were thus fully aware that Edith had been punished for her immorality, not for murder, and therefore played an important part in constructing an alternative truth about the case. But they did not yet have available a language in which to theorize their version of the 'truth'. It is at this point that the feminist contribution to the critical criminological imagination becomes most apparent because it has subsequently developed the tools with which to theorize Edith's punishment. As I have demonstrated, this theory has taught us not to underestimate the power of discourses around idealized femininity which in the cases examined in this chapter, overrode – at times even replaced – actual evidence, thus providing further evidence of the presence of judicial misogyny within the androcentric courtroom.

Conclusion

The cases of Swann/Gallagher and Thompson/Bywaters stand in

sharp contrast to the three previous cases since the *mere presence* of the two women during their husbands' murder was considered adequate proof of their guilt and subsequently led to their execution. Even Freddy's confession to the crime and denial of Edith's involvement could not save her; on the contrary, this was interpreted as yet further proof of her manipulative powers over him (Ballinger 2000: 230–1).

In order to understand the disparate outcomes of the above trials we return to the feminist challenge to law's truth-claims and its accompanying theoretical concepts of 'double standards', double deviance and judicial misogyny outlined earlier. A feminist analysis of these double trials has confirmed that, far from being blind, rational or objective, the law was deeply influenced by the discourses around idealized femininity – particularly those relating to respectability, sexuality, domesticity and motherhood – which consequently came to play an important role in determining the final punishment of the female defendants. Thus, rather than judging such cases according to available evidence, judgements were made according to the *type* of woman the offender was, as well as the *type* of crime committed. Did she conduct herself in accordance with idealized femininity, 'or was she unruly and devious – representing dangerous womanhood?' (Ballinger 2003: 224). Did she commit the type of 'feminine' crime which would allow her to be constructed as 'mad' or 'sick', such as infanticide, or did she kill in cold blood for personal gain or pleasure (Ballinger 1996)? In short, rather than being based on evidence tested in court, the final outcomes of these double trials were a reflection of the threat the women posed to a gender-based social order. As such, they demonstrate the presence of judicial misogyny within the courtroom – amplified through the double trial as a result of the close proximity of the two accused which provided unique and specific opportunities for constructing them against each other.

Double trials therefore took place on a terrain where double standards became uniquely visible due to the women being constructed through gender-specific discourses such as 'carer', 'mother', 'poisoner' and 'deceitful, scheming wife'. In turn, this impacted on the way in which they were constructed against their male partners, for it was the *lack* of discourses through which the men's criminality could be heard and understood which is most noteworthy.

Thus, despite spanning five decades, these cases were nevertheless united by the women's failure to comply with idealized femininity – while the social construction of masculinity simply did not allow for an equivalent level of failure by their male co-accused. The cases were thus also united by the lack of discourses through which men's 'failure' in the areas of fatherhood, domesticity, respectability and sexuality could be articulated; hence they could not be judged against such standards. Despite major social changes during specific historical moments – for example the introduction of female suffrage in 1928 – the social construction of femininity and masculinity has nevertheless proved remarkably resilient and – as such – has formed a strand of continuity during the first half of the twentieth century. Indeed we barely possess a vocabulary *today* in which to articulate men's 'failure' in the areas of domesticity, respectability or sexual conduct, and as noted by Cameron, when men kill children, we hear nothing about 'failure of fathering' unlike female child-killers whose crime will invariably be understood as transgressions of motherhood (1996: 27). Instead, a degree of criminality continues to be constructed as part of *normal* masculinity, with child-murder being constructed as an excessive form of masculinity – male criminality having gone too far. Moreover, as indicated above, the discourses of masculinity which *were* available through which the male accused were constructed, served to emphasize positive masculinity, generating sympathy and understanding. Such constructions of masculinity also served to emphasize the women's deviance, whose juxtaposition against their men ensured they were now 'doubly damned'.

In sum, the application of feminist theory and epistemology provides the basis for analysing the disparate outcomes of these trials as they are able 'to expose the gendered nature of both the courtroom and legal processes', which in turn demonstrates the state's ability and power to mobilize and establish a dominant truth based on gender-specific ideologies and discourses. As such, feminist analysis 'stands as a powerful challenge to … law's truth-claims regarding the delivery of objective and neutral justice' (Ballinger 2003: 236). Far from being a scientific process whose rational procedures generate indisputable 'facts' from available evidence, this chapter has demonstrated that in the above cases law drew heavily on assumptions, speculations and probabilities about 'the natural woman' and 'true' femininity and masculinity, to the point where they were allowed to be substituted for evidence.

However, having completed the process of exposing double standards in double trials, we are also able to appreciate the impact that feminism has had on the criminological imagination. Thus, feminist theory is now able to challenge the very foundations of the criminal justice system – due process, the rule of law, the right to a fair trial and presumptions of innocence – by exposing the close relationship between masculinity and the law, and by demonstrating that legal knowledge is androcentric in nature and 'grounded in patriarchy',[6] hence deeply implicated in the production and re-production of the gendered subject – yet without being perceived as such. Instead, it has been able to gain access to power by laying 'claim to a superior and unified field of knowledge, which concedes little to other competing discourses' (Smart 1989: 88). Thus, the cases analysed in this chapter are a stark reminder of the criminal justice system's ability 'not only to define itself but also the "truth" about the everyday lives of those who stand in the dock' (Ballinger 2000: 218). Yet, the feminist analysis presented here provides evidence of resistance to law's power to define reality, which in turn places limits on subsequent truth-claims. Hence, the valuable contribution that feminism has made to the criminological imagination since these cases were judged is made visible through its analytical framework. For example, this chapter has demonstrated that female violence can be discussed outside the 'mad *v.* bad' discourses and without resorting to pathological explanations of offending women's actions. In that sense the analysis presented here has answered the earlier, often voiced charge that feminism itself has been reluctant to address the issue of violent women for fear of harming the wider feminist cause (Kirsta 1994; Ballinger 1996). As I have illustrated through the case studies, feminist analysis has developed to the point where it is capable of taking account of the agency of violent women and the phallocentric nature of law *simultaneously*. In short, feminist analysis has now reached a level of sophistication where it has nothing to fear from acknowledging women's agentic involvement in violent crime. It is not a game of zero sum – the fact that some women engage in violent crime does not eliminate or diminish the hetero-patriarchal treatment they may experience when confronted with the legal process (Morrissey 2003).

A second important contribution that feminism has made is noteworthy for the fundamental impact it has had on the criminal justice system so far. It concerns the level of resistance immediately apparent in contemporary cases of women accused of violent crimes who are perceived to have been judged according to double standards. While there is plenty of evidence of women still being regarded as 'doubly deviant' by the criminal justice system, and hence judged and sentenced according to 'double standards' (see, for example, Roberts 2003), it is now almost inconceivable that such cases can pass through the legal process without vociferous resistance from both feminist activists and theorists (see, for example, Wistrich 2005). Indeed, the success of that resistance can be measured by the number of women whose cases have subsequently been revisited by the legal system, periodically resulting in a reduced charge or eventual release.[7]

The current work of both feminist theorists and activists thus provides evidence of how new discourses and – in turn – new knowledge can be created through resistance to the dominant truth. In deconstructing the dominant discourses through which historical cases were understood, and in reconstructing them through contemporary feminist discourses, feminist historians can help to strengthen arguments put forward by feminist activists and theorists who are engaged in present struggles to ensure that future cases of women judged according to 'double standards' will never again pass through the criminal justice system with the ease of the cases documented here. While such developments occurred too late to benefit the women discussed in this chapter, they should nevertheless receive recognition for the important role they have played in 'the retrieval of subjugated knowledge' from the past (Sawicki 1991: 57), which in turn helps to make new spaces available on which the criminal justice process can be challenged in the present and changed for the benefit of women defendants in the future.

Acknowledgements

Many thanks to Joe Sim for his support during the preparation of this chapter, and to the editors for their helpful comments on an earlier draft.

Notes

1   The term '"worse" of the two' is taken from the National Archives' file relating to the Williams case (HO144/280XC17335).

2   Faith has used a similar term 'idealized females' in a different context (1994: 58).

3   William had previously invested a £100 inheritance in a newsagent shop. The venture was unsuccessful and he was soon penniless again (HO144/280/A61654).

4   As quoted above (*The Times* 27 February 1936). Joe had been a friend of Dorothea's husband and came to live with them. When her husband died, he simply stayed on with Dorothea.

5   Space does not permit a review of this extremely complex case, details of which are still being discussed in academic work e.g. Twining and Hampsher-Monk (2003). For a detailed analysis of the case, see Ballinger (2000).

6   'as well as in class and ethnic divisions' (Smart 1989: 88).
7   That success has been particularly noteworthy in cases of battered women
    who eventually retaliate by killing their abuser. Well-known cases include
    those of Sara Thornton and Emma Humphrys (Bindel and Wistrich 2003;
    Ballinger 1996; 2000; 2005).

References

Adam, H.L. (1911) *Woman and Crime.* London: T. Werner Laurie.

Ballinger, A. (1996) 'The guilt of the innocent and the innocence of the guilty:
    the cases of Marie Fahmy and Ruth Ellis', in A. Myers and S. Wight (eds)
    No Angels. London: Pandora.

Ballinger, A. (2000) *Dead Woman Walking.* Aldershot: Ashgate.

Ballinger, A. (2003) 'Researching and redefining state crime: feminism and
    the capital punishment of women', in S. Tombs and D. Whyte (eds)
    Unmasking the Crimes of the Powerful. New York: Peter Lang.

Ballinger, A. (2005) '"Reasonable" women who kill: re-interpreting and re-
    defining women's responses to domestic violence in England and Wales
    1900–1965', *Outlines: Critical Social Studies,* 2: 65–82.

Benyon, J. (2002) *Masculinities and Culture.* Buckingham: Open University
    Press.

Bindel, J. and Wistrich, H. (eds) (2003) *The Map of My Life: The Story of Emma
    Humphreys.* London: Astralia Press.

Broad, L. (1952) *The Innocence of Edith Thompson.* London: Hutchinson.

Browne, D.G. and Tullett, T. (1987) *Bernard Spilsbury.* London: Grafton
    Books.

Cain, M. (1990) 'Towards transgression: new dimensions in feminist
    criminology', *International Journal of the Sociology of Law,* 18: 1–18.

Cameron, D. (1996) 'Wanted: the female serial killer', *Trouble and Strife,* 34:
    44–52.

Carlen, P. (1983) *Women's Imprisonment.* London: Routledge & Kegan Paul.

Carlen, P. (ed.) (1985) *Criminal Women.* Cambridge: Polity Press.

Carlen, P. (1988) *Women, Crime and Poverty.* Milton Keynes: Open University
    Press.

Collier, R. (1998) *Masculinities, Crime and Criminology.* London: Sage.

Du Cann, C.G.L. (1960) *Miscarriages of Justice.* London: Frederick Muller.

Edwards, S. (1987) '"Provoking her own demise": from common assault to
    homicide', in J. Hanmer and M. Maynard (eds) *Women, Violence and Social
    Control.* London: Macmillan.

Faith, K. (1994) 'Resistance: lessons from Foucault and feminism', in
    H.L. Radtke and H.J. Stam (eds) *Power/Gender: Social Relations in Theory
    and Practice.* London: Sage.

Heidensohn, F. (1986) *Women and Crime.* Basingstoke: Macmillan.

Howe, A. (2002) 'Provoking polemic-protocol killings and the ethical
    paradoxes of the postmodern feminist condition', *Feminist Legal Studies,*
    10: 39–64.

Huggett, R. and Berry, P. (1956) *Daughters of Cain*. London: Allen & Unwin.

Jones, A. (1991) *Women Who Kill*. London: Victor Gollancz.

Kirsta, A. (1994) *Deadlier than the Male*. London: HarperCollins.

Klein, D. (1973) 'The etiology of female crime', in J. Muncie *et al.* (eds) (1996) *Criminological Perspectives*. London: Sage.

Lees, S. (1993) *Sugar and Spice*. Hammondsworth: Penguin Books.

Lustgarten, E. (1960) *The Murder and the Trial*. London: Odhams Press.

Morris, A. (1987) *Women, Crime and Criminal Justice.* Oxford: Blackwell.

Morrissey, B. (2003) *When Women Kill*. London: Routledge.

Naffine, N. (1990) *Law and the Sexes*. London: Allen & Unwin.

Naffine, N. (1997) *Feminism and Criminology*. Cambridge: Polity Press.

O'Donnell, B. (1956) *Should Women Hang?* London: W.H. Allen.

Roberts, Y. (2003) 'Mad as a desperate woman', *Observer,* 18 May.

Sawicki, J. (1991) *Disciplining Foucault*. London: Routledge.

Smart, C. (1989) *Feminism and the Power of Law*. London: Routledge.

Smart, C. (1995) *Law, Crime and Sexuality*. London: Sage.

Smart, C. and Smart, B. (1978) 'Introduction', in C. Smart and B. Smart (eds) *Women, Sexuality and Social Control*. London: Routledge & Keagan Paul.

Stanko, B. and Scully, A. (1996) 'Retelling the tale: the Emma Humphreys case', in A. Myers and S. Wight (eds) *No Angels*. London: Pandora.

Sydie, R.A. (1987) *Natural Women Cultured Men*. Milton Keynes: Open University Press.

Twining, W. (1990) *Rethinking Evidence*. Oxford: Blackwell.

Twining, W. and Hampsher-Monk, I. (eds) (2003) *Evidence and Inference in History and Law*. Illinois: Northwestern University Press.

Watson, K. (2004) *Poisoned Lives*. London: Hambledon & London.

Wilson, P. (1971) *Murderess*. London: Michael Joseph.

Wistrich, H. (2005) 'Still taking abuse', *Guardian,* 14 July.

Worrall, A. (1981) 'Out of place: female offenders in court', *Probation Journal*, 28: 90–3.

Worrall, A. (1990) *Offending Women*. Routledge: London.

Young, F. (1923) *The Trial of Freddy Bywaters and Edith Thompson*. Edinburgh and London: William Hodge & Co.

Public Record Office Documents:

ASSI13/66XC6872
ASSI52/785
CRIM 1/59/4
HO29/229XC2573
HO291/230
HO144/20185
HO144/280XC17335
HO144/280/A61654
HO144/2685 PT 2 XC2501
HO144/736/113887XC2356

Chapter 5

'Talking about resistance': women political prisoners and the dynamics of prison conflict, Northern Ireland

Mary Corcoran

The stakes in embarking on prison resistance in pursuit of political status and conditions are high, and embroil prisoners, prison administrators and governments in a range of conflicts over legitimacy and power. The resistance of politically motivated prisoners is not only vested in challenging institutional authority, but in contesting the legitimacy of the state's right to punish. As a consequence, restoring discipline and order in prisons takes on a number of conflictual characteristics. This chapter explores the dynamics of prison punishment and resistance experienced by Republican women prisoners in Northern Ireland from the internment of women in 1972 until the years before the signing of the Belfast Agreement in 1998. Prison conflict is analysed as a dialectic which reflects the interplay between various prison powers and prisoners' resistance to them.

However, there is no simple connection between the political rationales of punishment and other forms of penal discipline and control. Political prisoners, like others in confinement, are bound by the many pains of imprisonment. The punishment of female prisoners was as much mediated through the structural, ideological and disciplinary techniques that are conventionally used in the control of women in prison as it was in restoring the kind of prison regimes that were consistent with security policy. In many ways, too, women political prisoners struggled against different kinds of invalidation from both the prison administration and their own organizations.

But talking about women in prison who directly confront state and penal controls as well as powerful gendered constraints means cross-cutting well established criminological traditions and debates. These 'traditions' include classical prison sub-cultural theories which either ignore the significance of gender in penal power relations and the formation of prisoners' collective experiences, or view 'gender' as pertinent to women's experiences only; the continued polarisation of women offenders into 'dangerous' or 'harmless' categories in penal discourse; the androcentric bias of political detention analyses; and the state's role in the discretion of prison policy. I have argued elsewhere that the women's prison campaign tested the almost exclusive concern with rebellion against the State as the primary basis of conflict with political detainees by exposing this dynamic to other structural influences such as gender, ethno-nationality and class (Corcoran 2006). I concluded that there is a need for an understanding of the multilateral punitive aspects of political imprisonment. Another theoretical 'home' in which women politicals can be situated is in the important feminist project of politicizing women's imprisonment more generally by insisting upon the authoritarian and socio-economic drives which legitimize women's incarceration as well as the forms their punishment takes. Thirdly, it must be noted that the resistance of the women here consolidated those relationships between state power, gender control and prison punishment which are implicitly acknowledged, if at all, in 'mainstream' criminology.

These are the background debates to the specific concerns of this chapter. The chapter itself focuses on three scenarios which reflect the wider interest of the collection with re-engaging Charles Wright Mills' 'sociological imagination' as a manifesto for probing the unsettling edges of disciplinary consensus and the role of professional criminology in articulating (and avoiding) issues of power and domination. They have also been selected because they show the intersection of the different forms of subordination with which I am concerned, and because these conditions provided the context for struggle and change. Thus, the chapter deals with questions that are already bounded by familiarity where they chime with existing precepts in the study of political imprisonment or women's punishment respectively, but are unfamiliar where the central tenets (and limitations) of each theme are brought together.

The opening discussion deals with the well established observation relating to the suppression of alternative analyses in state-defined descriptions of political imprisonment. This refers specifically to the governmental goal of securing a consensus for criminalizing illegitimate and extremist activities. The second part explores the problem already inherent in talking about women political prisoners, which is the estrangement of the 'other' from criminological definitions of political and collective agency in prison. The last section explores the political utility of functional criminology as prison administrators turned towards politically 'safer' and ideologically 'neutral' bureaucratic mechanisms for managing the later phase of political imprisonment in Northern Ireland.

Criminalizing political prisoners: state and penal interests

Defining political imprisonment in the UK has never been straightforward. A separate legal category of 'political prisoner' does not strictly exist in the English penal system. This is not to say that, historically or in the contemporary period, the penal system has failed to recognize or accommodate political or conscionable offenders (prisoners of conscience who usually, but not exclusively, adopt non-violent methods) for the purposes of convicting or punishing them. Instead, legislators and the courts have conventionally taken the position that political motives or objectives do not in themselves constitute a sufficient cause for separate treatment under the law, and accordingly, there should be no special dispensation available to offenders under these circumstances. Political offending has thus been dealt with as aggravated criminality; that is, as essentially criminal acts which are triable under the criminal law.

Criminalization is retained for a number of reasons. The first is that, until recently, the criminal law was thought to be appropriate and sufficient for dealing with political offending, and any shortfalls in the law could be supplemented by temporary emergency legislation. However, the enactment and annual renewal of the Emergency Provision(s) Act 1973 and Prevention of Terrorism Act 1974 in response to violence related to the Northern Ireland conflict meant that legislation against political crime began to take a more long-lasting form in the statute books. This process can be said to have continued with the passage of comprehensive and permanent legislation connected with the current 'war on terrorism', such as the Terrorism Act 2000, the Anti-Terrorism, Crime and Security Act 2001 and the Prevention of Terrorism Act 2005.

Second, the inadmissibility of a separate category of political prisoners derived from the principle of uniformity of treatment for all prisoners that emerged in the nineteenth century, which was resistant to separate or 'preferential' status or conditions in prison. Although many elements of standardized treatment have been whittled away in over a century of prison administration, vestiges of opposition to giving prisoners 'privileges' have been most conspicuous in relation to those who claim a political motivation (Radzinowicz and Hood 1979).

The third reason for criminalization was essentially concerned with upholding the legitimacy of the rule of law, in that any separate status or treatment afforded to political offenders might lend some validity to their cause. This reasoning was also related to concerns about the political dangers for governments in entering into a tainting compromise with those who seek to oppose the very state whose recognition they subsequently demand (Gardiner 1975).

What is also evident is that successive responses to protests in pursuit of political recognition in prisons in Britain and Ireland have altered some elements of these rules since they originally took shape. The uniformly harsh response to protesting or non-conforming political prisoners has been periodically circumvented in the form of interventions by Home Secretaries on humanitarian grounds in the cases of hunger strikes or other protests, by emergencies (such as internment in Northern Ireland) or by various 'pragmatic' arrangements at politically sensitive junctures such as those surrounding the Northern Ireland political process (McEvoy 2001; McConville 2003). Crucially, these compromises have followed protracted and agonizing campaigns by prisoners to achieve their goals. Furthermore, as O' Dowd *et al.* (1980: 193) have observed, an anomaly has also run through the treatment of defendants where '[t]errorist offences, defined in law as those involving violence for political ends, are considered as "political" in the courtroom, but "criminal" for the purposes of punishment'. Thus, the policy of criminalization rests on a fundamental inconsistency. In the first place, the tendency to enact more specialized anti-terrorism laws has given rise to even greater distinctions between 'ordinary' and 'political' crimes, and gives further definition to the legal reality of a category of 'political offender'. At the same time, prison administrators are obliged to disregard the political character of offenders, other than for security purposes, and to implement policies which compel them to accept the 'criminal' label and submit to regular prison discipline.[1]

Much of this suggests that the relationship between changes in the penal treatment of politically motivated offenders and their struggles to achieve their objectives are intertwined. However, one must be wary of evolutionary accounts which imply that prison campaigns, provided they are sufficiently well organized or are based on an element of 'justice', are likely to produce some improvement in prison conditions after an appropriate period of calm or official reconsideration. It must be noted that prison protests have often failed or led to greater coercion, at least in the short term, while more durable gains are dependent on political timing or expediency, or external constitutional or security factors. The following discussion examines how the vexed question of political legitimacy went from being a contested principle to becoming embedded in everyday correctional relationships in Northern Ireland's prisons.

Punishment and resistance in Northern Ireland's prisons: a dialectical approach

Although men and women Republican prisoners were involved in some form of protest for nearly three decades, they were only officially recognized as a separate category for four of those years, between 1972 and 1976.[2] 'Special-category status' had been introduced in 1972, a year after the introduction of internment for men, and following the extension of internment to women. The Republican campaign for the return of political status for much of the period after 1976 (outlined below) was characterized by its longevity, its relative coherence and the versatility of the prisoners' resistance to the policy of criminalization. Therefore, their campaign stands out from the more familiar pattern of short-lived prison mutinies or acts of defiance by individuals or small groups, which have engendered reactive and usually successful, official suppression (Adams 1992). Lawrence McKeown's (1998: 46) description of the successive protests conducted by male Republicans in the Maze Prison reflects this dialectical momentum: 'From the prison authorities' point of view their goal was the imposition of a "normal" prison regime ... For Republicans, their goal was to resist all such attempts to criminalise them and to bring about change in the prison regime and political policies that governed it.'

McKeown goes on to show how this dialectical struggle permeated prison relations, going beyond the original principle of opposing criminalization to incorporate a range of resistances into the symbolic and disciplinary consequences of the policy. As Sparks *et al.* noted (1996: 34), the maintenance of control and order in prisons relies on different mechanisms for restoring authority which include violence and coercion but, 'also incorporate countervailing impulses towards accommodation, co-operation and sociability, so that the dialectic between the potentialities for order and disorder is more nuanced and intricate than at first appears'.

Sparks *et al.* (1996) were referring here to the many dangers that are inherent in the deployment of power and authority in prison, and the consequences of the breakdown of legitimacy, consensus and justice in prisons. Their analysis is ultimately concerned with the conditions in which these discrepancies have been addressed, most notably through liberal (and more recently neoliberal) forms of 'social contract' based on the mutual rights and responsibilities of administrators and prisoners. The most conspicuous example of this approach is to be found in the conclusions of the Woolf Report (1991), which observed that the kind of conflicts that were found in the prison system in England and Wales in the late 1980s could be avoided by means of introducing incentives, procedural transparency, fairness and other mechanisms for securing a consensus with the confined. As discussed later, these precepts emerged as levers for reforming the Northern Ireland prison system in the 1990s.

Nevertheless, the drive to establish the legitimacy through such 'voluntary' arrangements obscures their instrumentally political function. In the case of political imprisonment in Northern Ireland, and especially with Republican prisoners, the most striking weakness of contractarianism was that the question of the validity of prison authority was already framed by a more fundamental conflict over the legitimacy of the state. Thus, the presumption that political prisoners might voluntarily accede to some quasi-criminal status was doubtful from the very point of removing special-category status. As a consequence, implementing the policy tended to rely on enforcement rather than persuasion.

At the same time, the material and practical contexts in which good order and legitimacy were conceived and implemented, and resisted, were not divorced from other systematic controls in prison. If the relationship between punishment and resistance was dialectical, it was also relational in that enforcing conformity meant incorporating methods for targeting political prisoners as women. As the following discussion shows, this intersection between the gendered and political conditions of imprisonment introduced additional levels of ambiguity to these categories of analysis.

Political or women prisoners? The estrangement of the 'other' in criminological discourse

One of the problems with talking about women political prisoners is that they occupy a contradictory place in analyses of both political and women's imprisonment. In the first instance, they are subsumed within conceptual frameworks which hold that political conflict in prison is primarily defined by resistance to the ideological and material power of the state. While this is observably true, this paradigm may conceal other, equally prominent, structures of control (racism, sexism, socio-cultural domination) that influence prisoners' consciousness and agency. Furthermore, as Brewer (2003: 11) observed, it is important to avoid the tendency, itself a product of political conflict, to reduce diverse power relationships to a singular, all-encompassing social cleavage. Instead, conflicts are plural and fluid, which prevents them 'from emerging solely around one axis of differentiation'. Whereas Brewer is referring to the primacy of sectarianism as the almost-exclusive signifier of conflict in Northern Ireland, his point is relevant for pinpointing the intersecting controls within which women political prisoners conducted their struggle. To put it another way, although the issue of 'legitimacy' captured the most manifest essence of the prison struggle in Northern Ireland, it did not exclude the position of women political prisoners in various group struggles. Analysing women who were also political prisoners means acknowledging their many affiliations as working class, as 'Catholic' or 'Protestant', as self-conscious resisters and as subjected to sectarian, class and paternalistic forces inside and outside the prison walls.

Unravelling these relationships also involves unpacking some of the binary values that normally occur in criminological analysis. For example, the most immediate distinction to emerge in the case of political detention is that between 'political' and 'criminal' offenders. Yet, as previously pointed out, this simply captures a hegemonic distinction between governments and their political 'others' while concealing other conflicts and power relationships. As we shall also see, women political prisoners disrupt paradigms of the victimized or subjugated 'criminal' woman. In this sense, women political prisoners transgress the categorical certainties that support the analysis of political and women's imprisonment. In fact, they belong to both categories while remaining estranged from each.

This cleavage is most obvious when one looks for a criminological framework for analysing political women's prison resistance. Feminist penologists have identified the experience of women in prison as one of profound subjectification, moral correction and compulsory feminization (Dobash *et al.* 1986; Hannah-Moffat 2001). 'Criminal women' have been assigned a special place in the history of prison administration as candidates for personal rehabilitation, psychiatric and medical intervention, and extraordinary levels of personal adjustment. Women in contemporary prisons continue to be enmeshed in a network of corrective prerogatives which seek to resocialize them into well adjusted womanhood.

Of course, these arguments have in the main been formulated in relation to 'criminal women' (a category which in itself is rightly subject to critical feminist deconstruction) imprisoned for 'ordinary' crimes. Certainly, the imprisonment of 'criminal' women, who were sentenced for 'regular' offences against property or the person, and who did not claim affiliation with any political group, continued to rise alongside the intake of politicals. Indeed, one of the distinguishing features of women's imprisonment in Northern Ireland was that these separate groups of women were held in greater proximity to each other in the same institutions than their 'ordinary' and 'political' male counterparts. Consequently, one of the outcomes of concentrating different categories of women prisoners in one establishment was the reliance on methods of control which were commonly experienced across the political/ordinary divide. Being political prisoners did not preclude being disciplined as women in prison.

Similarly, the position of women in the annals of prison resistance has been equally ambiguous. Accounts of male prisoners' resistance in Northern Ireland have been largely drawn from 'inmate subcultural' and 'adaptive' theories of the 1950s and 1970s (Crawford 1999; McKeown 2001). However, the classical accounts tend to lack an explicit analysis of the gendered constraints on the levels of 'autonomy' which are officially permitted or tolerated. Where these theories have been applied to women's prison communities, they have tended to reinforce essentialist paradigms wherein women's collective relationships in prison take the form of reconstituted 'pseudo-famil[ies]' which are grounded in 'women's psychological needs ... psycho-sexual needs and symbiotic needs' for stability and relationships (Ward and Kassebaum 1966: 73). Later, feminist revisionists of 'subcultural' theory have pointed to the overwhelming pressures on women's social relationships in prison, apart from those which are officially sanctioned and mediated through staff or 'appropriate' channels, which ultimately prevent them from sustaining coherent alliances (Heffernan 1972). As a consequence, the literature has tended to conclude that women's resistance is either restricted to individualistic, and ultimately ineffectual, subversion which invites further suppression, or confirms the narrow and tenuous character of their alliances (Mandaraka-Sheppard 1986).

More recently, Bosworth (1999: 156) has investigated women prisoners' resistance, arguing that while they are subject to race, class, gender and other normative controls, they consciously use identity as a 'crucial site' for contesting them. While women prisoners may appear to adhere to dominant penal values, these are reshaped and subverted by them. It follows that, '[a]though a hegemonic notion of passive femininity continues to underpin much of the management and criminological assessment of female imprisonment, thereby appearing as both the goal and the form of women's punishment, it does not pass unchallenged' (Bosworth 1999: 156). Here, Bosworth develops Foucault's (1990) observation that power relationships are contingent and contradictory, allowing the dominated to participate, however marginally, in resistance. This post-structural approach to the potential of mundane acts of resistance is also consistent with previous feminist observations that, far from being unimportant, they expose the acute levels of intimate controls that make up so much of the punitive apparatus in women's prisons. Thus, 'concepts of identity and resistance enable the criminologist to develop a feminist theoretical critique of imprisonment which can acknowledge the specificity of different experiences of punishment' (Bosworth 1999: 151).

However, such arguments have not convinced Carlen (1994, 2002), who contends that the objects of analysis ought not to be those of identity or agency, but the overwhelmingly punitive function of prison. Women's punishment originates in the panoply of 'discursive, ideological, and physical' controls for 'keeping women "in their place"' more generally, but these acquire a privileged function in penal institutions (Carlen 1998: 67). Carlen (1994: 137) has thus criticized inward-looking, micro-level theories of resistance that privilege ephemeral gains over structural penal power 'which exists and persists independently of the best attempts of (some) prisoners to defeat it via strategies of resistance'. While there is insufficient space here to engage fully with Carlen's objections to the 'insistence on resistance brigade' (1994: 133), it is suggested that analysing resistance need not be diametrically opposed to examining the 'political combat' which the denial of agency in prison actually entails. As Carlen (1994: 133: emphasis in the original) also notes:

full recognition of the complex power relationships and penal practices within which *women's imprisonment* is constituted as such is no more to *deny* women prisoners the power to resist than it is to *endow* them with that same power. For the effects of theories do not occur *sui generis*. They depend rather on the political calculations and conditions in which they are realised.

It follows from this that prison resistance is intrinsically a question of prison power because it invokes the material and ideological forces which shape these struggles. This does not deny the fact that 'resistance' and agency are plausible objects of analysis, but points to their emergence and growth within other relations of power. Just as importantly, Carlen's observation, although coming from a different perspective, reinforces the point made in the previous section that resistance, like punishment, is a political undertaking. The concern here, moreover, is to identify the intersections between these different punitive dynamics which created the 'political calculations and contexts' in which women political prisoners resisted.

Reconstituting community as collective and individual resistance

The administration of prisons in Northern Ireland developed through three phases during the conflict. These were 'reactive containment' from 1969 to 1976; 'criminalization' from 1976 to 1981; and 'normalization' from 1981 onwards (Gormally and McEvoy 1995). Reactive containment was characterized by internment, and the use of special powers of arrest, interrogation and detention in the context of mass civil disobedience and the rise of paramilitary violence. The prison population increased fourfold in the first half of the 1970s, largely as a result of offences connected with disorder and political violence. From 1970, incoming Republican sympathizers and women who had become politicized by their involvement in civil disobedience campaigns were involved in individual and collective challenges to the paternalistic and outdated prison regime. In 1972, men and women IRA prisoners held a cross-prison hunger strike for political status. This was granted in the form of 'special-category status'. Special-category status granted the conditions commensurate with 'political status', but fell short of creating a separate legal category. In practice, it entitled political prisoners to wear their own clothes, receive food and parcels above the legal statutory limits, the right not to do prescribed prison work and political association and segregation.

The new arrangements also enabled Republican women to establish the 'A' Company of the IRA, Armagh Prison, which was recognized as the political structure through which prisoners mediated with the authorities. Their elected commanding officers (OCs) represented prisoners in all aspects of negotiating with the prison administration and staff, allocated prison work to members of the group and conducted roll-calls and wing inspections. Their system worked in parallel with the official regime. Eilís, a former internee in Armagh prison, explained:

> by ten o' clock [a.m.] we had our own regime, between ourselves. Your cells ... you had them ready and we inspected them ourselves. The OC would come down and go in and inspect it, make sure it was clean. The people who were in charge of cleaning the wings would be inspected. After that you did drill for about half an hour, and then directly after that you had all sorts going on. You had your time filled, literally.[3]

Their collective structure fulfilled a number of functions. If subcultural theory holds that prisoner 'communities' assist with adaptation and survival or shielding individuals from full exposure to the alienating effects of imprisonment, it also needs to address the inscription of gender discipline within these relationships. This emanates from within groups themselves, as well as from the official prison regime. Clearly, the preservation of boundaries and the exclusion of disciplinary or political 'others', such as staff, and 'ordinary' or Loyalist prisoners, supported the maintenance of ideological orthodoxy and internal discipline, as well as preventing individuals from becoming unwitting informants or involved with compromising relationships outside the group. Additionally, the strategy of disengagement from staff was also based on more pragmatic precautions against the realities of surveillance and the monitoring of mail, correspondence and visits, and other means by which the authorities control prisoners individually, and as a group.

However, self-segregation was equally concerned with confronting the alienating controls that are usually legitimized in women's prisons. Crucially, the kinds of intensive personal demands that are placed on women to subscribe to the values of rehabilitation, refrain from voicing criticism and establish 'constructive' relationships with staff are closely tied to maintaining them in a state of perpetual atomization and dependency. As Carlen (1983: 102) noted, individualization reflects a more pervasive 'resentment and suspicion of the women developing a private realm of consciousness, yet at the same time there are bars to sociability which prevent them developing a public realm of consciousness'. Clearly, too, individualization had additional ramifications for undermining what was, in administrators' eyes, a rival and destabilizing counter-authority in the prison. As one sentenced prisoner commented, much of the mundane work of resistance involved challenging these mechanisms:

> It was a constant battle to see who was going to get the upper hand all the time. We did quite a few times. They did quite a lot of the times. But it was a constant battle. The thing about when you go on protest is this feeling of family. You're with your own, and as long as you're with your own, nothing can touch you.

Criminalization and resistance, 1976–81

The period of conflict associated with the return of criminalization as official policy commenced in March 1976 and came to an end, or at least took a different direction, in 1981, after five years of Republican protest. The removal of differential status for prisoners sentenced after March 1976 followed the Gardiner Report, which found that the introduction of special-category status in 1972 'was a serious mistake', was possibly illegal and supported the view among prisoners 'which society must reject, that their political motivation somehow justifies their crimes' (Gardiner 1975: para. 107). Special-category status, the report concluded, had enabled paramilitary prisoners to consolidate their subversive aims, allowed individuals to avoid full prison punishment, impeded rehabilitation and, by enabling factions to recruit and school members in prison, posed a serious threat to future security. Consequently, the report recommended that the paramilitary influence in prison should be broken up and differential treatment brought to an end. In response, male Republican prisoners started a 'blanket' strike in 1978, in which they initially refused to wear the non-compulsory prison uniform, preferring to drape prison blankets over their naked bodies, and a no-wash protest. These protests culminated in two hunger strikes, the first of which, in 1980, involved both men and women and a second in 1981, which led to the deaths by starvation of ten Republican men (Beresford 1987).

Women prisoners sentenced after March 1976 embarked on a campaign of non-cooperation with the regime by refusing to engage in compulsory activities, withdrawing from educational programmes and refusing to obey prison rules or instructions that were not passed through their selected commanding officers. This was initially dealt with by the prison authorities as a disciplinary problem. Criminalization had returned to the prison authorities the means to exercise their full disciplinary powers. Senior officers had previously argued that political prisoners had been shielded from proper discipline during the 'status' years to the detriment of good order. The first sign of the return to 'normal' discipline was immediate and dramatic, with the number of prisoners who were brought before the Governor for adjudication for a variety of breaches of the rules connected to their protest rising 23-fold in 1976, the first year of the non-cooperation protest, and it remained high for the following two years (NIPS 1979). Anna, who was sentenced without political status, argued that greater punishment was:

> part of the idea in taking away the status. It was to make it a more or less strict regime to deter [us]. Because imprisonment wasn't a deterrent. There were a lot of women back in for the second time, so they [the authorities] saw [that] it wasn't acting as a deterrent.

Others argued that criminalization was at best a political miscalculation, and at worst a conclusive effort to achieve the moral defeat of Republicanism:

> I don't really understand their thinking. If they [the authorities] don't realise [that Volunteers] first join the struggle, and they know that they're either going to go to prison, or they're going to die, why did they think that any sort of measures that they bring in are going to stop people? (Meg, internee, Armagh).

A number of factors influenced the change in direction towards more extreme and confrontational tactics in Armagh in 1980. Republican prisoners had acknowledged that the non-cooperation campaign of the previous four years had been generally contained by the use of the disciplinary system. However, women were discouraged from taking a part in a hunger strike which was being proposed by prisoners in the Maze. The Republican leadership outside was sensitive to charges that they would be exploiting women by 'forcing' them on protest, or that they would take the dubious and potentially retroactive risk that the government would respond more rapidly to the moral pressures posed by the presence of women on an extreme form of protest. Nevertheless, the women's decision to act against this order had more complex origins. On the one hand, women prisoners wanted to open up another strategic front in a cross-prison protest, with the view to weakening the capacity of the authorities to concentrate its resources in any one prison. They had also recognized the dangers of becoming peripheral to the momentum that was being driven by events in the Maze Prison.

Winnie, who was sentenced after 1976 and participated in the no-wash protest, recalled: 'we fought very hard to get [clearance from the Army Council] and they wouldn't allow us to do anything. It was as if [the men] were out there fighting for us and we weren't doing very much for ourselves.' She also observed that, although the women had argued that their presence could have placed the government in a more invidious position, they were overruled as much by protectionist attitudes within the Republican prison structures as by the tactical caution of the leadership:

> Obviously the no-wash protest was difficult for men, but it was much more difficult for women because of their biological make up. I think no matter what country you go to, whether it's the oppressed or the oppressor, everyone has this thing about the women being the mainstay or the support. Men are expected to go to jail, men are expected to fight, men are expected to die, men are expected to get battered. But when a woman does this, it's something different. *So everybody uses that.* I also think that people in struggle use that also, I mean, 'our women are being treated like this'. On the other hand, the oppressors could say, 'we'll take it easier on the women as a concession' (emphasis added).

Yet, the outbreak of outright conflict in 1980 also had its origins in the paternalistic order of authority in the prison in the form of minor challenges to the personal authority of staff and the male Governor. Anna, who was involved in the protest said: 'it was this type of "on-off" all the time, with us trying to get one over on them, and them trying to get one over on us. This was constant.' The cycle of routinized confrontation was short-lived. On 8 February 1980, a disturbance broke out after the Governor announced a wing and cell search while Republican prisoners were queuing up for their midday meal. Male officers from the Maze were called in to assist with the search, and it later emerged that male maintenance staff were also involved in the incident:

The riot was on a Friday, and I had a visit on a Saturday. My sisters came up and saw me, and I was covered in bruises. My older sister went ballistic in the visiting room. I said, 'you go out and tell them all what happened'. So I came back up from the visit and I was put on report. I was brought up in front of the Governor for grievous bodily assault of five prison officers. One of them was charging us [with assault], so they brought in the police to take statements from us. They wanted to take statements and we told them where to go. We got the crap beat out of us but they charged us with assault (Winnie, no-wash protester, Armagh).

After the disturbance, the sentenced Republican prisoners were locked in their cells without access to toilets or other facilities. This started the 'no wash' protest in which the prisoners were compelled to smear their excreta on to the ceilings and walls of their cell and disrupt the prison through a strategy of degradation (D'Arcy 1981). In December, three of the women on that protest joined men in the Maze in a hunger strike. All protests were suspended at the end of 1980, but following a dispute over the terms of agreement, the second, and more widely known, hunger strike, involving men only, resumed in the Maze in 1981.

'Normalization' and continued resistance: Maghaberry, 1986–1990s

Charles Wright Mills said that there were three developments in professional sociology which betrayed the goals of the 'sociological imagination'. These were grand, universalizing theory-making, abstracted empiricism and 'research for bureaucratic ends' (Mills 1959: 117) which 'deliver[ed] the sociologist from any concern with power' (1959: 35). The final section uses Mills' comments to foreground the technicist turn in prison administration in Northern Ireland and its implications for further relegating the presence of women (political and 'ordinary') to the margins of 'historical' political reforms. From the official perspective, the period after the hunger strikes to the signing of the Belfast Agreement (1998) amounted to a successful transition from confrontation to one in which administrators would engage in some form of tacit engagement with and recognition of political prisoners. 'Normalization', as this new departure was known, involved a series of initiatives which would bring the

Northern Ireland Prison Service closer to the goals of 'constructive' and 'positive regimes', 'safe and secure custody' and 'rehabilitation', and had a number of predominant characteristics.

The new approach involved the greater influence of a managerialist ethos in public administration, with its emphasis on operational efficiency, rationalized staffing, budgetary management, performance indicators, and fiscal and operational transparency and accountability. It assigned a more prominent role to social contractarianism in promoting the balance of 'rights and responsibilities' as common interests of prisoners and the administration. Finally, as McEvoy (2001: 250–313) argues, 'normalization' was a more sophisticated example of state management whose underlying concerns were directed towards restoring the public legitimacy of prison policy, and integrating the gaols of containment and conflict management into prison reform. Thus, a key objective was reducing the politically contentious effects of certain key symbolic or material issues in the prisons by reshaping them as technical, rather than 'ideological', matters. Potential conflicts over conditions or treatment, for example, could be circumvented by treating them as minor managerial issues which were resoluble by adjusting operational, resourcing and distributional systems.

However, the language of personal rights and responsibilities, transparency and procedural fairness failed to obscure the point that the very goal of 'depoliticizing' prison policy was likely to be interpreted by prisoners and their supporters as a political manoeuvre. Clearly, too, these objectives reflected broader priorities with minimizing the potential of the prisons to reignite the kind of political crisis brought about by earlier protests. Rather, the thrust of the new prisoner management agenda, with its emphasis on separating prisoners as individuals from the political context of their imprisonment, submission to professional authority and the prerogatives to take responsibility for productively managing their sentences, revived in political prisoners the belief that criminalization – albeit in an administered and technocratic form – was still a significant element of political and administrative thinking.

Yet the full consequences of these changes were not observable for much of the 1980s. On the contrary, the years immediately after the hunger strikes were marked by renewed confrontation over the introduction of an integration policy. This sought to terminate the system of allowing Loyalist and Republican prisoners to live separately. The attempts to implement integration led to a decade of violence inside and outside the prisons. Another point of contention was the introduction of more stringent security after two major escapes by Republican prisoners from Belfast Prison in 1981 and the Maze Prison in 1983. Moreover, the greatest potential for politically damaging controversy about prison conditions resurfaced in Armagh women's prison where reports of the disturbing increase in the use of strip searching generated considerable protest from civil liberties groups, politicians, women's groups, the churches and trade unionists (NCCL 1986).

Although strip searching had been a part of the reception process for new and incoming prisoners, the implementation of 'routine' strip searching in Armagh in November 1982 appeared to have a superficial foundation in risk assessment, and lacked appropriate systems of scrutiny. Some well publicized allegations of assault and the use of force by officers underlined the suspicion that strip searching was being used as a form of generalized deterrence, and reinforced the incorrect belief that the procedure was disproportionately used against Republican prisoners. Nevertheless, it would be equally wrong to remove strip searching from the political context of sporadic protest in Armagh against integration, or from the human costs of continuing antagonism between political prisoners and staff after years of traumatic conflict. Elizabeth, a former remand prisoner in Armagh, argued that strip searching was symptomatic of a determination to impose the new order initially on the 'softer' prisoner groups:

> You had the introduction of strip searching, you had enforced integration, so all that came in the backlash after the hunger strikes and Blanket protests … At that stage, you had a bigger number of prisoners in on supergrass[4] evidence, you had a bigger number of prisoners on remand than there had been for a long time … Also, it was like the pound of flesh, 'we have [yet] to change things in the 'Blocks but we can still get in here and come down on them'.

From the end of the 1980s, the policy of normalization had, to all appearances, achieved a number of its objectives, so that Gormally and McEvoy (1995: 297–9) were able to claim that administrators and prisoners had moved some way towards mutual, 'pragmatic' accommodation. The new style of prison administration had made some inroads into containing potential flashpoints through practical flexibility on the issues of segregation, and negotiation and consultation with prisoners. Furthermore, they continued, conflict around the issue of political recognition seemed to have receded in favour of the protection by prisoners of their improved conditions: 'From the management's point of view, the narrower the range [of issues], the more discussions centre on the practical details of prison life, the more prisoners are accepting the legitimacy of the prison system' (1995: 298).

The participation of Republicans and Loyalists offers some evidence that managerialism had achieved what previous strategies had failed to do. What is less assured is whether this amounted to a relinquishment by prisoners of the symbolic or substantive weight of their demands, or even whether administrators fully appreciated the consequences of channelling the style and methods by which prisoners pursued their demands into more 'manageable' legalistic and technical forms. Republicans argued that their participation concentrated official minds on the needs of prisoners, their families and communities, which inevitably involved addressing the political dimensions of prison policy. Similarly, the prisoners acquired a formidable level of proficiency in selecting test cases for judicial review, and made substantive gains in the areas of life-sentence review, parole and temporary release licensing procedures, and overturning internal disciplinary decisions.

Yet again, the position of women prisoners in these developments remained far more problematic. The reforms associated with 'normalization' did not even begin to apply to women's imprisonment until after Armagh Prison was closed and all women prisoners moved to Mourne House, the women's section of Maghaberry Prison, in 1986. There, women Republicans focused on strategies of negotiation, internal appeal and the use of judicial review of sex discrimination in the provision of education, medical facilities, association and visiting facilities. However, women prisoners in general, and those viewed as claiming political 'privileges' in particular, were regarded as being too few to count when it came to providing 'special' facilities or the development of gender-appropriate pre-release or other training programmes. Their campaign was thus generally impeded by the official belief that their actions amounted to vexatious litigation by a resource-draining minority in furtherance of illegitimate political goals.

Furthermore, the signature of previous patterns of control resurfaced during an enforced strip search of 34 women prisoners on 2 March 1992 by female officers assisted by male riot officers (CRSS 1993). The violence of the incident, which took place over ten hours, was clearly related to the refusal by the 21 Republican prisoners to co-operate with a full cell and wing search. The basis of the original decision to conduct a full search, which was uncommon on the women's side of Maghaberry, and the failure to investigate allegations about staff behaviour and the injuries received by some prisoners, have never been adequately explained. As Hanna, who was one of the strip-searched prisoners commented, the claim that there was an ongoing process of liberalization and constructive engagement was far more tenuous for women prisoners:

> The men were always OK in Long Kesh because there's a bigger number.[5] There's over 300 prisoners. So you got more power there. But, when I walked in to Maghaberry there was only 24 women, and they were split up into three wings. Eight into each wing. So that's what gives the Maze power. And at that stage we weren't getting any association, only in the yard or in education. So that broke down our power. We got inter-wing association … we campaigned for that, it was ours. Anything we wanted we had to fight for, even for a bottle of perfume, for extra stamps, or something in our tuck-shops. Everything, food, clothing – everything was just a constant fight, twenty-four hours a day. You were constantly in with the Governor all the time. With the 'Kesh[6] it was different. They could just sit down with the Governor and say, 'here it is, what are you going to do about it?'

Conclusion: talking about gender, resistance and political imprisonment

Hanna encapsulates the dilemmas of struggle in the context of the many incongruities of women's political imprisonment. Political detention for women in Northern Ireland developed along the fault lines of gender, state power and prison punishment, and was marked by serial ideological, structural and correctional contradictions. As a consequence, their experiences were shaped by their position relative to the male majority, and by conditions and terms of treatment which were little more than *ad hoc* modifications to generalized penal and security policies. Prison resistance by women thus involved negotiating a variety of controls which threatened to invalidate them as political actors within their own structures, marginalize them as exceptions to the general rules of prison administration, disregard them as having needs as women in prison yet fetishize them as objects of security because of their political status.

Their case also points to the analytical usefulness of talking about political imprisonment in relation to localized practices and specific prisoner groups. This is evident, for example, in the inconsistencies and problems that appeared when administrators integrated various gendered, regulatory and political controls for a prison population which appeared to fall between existing correctional norms. It is useful, too, for considering the areas of overlap between 'ordinary' and 'special' detention. The latter reshaped and extended the distribution of 'regular' prison powers as special search and security practices, regulation and punishment, and isolation and segregation were justified and normalized. Arguably, too, this mesh of penal discourses and deterrents led to the further specification of a distinctive disciplinary subject – the dangerous and subversive female prisoner.

A subtext of this chapter, the brevity of which permits only a brief comment, is that examining the political detention of women moves the critical focus beyond the more usual scholarly narrative about them as exceptional, awkward adjuncts to the main drama of men's political struggle. There are epistemological implications to this too, in that the ideological construction of women as political offenders and prisoners, and the distinctive organization of penal repression they experienced, calls into question the unity of conventional definitions of political imprisonment. Rather, it causes us to focus on the development of political detention from below as it was observable in practices and attitudes, and in the responses of prisoners, as elements in the way prison rule was shaped. In short, the way political imprisonment is conceived of, worked out and practised is as important to understanding the phenomenon as analysing judicial or political definitions of detention in times of conflict. These concerns may well be relevant to the intersection of racial and religio-secular tensions, fears about global migration and security discourses which inform the current phase of internment and 'special detention' policy in the UK.

Notes

1   While this central tension generally holds, the rapid succession of emergency laws in the UK in recent years has supported the development of isolated regimes in Belmarsh and Woodhill Prisons for those detained under the new measures. Similarly, judicial reviews such as House of Lords ruling of December 2004, which found that indefinite detention

of 'foreign' terrorists to be illegal, prompted the introduction of control orders and curfews to be issued against those released from custody. Breach of orders incur an immediate return to custody. Thus, the prison system has been obliged to make special provision for what has become, ipso facto, a recognizably distinctive group of 'political prisoners'.

2   Although Loyalist organizations were also opposed to criminalization, they were equally concerned with distancing themselves from any tacit support for Republicans. The very few Loyalist women prisoners tended to be isolationist, segregating themselves from other women prisoners and staff, and avoiding direct confrontation with the prison administration.

3   All respondents have been given aliases.

4   The practice between 1981 and 1986 of using 'converted' Loyalist and Republican paramilitaries as prosecution witnesses.

5   The interview was conducted before the release of prisoners under the terms of the Belfast Agreement.

6   The Maze was also known as 'H-Blocks' or 'Long Kesh'.

References

Adams, R. (1992) *Prison Riots in Britain and the USA*. Basingstoke: Macmillan.

Beresford, D. (1987) *Ten Men Dead: The Story of the 1981 Hunger Strike*. London: Grafton.

Bosworth, M. (1999) *Engendering Resistance: Agency and Power in Women's Prisons*. Dartmouth: Ashgate.

Brewer, J.D. (2003) *C. Wright Mills and the Ending of Violence*. London: Palgrave/Macmillan.

Carlen, P. (1983) *Women's Imprisonment: A Study in Social Control*. London: Routledge & Kegan Paul.

Carlen, P. (1994) 'Why study women's imprisonment? Or anyone else's?', *British Journal of Criminology*, 34: 131–9.

Carlen, P. (1998) *Sledgehammer: Women's Imprisonment at the Millennium*. Basingstoke: Macmillan.

Carlen, P. (2002) 'Carceral clawback: the case of women's imprisonment in Canada', *Punishment and Society*, 4: 115–21.

Christian Response to Strip Searching (CRSS) (1993) *The General Strip Search in Maghaberry Women's Prison, Monday March 2, 1992*. Belfast: CRSS.

Corcoran, M.S. (2006) *Out of Order: The Political Imprisonment of Women in Northern Ireland, 1972–1998*. Cullompton: Willan Publishing.

Crawford, C. (1999) *Defenders or Criminals? Loyalist Prisoners and Criminalisation*. Belfast: Blackstaff Press.

D'arcy, M. (1981) *Tell Them Everything*. London: Pluto.

Dobash, R.E., Dobash, R.P. and Gutteridge, S. (1986) *The Imprisonment of Women*. Oxford: Blackwell.

Foucault, M. (1990) *The History of Sexuality. Vol. 1. An Introduction*. Harmondsworth: Penguin Books.

Gardiner, Lord (1975) *Report of a Committee to Consider, in the Context of Civil Liberties and Human Rights, Measures to Deal with Terrorism in Northern Ireland* (Cmnd 5847). London: HMSO.

Gormally, B. and McEvoy, K. (1995) 'Politics and prison management: the Northern Ireland experience', in L. Noaks *et al.* (eds) *Contemporary Issues in Criminology*. Cardiff: University of Wales Press.

Hannah-Moffat, K. (2001) *Punishment in Disguise: Penal Governance and Federal Imprisonment of Women in Canada*. Toronto: Toronto University Press.

Heffernan, E. (1972) *Making it in Prisons*. New York, NY: Wiley.

Mandaraka-Sheppard, A. (1986) *The Dynamics of Aggression in Women's Prisons in England*. Aldershot: Gower.

McConville, S. (2003) *Irish Political Prisoners, 1848–1922: Theatres of War*. London: Routledge.

McEvoy, K. (2001) *Paramilitary Imprisonment in Northern Ireland: Resistance, Management and Release*. Oxford: Oxford University Press.

McKeown, L. (1998) '"Unrepentant Fenian bastards": the social construction of an Irish Republican prison community.' PhD dissertation, Queen's University, Belfast.

McKeown, L. (2001) *Out of Time: Irish Republican Prisoners, Long Kesh, 1972–2000*. Belfast: Beyond the Pale Press.

Mills, C.W. (1959) *The Sociological Imagination*. New York, NY: Oxford University Press.

National Council for Civil Liberties (NCCL) (1986) *Strip Searching: An Inquiry into the Strip Searching of Women Remand Prisoners at Armagh Prison between 1982 and 1986*. London: NCCL.

Northern Ireland Prison Service (1979) *Annual Report of the Prison Service for 1978* (Cmnd 250). Belfast: HMSO.

O'Dowd, L., Rolston, B. and Tomlinson, M. (1980) *Northern Ireland: Between Civil Rights and Civil War*. London: CSE Books.

Radzinowicz, L. and Hood, R. (1979) 'The status of political prisoner in England: the struggle for recognition', *Virginia Law Review*, 65: 1421–81.

Sparks, R. (1994) 'Can prisons be legitimate?', *British Journal of Criminology*, 34: 14–29.

Sparks, R., Bottoms, A. and Hay, W. (1996) *Prisons and the Problem of Order*. Oxford: Clarendon Press.

Ward, D.A. and Kassebaum, G.E. (1966) *Women's Prison: Sex and Social Structure*. London: Weidenfeld & Nicholson.

Woolf, Lord (1991) *Prison Disturbances, April 1990 Report of an Inquiry* (Cmnd 1456). London: HMSO.

Worrall, A. (1990) *Offending Women: Female Lawbreakers and the Criminal Justice System*. London: Routledge.

Chapter 6

Changing focus: 'drug-related crime' and the criminological imagination

Margaret S. Malloch

Introduction

The introduction of a range of disciplines into strategic responses to drug use has led to the expansion of the parameters of criminological knowledge through the incorporation of theories, debates and concepts from within and outside criminology. However, there has been little critical dissent to current policies and practices largely due to a consensus that 'something needs to be done' to address the damage caused by drug use and 'addiction': a consensus that has resulted in considerable emphasis, in research terms, on establishing 'what works.' Nevertheless, a critical theoretical framework provides an opportunity to present new insights to the dynamics of power. This requires a focus, not on crime and deviance as behaviours, but on understanding social order and the use of power to criminalize and control.

In recent years, there has been a great deal of interest in drug-related crime: in terms of extent, nature and ways of reducing it. Current criminal justice policies place considerable priority on responding to drug use as a way of reducing drug-related crime and this has become a key issue for both policymakers and practitioners. This focus has resulted in the development of a number of initiatives, many of them aimed at providing a multi-agency approach to drug users who come into contact with the criminal justice system – for example, arrest referral schemes, drug treatment and testing orders;

drug courts and prison-based initiatives (particularly those aimed at linking the transition between prisons and local communities).

While traditional approaches have focused on legal and/or medical responses to this issue (legislation, responding to 'crime', 'punishment', 'treatment'), a critical criminological perspective provides an opportunity to go beyond this restrictive view. A critical criminological perspective enables an examination of the social, political and economic context of drug use (socio-economic context of international supply and demand), of drug users (socio-economic context of drug-related crime) and of processes of marginalization that dominate the experiences of many individuals (the punitive ethos and attempts at control; impact of relations of class, ethnicity and gender) (Hudson 1993; Parenti 1999; Malloch 2000; Duke 2003). Critical *criminology* is fundamental in locating responses to drug use within structures of law enforcement and the socio-legal context of contemporary society. By examining the emphasis on criminal justice, critical criminology paves the way for recognition of the need for a strategy based on social justice.

Critical reflections on social, political and economic responses to drug use provide an opportunity to redefine the problem and to contextualize issues and potential solutions. Critical perspectives draw on a range of theories: abolitionist, Marxist, feminist, anti-colonialist and anti-racist, and transformative justice approaches. In particular, criminological theory and research that are informed by a critical approach enable an analysis of the relationship between the individual, society and the state in terms of law and legal practices and structures.

This chapter will contextualize responses to drug-related crime and drug users, in the current political, economic and social climate. The historical shifts between medical and legal responses to the issues will be considered and the way in which drug use has come to be perceived as a 'criminal justice problem' will be examined. The main focus of the chapter is to consider the distinctive analysis that can be provided by developing a critical criminological approach. This will involve an examination of penal processes and criminal justice practices, as well as theoretical considerations. The development of different ways of understanding and responding to drug-related crime (and accordingly to drug users) is considered alongside the response of state institutions and agencies, notably the criminal justice system.

Defining the issue

While orthodox approaches begin from the acceptance of legal categories of crime, a critical approach requires a consideration of the meaning and values attached to definitions and categories of 'crime.' This is particularly true of drugs and drug use and is indicative of the social and cultural constructions which lead to certain substances being acceptable or proscribed. As McDonald (1994: 11) states: 'A substance's meaning or reality, its capacity to attract or repel, varies according to the cultural context in which it is placed.'

A variety of factors affect the legal status of a drug, including the properties of the drug itself, country of origin and the current social/ historical climate. In the UK, certain substances are controlled and/or prohibited under the Misuse of Drugs Act 1971. Drugs are classified (Class A, B or C) with specific regulations and punishments applied accordingly.[1] However, a drug's potential for harm clearly does not determine legal status. Many drugs which can in certain circumstances be harmful are acceptable if use is medically regulated while others are available with relatively few restrictions. Cigarette and alcohol use are both legal[2] but are responsible for considerably more deaths than any other substances. It is estimated that around 114,000 smokers die each year in the UK as a direct result of smoking (Action on Smoking and Health 2005) while over 5,000 deaths were directly attributable to alcohol in England and Wales alone (Alcohol Concern 2002). The implication of both alcohol and tobacco in significant numbers of deaths illustrates that the legal status of a drug is instead closely linked with social and cultural influences (see Szasz 1974; Boyd and Lowman 1991; Strausbaugh and Blaise 1991; Kohn 1992).

The control and/or prohibition of certain substances is not static but changes with and within different cultures and in different historical periods. Many drugs which are proscribed today were considered acceptable in the past (Strausbaugh and Blaise 1991), while alcohol has been prohibited in certain times and places. Opiates and cocaine, which are presently Class A drugs with penalties of up to life imprisonment for supply, could be purchased with relative ease up until the Dangerous Drugs Act 1920. Indeed, opiate use was common during the nineteenth century and was eaten, drunk as tea and administered for medical purposes. Cannabis has recently been relegated from a Class B to a Class C drug.

The development of legislation governing the use of certain substances has arisen within specific cultural contexts, usually with particular intent. Attempts to regulate the use of specific drugs can be linked with attempts to regulate particular populations. This was evident in attempts to control immigrants following World War One in the context of disappearing labour shortages and increased competition for jobs. The legislation which developed led to the criminalization of certain substances, particularly opiates, cocaine and, in 1925, cannabis. Many of these substances were linked with immigrant communities, notably opium with the Chinese, and cocaine and marijuana with black immigrants. The implicit racist connotations associated with legislative controls on drug use have been outlined by several authors (Szasz 1974; Kohn 1992; McDermott 1992; McDonald 1994).

Kohn (1992: 176) demonstrates how the sale of narcotics became enmeshed in a 'moral campaign' leading to the extension of the power of the state over private lives and personal choices:

In this state of tension, drugs presented themselves as an explanation for some of these disturbing developments, and as a way of expressing profound anxieties about the social order as a whole. Alien, in nature, dope was invested with magical properties by being prohibited. Existing in marginal zones of society where conventional boundaries were unstable, it was understood as the agent which dissolved these boundaries, rather than as a symptom of instability.

Social attitudes toward 'drugs' are not based on scientific classification but on moral and/or political evaluations (Lidz and Walker 1980; Husak 1992; McDonald 1994). Boyd and Lowman (1991) (see also Sumner 1990) point out that the criminalization of certain drugs enables 'moral' values to be levelled at those who use particular substances: 'A practice of social censure distances the legal smoker from the illegal drug (ab)user' (Boyd and Lowman 1991: 114). For Sumner (1990: 28), moral censure is a technique which forms part of the process of 'normalization.' Moral regulation follows through governmentality (Foucault 1979). In this way, the surveillance and management of particular individuals and groups through government 'infuses the social and penetrates the self. It radiates in all directions' (McLaren et al. 2002: 14).

The situational context of social anxieties continues to influence the development of drug policies to the present day, both internationally and nationally. How the 'drugs problem' is defined and the attempts made to control it reflect overt and insidious methods of controlling both individuals and populations considered to pose a threat to the stability of the social order. Critical criminology, with the emphasis it places on the relationship between structure and agency within legal and social contexts, is useful in linking these different levels, thus providing an understanding of the impact at the individual level of broader social, economic and political responses (Cohen 1985; Malloch 2000; Walters 2003).

International controls, national responses: the political and economic context

At an international level, the development of drug control has enabled certain countries to adopt the self-claimed right to interfere in the affairs of other nations in much the same way as individual states use the threat of drugs to intervene in the lives of individual citizens. US drugs intelligence has been linked with foreign policy, or at least closely related to it. When the USA was politically involved in the Far East during the 1960s and 1970s, heroin was the focus of 'enforcement efforts.' The focus on cocaine throughout the 1980s paralleled concern with South America. Indeed, as Dorn (1992) argues, the American fear of moves towards 'independence' by certain South American countries has often been pursued by the redefinition of the seriousness of the drugs which they produce, most notably cocaine. Nevertheless, it has been suggested that the US government in particular has not been averse to supporting political groups who fund their struggles through the drug trade, notably in Afghanistan, the Far East and Panama (Chomsky 1992; Chambliss 1994; Young 2002). In Afghanistan, Hallam (2004) suggests that US militarized strategic politics have 'dovetailed' with the strategic politics of drug control. Indeed it would appear that the USA has synthesized the so-called 'wars' against terrorism, crime and drugs.[3]

Technological developments have also been brought into this arena. The use of intrusive surveillance measures which clearly infringe on the rights of an individual or group is justified by the creation of a discourse on the 'dangerousness' of particular drugs. At an international level, government commitment to fighting the 'war against drugs' has led to a massive expansion in police powers, both nationally and internationally. In response, contemporary policing methods include the use of high-tech surveillance and co-operation between regional and international police forces. There has been increased support for joint operations between customs and police both nationally and internationally and agreement over the need for the maintenance of frontier checks (Roberts *et al*. 2004).[4]

Many of the measures taken to control the production and movement of drugs have wider and more profound implications for the rights of citizens and individuals. In particular there is evidence of the targeting of people from countries characterized by both the production of drugs and/or social and economic unrest. The perceived threat of drug traffickers, 'terrorists' and 'illegal immigrants' being afforded easy access to Europe has led to persuasive arguments for the expansion of policing and law enforcement (Malloch and Stanley 2005). Indeed, such efforts can be likened to an industry which continually reinforces and extends its powers and resources (Chambliss 1994; Christie 1994; Parenti 1999).

While international efforts to control drugs operate within and between national boundaries, specific methods apply to the mobilization of individuals from one country to another in terms of trafficking but also in terms of migration. The lengthy sentences used to deal with foreign 'couriers' raise fundamental issues. While this form of punishment is intended to illustrate the severity of the offence, social revulsion towards it and to act as a deterrent to others, it is widely accepted that the effect of deterrence is limited. The people who are presently held in British prisons for drug smuggling are rarely the organizers of trafficking cartels and it is doubtful that their imprisonment will have any noticeable effect on the drug trade.

Similar ideologies operate at a national level. While law enforcement is extended and increased to 'control' drugs, individuals become targeted and criminalized as a direct result of their drug use. Both nationally and internationally, individuals who consume particular substances are the focus for social controls. As Husak (1992: 2) discusses in relation to the 'war on drugs': 'The war, after all, cannot really be a war on drugs, since drugs cannot be arrested, prosecuted or punished. The war is against persons who use drugs ... And unlike previous battles in this apparently endless war, current campaigns target casual users as well as drug abusers.' It has also been defined as a 'war on women', particularly black and ethnic minority women due to the impact this response has had on the criminalization of women, and the increase in female prison populations internationally (Campbell 2000; Boyd 2004; Sudbury 2005). In the UK, 37 per cent of black prisoners, 25 per cent of Asian and 28 per cent of 'other' minority ethnic group prisoners were serving a sentence for drug offences in 2002, compared with 13 per cent for white prisoners (Home Office 2004a). In June 2002, 75 per cent of sentenced black women in prison were held for drug offences compared with 41 per cent of all sentenced women in prison for drug offences (Home Office 2004b).

When action is taken to respond to a 'social problem' the intervention which arises is frequently targeted at particular groups or communities, generally towards those already marginalized by relations of production and neo-colonialism. Campbell (2000) argues that the US has witnessed a shift from the *discipline* of unregulated drug users to *punishment*, a shift that emanated from the increase of crack use in the mid-1980s. Chambliss (1994: 118) demonstrates how law enforcement operates against particular groups in the USA:

> And when the laws are blatantly racist to the extent that possession of a small amount (five grams) of crack cocaine, the drug of choice of people in the Black ghetto, carries a mandatory five-year prison sentence without the possibility of parole but possession of a hundred times that amount of cocaine powder (the drug of choice of the white middle class) has no mandatory sentence, any illusion of an impartial judicial system is permanently shattered.[5]

Social or criminal justice?

Historically, control of drug users has been advocated, whether medical or legal, in an attempt to prevent the perceived threat of crime and disorder and the spread of disease. Singer (1993: 43) notes:

> Both criminality and disease are conceived as outlaws, invaders with secret ways, as well as forces of disorder. Both criminality and disease (and their postulated equivalence) are used to rationalise forms of power in the name of maintaining a healthier, that is, crime-free and disease-free, society. Both rationalise power as management.

How behaviour (or people) become defined and managed as a 'social problem' has to be understood within a broader context, the way in which 'official' definitions become institutionalized and operate as ideologies. This is clear with regard to drug use and drug users where a myriad of negative images and reputations exist. McDermott (1992: 197) argues that a split occurred with the development of legislation on drug use between '"respectable" therapeutic addicts and hedonistic or recreational drug use. These definitions have an explicit class basis; it was acceptable behaviour for the well-to-do, but there was always a concern to regulate the pleasures of the "dangerous classes".'

Drug enforcement policy is thereby used to legitimate the further criminalization of already marginalized groups. As Scraton and Chadwick (1987: 213) point out: 'the intervention of the state's institutions – its very political management – reflects, transmits and reinforces the ideological construction of identities and reputations. It is this *range* of responses – economic, political and ideological – which cuts into people's daily lives and which, taken together, forms the process of marginalization.' Once marginalized from society, the operation of law enforcement agencies will be instigated in an attempt to regulate and control those deemed to require it, in this case drug users (Collison 1993, 1994). In this context, marginalization is closely tied to the process of criminalization, affecting policing and law enforcement. Ultimately, this affects the ability of those involved in their negotiation with state agencies.

McConville *et al.* (1991) provide some explanation as to how this operates with regard to police perceptions of what they term the 'suspect' population.[6] They argue that the 'suspect' population is a police construct of which the 'criminal' population is merely a subset: 'The suspect population is constructed on the basis of a complex interaction of rules and principles. But they are *police* – rather than *legal* – rules and principles' (1991: 15). These rules and principles are heavily weighted by wider structures of class, race and gender. In this way, McConville *et al.* (1991: 15) argue that the major contentions of labelling theory are correct: 'that suspicion, accusation, conviction and criminal self-identity are not objective characteristics of "criminals", but they are the products of law enforcers as well.'

The supposed relationship between drugs and crime has already been identified as an influential factor in developing strategies of drug control. Government estimates of the costs of drug-related crime are significant as it is implied that drug 'addicts' engage in crime as a means of 'feeding their habit' (Bennett 1998). It is clear that the illegal status of drug use enables a thriving illicit economy to operate. This has been reluctantly admitted by the Prime Minister's Strategy Unit (Strategy Unit 2003) as well as more radical organizations (TRANSFORM 2004).

However, law enforcement has continued to be prioritized with a growing emphasis on the need for preventative and treatment interventions. The 1995 white paper *Tackling Drugs Together*, which established the basis for all subsequent policies (Scottish Office 1999; Scottish Executive 2000; Home Office 1998, 2002, 2004c), set out a new agenda for dealing with drug use with less emphasis on harm reduction, and more on abstinence and overall prevention. The emphasis given to crime prevention and 'community safety' illustrates a clear 'anti-drugs' policy aimed at reducing drug-related crime.[7] The White Paper (Home Office 1995: 1) sets out its strategy: 'To take effective action by vigorous law enforcement, accessible treatment and a new emphasis on education and prevention to increase the safety of communities from drug-related crime; reduce the acceptability and availability of drugs to young people; reduce the health risks and other damage related to drug misuse.'

This illustrated a focus on community safety through the targeting of individual drug-using offenders who would be 'fast-tracked' into treatment services through the criminal justice system (Home Office 1995, 1998, 2002, 2004c). Subsequent legislation put this in place: the Criminal Justice Act 1991 allowed for treatment requirements to be made a condition of a probation order; drug treatment and testing orders were introduced with the Crime and Disorder Act 1998; and drug testing was further extended with the Criminal Justice Act 2003. The criminal justice system as a gateway to drug treatment continues to be a key component of government drug strategies, further evidenced by the establishment of the Criminal Justice Interventions Programme in April 2004. This programme was introduced in 'high-crime areas' with the aim of targeting problem drug users and guiding them into treatment. Current legislation would appear to be continuing this trend.

The emphasis given to provisions within the criminal justice system is likely to have an impact on community-based services which are expected to provide a 'fast-track' resource to the courts (Barton 1999; Turning Point 2004; Holloway *et al.* 2005). Some involve criminal justice referrals to treatment agencies (Rumgay 2000; NACRO 2003), including drug treatment and testing orders (Turnbull *et al.* 2000; Eley *et al.* 2002a), while others such as the drug courts in Scotland provide dedicated treatment and supervision teams within district court settings (Eley *et al.* 2002b; Malloch *et al.* 2003). Drug testing plays a key feature in these disposals, intended to encourage motivation and assess levels of compliance.

Importantly, this approach is based on a recognition that relapse is a potential element of drug treatment and is recognized as such within the operation of the orders. These initiatives are presented as important opportunities to provide drug users with an opportunity to access a range of services and supports, within the context of a court-mandated order and all the possible consequences that non-compliance will entail. Change is expected and required and failure to comply will result in a breach and the possibility of a custodial sentence.

One of the important principles which form the crux of court-based interventions is to enable drug-dependent offenders to cease from offending behaviour and to reduce or end their use of illicit drugs. While these initiatives are still at a relatively early stage of operation, the evidence available to date suggests that these objectives are entirely plausible. While ending an individual's drug use may have variable success rates, the reduction in offending behaviour appears to be a consistent feature of evaluations (Eley *et al.* 2002a, Eley *et al.* 2002b; Hough *et al.* 2003; Malloch *et al.* 2003; McIvor 2004) – but a feature for those who are retained on orders.

A broad range of research, from both the criminal justice and addiction studies fields, has illustrated that 'coerced treatment' is an important way of bringing people into treatment services who may not otherwise access them (Hough 1994; Holloway *et al.* 2005). Once that contact has been made, it is assumed that individual motivation to end or reduce substance use may be developed. Continued emphasis has been given in successive policies to protecting communities by targeting individuals in this way (Home Office 2004c). This approach has not been without criticism. The important element in effective treatment is not the emphasis on coercion, but on engagement with services (Hough *et al.* 2003; Ashton and Witton 2004; Holloway *et al.* 2005). Any mechanism for linking individuals who require support is to be welcomed. However, the emphasis on mandatory treatment, particularly where voluntary resources are limited due to the impoverishment of community resources, removes any focus on broader structural issues (Malloch 2004b). As Campbell (2000: 222) notes: 'the emphasis on personal responsibility creates an atmosphere of public surveillance and minimises public responsibility for structural change and redistributive social policy.' Making resources available in local communities may prove to be more effective than the current discriminatory practice of providing specific services for 'offenders' in communities where resources for drug users in general are limited (Rumgay 2000; Audit Commission 2002; Rethinking Crime and Punishment 2004; Donmall *et al.* 2005).[8]

Identifying 'effective' resources can be problematic. Much of the research conducted in this area is funded by government agencies and there is often an absence of clear objectives with which to assess policy initiatives (Trace *et al.* 2004). Critical research provides an important opportunity to represent individuals' views and to obtain knowledge that is not always accessible from a 'top-down' definition of a social problem. While the purpose of evaluations is to measure how services operate and their 'effectiveness', the real opportunity with critical work is to identify the views of a marginalized and criminalized group of people, diverse though these views may be. This opportunity goes beyond an examination of the impact of services to investigate the broader social, political and economic contexts of drug users' lives and circumstances. This also requires the identification of broader structural issues which may need to be addressed (Spooner and Hetherington 2004). This provides a broader structural analysis which comes from recognizing that focusing on illegal drugs as the cause of 'pathology' and 'deviant behaviour' in society obscures the responsibility of global capitalism and its contribution to the destruction of individuals and communities (Chomsky 1994).

The development of the 'criminological imagination' requires the collection of alternative forms of knowledge – in particular, the views, perceptions and knowledge obtained from those directly affected. Service evaluations can provide important information in this respect (Addaction 2004; Turning Point 2004). Service providers are often ideally placed to identify some of the contextual issues which determine individual experiences. Nevertheless it is important to acknowledge that professionals are themselves located within the determining contexts of 'structure' and are required to negotiate power as it operates through institutionalized practices (Cohen 1985). In this respect, structural contradictions are managed through the process of criminalization which operates through the re-presentation of individuals and groups.

From the narratives of drug-using respondents themselves, and professionals involved in providing interventions, it is evident that individual, social and structural factors have a significant influence on clients' ability to 'succeed' (to comply with mandated directives, to reduce or end drug use). Importantly it illustrates the importance of context. While individual agency is a key determinant of success, the broader issues of resources, multi-agency co-operation and social and economic factors have very real consequences for individual clients. By focusing on the experiences of individuals within the criminal justice system, through critical research, it is possible to consider how official discourse is translated into practice (by service providers) and the consequences for those affected by policies and practices (service users). It is evident that policies and operational practices are imbued with distinct priorities and objectives which reflect values and meaning throughout their implementation. Thus, to link individual experiences into broader socio-economic structures is to develop new forms of knowledge which have the *potential* to challenge orthodox perceptions and, subsequently, the status quo.

Linking agency to structure

There are a range of issues which have been identified which can impact on the ability of an individual to 'succeed.' While some of these features can be linked into the individual client's lifestyle (which may be 'chaotic') or to his or her motivation (which may be simply to stay out of jail for as long as possible) at least some of the obstacles arise from the operation of court-mandated orders themselves and their structural location, and which can ultimately hinder the innovative 'rehabilitative treatment' which they claim to make available.

Gossop *et al.* (1998) illustrate the range of difficulties that people with drug problems often have in their lives. This can include housing, family relationships, employment and debt. These problems appear to be increased and magnified for women (Malloch 2004a, 2004b). This is not to suggest that these issues are necessarily causes of crime or drug use; rather they are factors which frequently need to be addressed when responding to problem drug use/drug-related offending.

Multi-agency and inter-professional working are increasing features of the New Labour response to social problems. In the field of 'addiction', criminology, medicine, psychiatry, social work and sociology have all developed new forms of knowledge and methods geared towards the identification, surveillance and management of particular populations. In a sense, the different disciplines compete for ownership of the drug problem and how to manage it. This has consequences for individuals caught up in this complex system. Ineffective multi-agency working can have repercussions which may have the potential to reduce the scope and quality of care for individual clients. As one worker associated with one of the Scottish Drug Courts indicated: 'Yes, I think the difficulty with multi-agency working is that in principle it's an excellent idea drawing on people's experiences, the difficulty is that no-one's really told anybody how to do it' (Malloch *et al.* 2003: 39).

While initiatives such as drug treatment and testing orders and drug courts are intended to lessen the number of drug users sentenced to custody, the success of such initiatives is obviously dependent on available community resources. Regional variations in resources can result in a geographical lottery in accessing services, which is clearly of particular importance where criminal justice agencies refer clients to external service providers (Scottish Drugs Forum 2003). As a drug court worker observed: 'If there is a range of limited services, then there is a danger that what you're actually doing is feeding people through what's available, rather than linking people up with what's actually matched to their needs' (Eley *et al.* 2002b: 40). Follow-up support and after-care are crucial for those who do near the end of court-ordered services, but they are often extremely limited in practice, with support often weighted towards the initial stages of intervention (Effective Interventions Unit 2002).

A range of structural issues (social, economic, political) can be identified as impinging on the lives of criminal justice clients, notably the economic context. It is therefore important that the broader issues are recognized to avoid decontextualizing individual experiences. The poverty and social deprivation that characterize the lives of many individuals in the criminal justice system illustrate the importance of engaging with services beyond the criminal justice system. These factors are underpinned by contexts of gender, class and ethnicity (Howard League 2000; Turnbull *et al.* 2000; Malloch 2000, 2004a, 2004b):

> The biggest problem with most of the people we have here anyway – their drug problem – I think it is because they have no self-respect. No self-worth. They're likely to have been unemployed for however long. Left school, never worked. They've got no prospect of ever working, they live in poverty, they live in hellish circumstances, they mix in a circle of friends, all in exactly the same position, you know. There is no light on the horizon for them. Day just goes into day, you know. If they commit an offence and go to jail, generally speaking, what have they got to lose exactly? (drug support worker quoted in Malloch *et al.* 2003: 80).

Recurrent calls to develop new approaches to dealing with drug-related crime have come from a wide range of sources (Association of Chief Police Officers 2002; Scottish Consortium on Crime and Criminal Justice 2002; NACRO 2003). It is notable that an organization such as ACPO should be among the most vocal in challenging current policy and practice in this area. Suggestions that an overemphasis on law enforcement should be replaced by a more 'rehabilitative' response to drug use have been prevalent, notably towards the adoption of policy that is able to tackle the broader social, political and economic consequences of drug dependency.

While it may be appropriate to focus on individual behaviour in the context of a court-mandated sentence, it is often impossible to alter the restrictions placed on the individual by institutional bureaucracy, lack of adequate resources or broader social and political determinants. It might be recognized that many problems associated with drug use are structural; however, services remain limited in directing their response towards the individual.

The depiction and creation of reputations for drug users remain ideological and political, defining and sustaining the methods that are required to deal with the 'problem' as defined by popular ideologies and official discourse. The importance of popular discourse in the creation and maintenance of 'negative' reputations is used to support official responses, and provide justification for the state to control drug users. The methods employed, be they 'welfarist' or punitive, are aimed at bringing those who fail to conform within the auspices of the state. The fears which are fuelled by drug use in terms of the perceived links with crime and disease are used to justify these measures as 'necessary' by ensuring that those who use drugs illegally are portrayed as quite distinct from the typical 'law-abiding' citizen.

Concluding points

Critical theory aims not only to understand society but also to change it. In research terms, this requires the development of different forms of knowledge, different experiential accounts, which may challenge the status quo and provide a different way of looking at social life. C.W. Mills (1975: 8) identified the relationship between personal context and the interrelationship between biography and history: the 'personal troubles of milieu' and the 'public issues of social structure.'

While personal troubles are located with the 'self' (for example, drug use and 'addiction') and characterized by interpersonal relationships, public issues, derived from the larger structures of social and historical life, go beyond the 'local environments of the individual' (criminal justice responses, issues of enforcement). For Mills (1975), to be aware of the social structure and interconnections of institutional arrangements while being critically self-reflective of personal context is to 'possess the sociological imagination.'

In order to understand and analyse issues of power, legitimacy and authority, contemporary social and cultural relations need to be contextualized in their material history and political-economic present (Scraton 2002). To understand social action requires the 'interweaving' of the 'personal', 'social' and 'structural' and the challenge for a critical criminology is to provide knowledge which engages with the prevailing social structures. The difficulties for any marginalized group are that dominant discourses about them have already been established. So, for example, 'drug users' or 'offenders' as a group are frequently defined, condemned and denied credibility through political opinion, the media and other social avenues.

Social critique (derived from research and theory) is a force for social change in that it challenges dominant social ideologies that present the existing society as natural and morally beneficent. Social critique has the potential to challenge the socially constructed character of society, to reveal the existence of unequal and unfair social arrangements, and to reveal the insidious nature of social control where appropriate. For critical theorists, 'knowledge', including academic knowledge, is neither value free nor value neutral. It is produced and reproduced within structural relationships which establish a particular social order. By providing the 'view from below', critical social analysis can set an oppositional agenda. It can ensure that the voices and experiences of those who are marginalized by state practices can be heard and represented. 'Cases' can be turned into social issues. Personal troubles can be viewed as public issues.

The images and ideologies which pertain to the use of proscribed substances contribute to the processes of criminalization which operate in relation to drug users. This results in the marginalization of drug users. These processes of marginalization are reinforced by prohibition and legislation. This process is crucial to an understanding of the nature of marginalization and its more structural manifestations. This also requires the recognition of the effects this has at an individual level.

The involvement of a range of agencies has brought with it the emergence of a spectrum of critiques and the presentation of different forms of knowledge. This, in turn, has provided critical criminology with the opportunity to draw on the work of other disciplines which focus on the individual (in terms of 'treatment', support and attainment of rights) and to provide a theoretical analysis which can synthesize this approach. Social control is an organized response to behaviour and people which society views as being in some way threatening or undesirable. This control operates through various disciplines: social work, criminology, psychology, the judiciary. The use of power in obtaining social control is a complex phenomenon and power does not emanate solely from above, or from social institutions. However, in relation to responses to drug use and drug users it is clear that state agencies and the criminal law have a significant role to play. This can be identified through a critical criminological perspective which is also capable of shifting the focus from criminal justice to social justice responses aimed at the transformation of social-structural conditions and the elimination of social inequalities.

Notes

1   This is dependent on the class of drugs, value, amount and whether or not the drug was intended for personal use or supply.

2   But tobacco and alcohol have both been prohibited in different countries during different historical periods (see Szasz 1974).

3   There are problems in the development of longer-term strategies as evidenced by the publication of a 10-year National Drugs Strategy in 1998 by the Clinton administration which set targets to focus on crime, public nuisance and health. This strategy was abandoned in 2002 with the election of George W. Bush and the establishment of different priorities. This situation was not so obvious with changes of government in the UK, where New Labour has developed many of the policies established by the previous Conservative governments.

4   The Government white paper (1995) Tackling Drugs Together outlines the responsibilities of the police and Customs and Excise in enforcing anti-drugs legislation.

5   The enforcement of this legislation has not been without criticism. Judges themselves have been outspoken in opposing mandatory drug sentencing. Judge Harold H. Greene rejected the use of a 30-year mandated sentence for a repeat offender stating: 'We cannot allow justice and rationality to become casualties of a war on drugs being waged with Draconian, politically expedient sentences.'

6   See Hillyard (1993) for his study of people's experiences of the Prevention of Terrorism Acts in Britain. While the context is very different, similar constructs apply.

7   This differs somewhat from the white paper's counterpart in Scotland (Ministerial Drugs Task Force 1994) which gave greater encouragement to reducing harm from drug misuse. Clearly the national contexts have contributed to this disparity. While the English report addresses voters' fears over drugs and crime, the Scottish Task Force had to address significant rates of HIV infection in some of Scotland's major cities, and an extremely high death rate among injecting drug users in Glasgow.

Scottish policy does, however, reflect concerns about the relationship between drug use, crime and community safety (Scottish Office 1999; Scottish Executive 2000).

8 While engagement with services is recognized as crucial, this can be severely limited if services are not available when an individual seeks help. In Donmall *et al.'s* study (2005), clients could expect an average waiting time from referral to treatment of 12 weeks. Much longer waiting times were reported in certain areas.

References

Action on Smoking and Health (2005) *Smoking Statistics: Basic Facts* (http://www.ash.org.uk).

Addaction (2004) *Collecting the Evidence: Clients' Views on Drug Services*. London: Addaction.

Alcohol Concern (2002) *Your Very Good Health?* London: Alcohol Concern.

Ashton, M. and Witton, J. (2004) 'The power of the welcoming reminder', *Drug and Alcohol Findings*, 11: 4–18.

Association of Chief Police Officers (2002) *A Review of Drugs Policy and Proposals for the Future*. London: ACPO.

Audit Commission (2002) *Changing Habits: The Commissioning and Management of Drug Services for Adults*. London: Audit Commission.

Barton, A. (1999) 'Breaking the crime/drugs circle: the birth of a new approach?', *Howard Journal of Criminal Justice*, 39: 144–57.

Bennett, T. (1998) *Drugs and Crime: The Results of Research on Drug Testing and Interviewing Arrestees*. London: Home Office Research.

Boyd, N. and Lowman, J. (1991) 'The politics of prostitution and drug control', in K. Stenson and D. Cowell (eds) *The Politics of Crime Control*. London: Sage.

Boyd, S. (2004) *From Witches to Crack Moms: Women, Drug Law and Policy*. Durham, NC: Carolina Academic Press.

Campbell, N. (2000) *Using Women: Gender, Drug Policy and Social Justice*. New York, NY: Routledge.

Chambliss, W. (1994) 'Don't confuse me with facts: Clinton "just says no"', *New Left Review*, 204: 113–26.

Chomsky, N. (1992) *Deterring Democracy*. London: Vintage.

Chomsky, N. (1994) *World Orders Old and New*. New York, NY: Columbia University Press.

Christie, N. (1994) *Crime Control as Industry*. London: Routledge.

Cohen, S. (1985) *Visions of Social Control*. Cambridge: Polity Press.

Collison, M. (1993) 'Punishing drugs', *British Journal of Criminology*, 33: 382–99.

Collison, M. (1994) 'Drug offenders and criminal justice', *Crime, Law and Social Change*, 21: 49–71.

Donmall, M., Watson, A., Milar, T. and Dunn, G. (2005) *Outcome of Waiting Lists (OWL) Study*. London: Department of Health and NHS National Treatment Agency.

Dorn, N. (1992) 'Clarifying policy options on drug trafficking', in P. O'Hare *et al.* (eds) *The Reduction of Drug-related Harm*. London: Routledge.

Dorn, N. and South, N. (1991) 'Drugs, crime and law rnforcement', in F. Heidensohn and M. Farrell (eds) *Crime in Europe*. London: Routledge.

Duke, K. (2003) *Drugs, Prisons and Policy-making*. Basingstoke: Palgrave/ Macmillan.

Effective Interventions Unit (2002) *Integrated Care for Drug Users: Principles and Practices*. Edinburgh: Scottish Executive.

Eley, S., Gallop, K., McIvor, G., Morgan, K. and Yates, R. (2002a) *Evaluation of Pilot Drug Treatment and Testing Orders*. Edinburgh: Scottish Executive Central Research Unit.

Eley, S., Malloch, M., McIvor, G., Yates, R. and Brown, A. (2002b) *The Glasgow Drug Court in Action: The First Six Months*. Edinburgh: Scottish Executive (http://www.scotland.gov.uk).

Foucault, M. (1979) *Discipline and Punish: The Birth of the Prison*. New York, NY: Vintage Books.

Gossop, M., Marsden, J. and Stewart, D. (1998) *The National Treatment Outcome Research Study: Changes in Substance Misuse, Health and Criminal Behaviour One Year After Intake*. London: Department of Health.

Hallam, C. (2004) *Afghanistan: New Front Line in the War on Drugs*. London: RELEASE.

Hillyard, P. (1993) *Suspect Community*. London: Pluto Press in association with Liberty.

Holloway, K., Bennett, T. and Farrington, D. (2005) *The Effectiveness of Criminal Justice and Treatment Programmes in Reducing Drug-related Crime: A Systematic Review*. London: Home Office (Online Report 26/05).

Home Office (1995) *Tackling Drugs Together*. London: HMSO.

Home Office (1998) *Tackling Drugs to Build a Better Britain*. London: Home Office.

Home Office (2002) *Updated Drug Strategy 2002*. London: Home Office.

Home Office (2004a) *Statistics on Race and the Criminal Justice System*. London: Home Office (online report).

Home Office (2004b) *Statistics on Gender and the Criminal Justice System*. London: Home Office.

Home Office (2004c) *Tackling Drugs. Changing Lives: Keeping Communities Safe from Drugs*. London: Home Office.

Hough, M. (1994) *Problem Drug Use and Criminal Justice: A Review of the Literature*. London: South Bank University.

Hough, M., Clancy, A., McSweeney, T. and Turnbull, P. (2003) *The Impact of Drug Treatment and Testing Orders on Offending: Two Year Reconviction Results*. London: Home Office (Findings 184).

Howard League for Penal Reform (2000) *A Chance to Break the Cycle: Women and the Drug Treatment and Testing Order*. London: The Howard League.

Hudson, B. (1993) *Penal Policy and Social Justice*. London: Macmillan.

Husak, D. (1992) *Drugs and Rights*. Cambridge: Cambridge University Press.

Kohn, M. (1992) *Dope Girls: The Birth of the British Drug Underground*. London: Lawrence & Wishart.

Lidz, C. and Walker, A. (1980) *Heroin, Deviance and Morality*. Beverly Hills, CA and London: Sage.

Malloch, M. (2000) *Women, Drugs and Custody*. Winchester: Waterside Press.

Malloch, M. (2004a) 'Not fragrant at all: criminal justice responses to women drug users', *Critical Social Policy*, 24: 385–405.

Malloch, M. (2004b) 'Missing out: gender, drugs and justice', *Probation Journal*, 51: 295–308.

Malloch, M., Eley, S., McIvor, G., Beaton, K. and Yates, R. (2003) *The Fife Drug Court in Action: The First Six Months*. Edinburgh: Scottish Executive (http://www.scotland.gov.uk/cru/resfinds/crf69-00.asp).

Malloch, M. and Stanley, E. (2005) 'The detention of asylum seekers in the UK: representing risk, managing the dangerous', *Punishment and Society*, 7: 53–71.

McConville, M., Saunders, A. and Leng, R. (1991) *The Case for the Prosecution*. London: Routledge.

McDermott, P. (1992) 'Representations of drug users', in P. O'Hare *et al.* (eds) *The Reduction of Drug-telated Harm*. London: Routledge.

McDonald, M. (ed.) (1994) *Gender, Drink and Drugs*. Oxford: Providence.

McIvor, G. (2004) *Reconviction Following Drug Treatment and Testing Orders*. Edinburgh: Scottish Executive Social Research.

McLaren, J., Menzies, R. and Chunn, D. (eds) (2002) *Regulating Lives: Historical Essays on the State, Society, the Individual and the Law*. Vancouver: University of British Columbia Press.

Mills, C.W. (1975) *The Sociological Imagination*. New York, NY: Oxford University Press.

Ministerial Drugs Task Force (1994) *Drugs in Scotland: Meeting the Challenge*. Edinburgh: Scottish Office.

NACRO (2003) *Drugs and Crime*. London: NACRO.

Parenti, C. (1999) *Lockdown America: Police and Prisons in the Age of Crisis*. London: Verso.

Rethinking Crime and Punishment (2004) *Searching for a Fix: Drug Misuse, Crime and the Criminal Justice System*. London: Esmee Fairbairn Association.

Roberts, M., Klein, A. and Trace, M. (2004) *Towards a Review of Global Policies on Illegal Drugs. Report One* (Beckley Foundation Drug Policy Programme). London: Drugscope.

Rumgay, J. (2000) *The Addicted Offender: Developments in British Policy and Practice*. Basingstoke: Palgrave.

Scottish Consortium on Crime and Criminal Justice (2002) *Making Sense of Drugs and Crime: Drugs, Crime and Penal Policy*. Edinburgh: SCCCJ.

Scottish Drugs Forum (2003) *Submission to the Scottish Executive Review of Treatment and Rehabilitation Services*. Edinburgh: SDF.

Scottish Executive (2000) *Drugs Action Plan: Protecting Our Future*. Edinburgh: Scottish Executive.

Scottish Office (1999) *Tackling Drugs in Scotland: Action in Partnership*. Edinburgh: HMSO.

Scraton, P. (2002) 'Defining "power" and challenging "knowledge": critical analysis as resistance in the UK', in K. Carrington and R. Hogg (eds) *Critical Criminology: Issues, Debates, Challenges*. Cullompton: Willan Publishing.

Scraton, P. and Chadwick, K. (1987) 'Speaking ill of the dead' in P. Scraton (ed) *Law, Order and the Authoritarian State*. Milton Keynes: Open University Press.

Singer, L. (1993) *Erotic Welfare*. London: Routledge.

Spooner, C. and Hetherington, K. (2004) *Social Determinants of Drug Use*. Sydney: National Drug and Alcohol Research Centre, University of New South Wales (Technical Report 228).

Strategy Unit (2003) 'Phase 1 – understanding the issues.' Unpublished policy document, available from Transform Drug Policy Foundation: www.tdpf. org.uk.

Strausbaugh, J. and Blaise, D. (eds) (1991) *The Drug User*. Baltimore, MD: Dolphin-Moon Press.

Sudbury, J. (2005) 'Celling black bodies: black women in the global prison industrial complex', *Feminist Review*, 80: 162–79.

Sumner, C. (ed) (1990) *Censure, Politics and Criminal Justice*. Milton Keynes: Open University Press.

Szasz, T. (1974) *Ceremonial Chemistry: The Ritual Persecution of Drugs, Addicts and Pushers*. London: Routledge & Kegan Paul.

Trace, M., Roberts, M. and Klein, A. (2004) *Assessing Drug Policy Principles and Practice*. London: Drugscope (Beckley Foundation Drug Policy Programme).

TRANSFORM (2004) *After the War on Drugs: Options for Control*. Bristol: Transform Drug Policy Foundation.

Turnbull, P., McSweeney, T., Webster, R., Edmunds, M. and Hough, M. (2000) *Drug Treatment and Testing Orders: Final Evaluation Report*. London: Home Office (Research Study 212).

Turning Point (2004) *Routes into Treatment: Drugs and Crime*. London: Turning Point.

Walters, R. (2003) *Deviant Knowledge: Criminology, Politics and Policy*. Cullompton: Willan Publishing.

Young, J. (2002) 'Critical criminology in the twenty-first century: critique, irony and the always unfinished', in K. Carrington and R. Hogg (eds) *Critical Criminology: Issues, Debates, Challenges*. Cullompton: Willan Publishing.

Chapter 7

Taking crime seriously? Disaster, victimization and justice

Howard Davis

Introduction

Individual crime and even 'anti-social behaviours' stand at the forefront of political, professional and public concern. They usually involve loss or harm that, in quantitative terms, is relatively minor. While their prevention, detection, prosecution and punishment are framed as key responsibilities of the liberal democratic state, deaths that result from the acts or omissions of corporations and state institutions seldom result in severe punishment (Slapper and Tombs 1999; Tombs 1999, 2002; Bergman 2000). Many such harms pass almost unnoticed by the media. By contrast, cases of multiple or mass fatality can become major stories and the subject of fierce political debate. As critical criminology has contested the legal straitjacket of 'crime' and moved beyond 'common sense', major disasters have received increasing attention (Coleman *et al.* 1990; Scraton *et al.* 1995; Davis and Scraton 1997, 1999; Scraton 1999; Slapper and Tombs 1999; Bergman 2000). Disasters, although often framed as 'accidents' rather than crimes, raise questions of culpability, responsibility and injustice that should be of serious concern to criminologists.

Defining 'disaster' is not merely an academic exercise. The term suggests that harm is severe in intensity, extent, or both. It often carries the connotation of official failure and as such poses a threat to authorities charged with ensuring public safety and politically dependent upon the maintenance of legitimacy ('t Hart 1993). The almost reflexive question, 'how did it happen?' easily elides into 'how was it allowed to happen?' Uncomfortably for the state and its powerful corporate allies, such questions increasingly extend towards the broader social, political and economic contexts that underpin such tragedies. Moreover, the failure to prevent harm, if construed as culpable, may threaten the positions of powerful individuals, organizations and sometimes even governments. 'Disaster', then, may be a label that those 'in the frame' would seek to avoid or deflect.

Disaster does not strike randomly. Globally, it disproportionately affects the marginalized. It impacts upon individuals and communities in various ways and harm takes a multitude of forms, from bereavement through material loss to psychological trauma. Moreover, victimization does not derive solely in the direct experience of disaster itself. It has become clear that the actions of responders, often official agencies, may be harmful. In the longer term, the characteristic contestation of the 'truth' of disaster presents those already traumatized or bereaved with the prospect of years of conflict, often against heavy odds.

Many disasters are the consequence of acts or omissions on the part of large organizations or states themselves. Frequently they are the result of the subordination of health and safety to other goals. For critical criminology specifically, the 'criminalization' of disaster raises difficult issues. Attempts to 'expand the criminological imagination' suggest the efficacy of an approach that engages 'social harm' rather than 'crime', *per se*. Yet there are clearly dangers in arguing that some forms of harm not presently criminalized should be treated as crimes (Alvesalo and Tombs 2002). Criminalization may lead to the extension of surveillance and the punishment of relatively 'low-level operators' as scapegoats (Horlick-Jones 1996).

This chapter describes how, within present arrangements, there is a clear double standard: events and processes that are massively harmful, and that are the consequence of intent and/or 'criminal' negligence, are not constructed as crimes, while minor acts are. This double standard cannot be justified by a lack of blameworthiness in the origins of disaster. Yet, in terms of criminal justice as it is presently framed and administered, the victims of such harms are denied the 'justice' accorded to (some) others. Powerful organizations are protected by blurred lines of responsibility, inadequate law and a reluctance or inability on the part of the authorities to investigate and prosecute successfully.

The chapter draws upon work from a variety of academic disciplines. While criminologists have produced key research interventions, so too have sociologists, geographers, historians, psychologists, lawyers, engineers and others. Disaster researchers have the opportunity to draw upon a breadth of work, some critical, some less so, to explore the continuities and discontinuities of disaster. Whether considered as 'crime' or 'harm' or both, disasters exemplify inequality and injustice. As such they should be considered to be well within whatever province criminology defines for itself.

Defining 'disaster'

Whatever the merits and demerits of particular conceptions of 'disaster' and 'crime', it is important to recognize that the construction of such categories is contextualized by pervasive relations of power. These find their expression in the primacy of official accounts but are also reproduced within media-led 'common sense'. 'Disaster' is a term whose use is usually restricted to the acute and visible, rather than the chronic and obscured. Neither the 'disaster' nor the 'crime' label is politically neutral. Both imply issues of responsibility.

While criminologists are concerned with the 'excessive imagination' extended towards traditional conceptions of crime, disasters present a contradictory picture. On the one hand the dangers of the 'terrorist' disaster are highlighted. The British state has aggregated to itself a wide range of draconian powers for use in emergency[1] and the disastrous potential of terrorist attack is used to justify derogation from basic human rights standards. On the other hand, corporate and state harms are underplayed and may not be understood as 'crimes' at all. While companies have been prosecuted for health and safety offences, only comparatively recently have criminal investigations more routinely begun to consider more 'serious' offences, such as corporate homicide.

There are a variety of definitions for disaster. Most incorporate the notions of extensive damage or harm and a 'suddenness' of onset that results in the overwhelming of response capacity (Taylor 1987; Tierney 1989; Quarantelli 2001; Shaluf *et al.* 2003). Often, therefore, what 'counts' as disaster depends upon the recognition, by official bodies or 'experts', that they have been unable, in *their* terms, to 'cope'. Disasters in this view are often misleadingly restricted to a 'moment' or a short period of time at a specific location. Famine and disease develop and reproduce over lengthy periods. Environmental disasters may take many years to become evident, regionally or globally. Disastrous consequences may remain unrecognized when they are not sudden or 'overwhelming' – at least in the terms of official agencies. Where recognized they may be 'normalized' as routine problems to be 'put up with' (Gephart 1984). Over the next 25–30 years it is estimated that 250,000 men will die from mesothelioma due to asbestos exposure across Western Europe, representing 1 in 150 of all men born between 1945 and 1950 (Peto *et al.* 1999). The 'sudden impact' approach understates such 'chronic' long-term exposures and the impact they have upon communities. Indeed, dominant discourses on disaster fail to recognize that some disasters are complex and, effectively, permanent (Slim 1995). Holding those responsible to account becomes inherently difficult where 'causes' are multifactored, contested or obscure.

Sudden 'losses', too, may remain unacknowledged by official frameworks. Fordham (1998: 129), for example, argues that, in the UK, floods may be denied 'disaster status' despite their subjective impact. She contends that 'this simply underlines the ambiguity and value-laden nature of the term "disaster" for which "objective" measurements and definitions are meaningless in the light of individual victims and survivors' levels of distress'. This raises the question, as Hewitt (1995: 333) suggests: "disaster sociology' for whom?' Dominant constructions frame disaster in terms of the interests, expectations and values of officials and experts, frequently at the expense of 'those in hazard' themselves (Hewitt 1995: 330):

> In this context, the social problem of disaster is not primarily one of, say, crisis, devastation, extreme experience and emiseration, let alone of tragedy, violence or misrule. It is all about (loss of) control – meaning control ... within a particular kind of public order. Problems are constructed as the absence, limitations or failures of police and discipline, as defined by Michel Foucault, and as demonstrating the need for more of them (1995: 332).

Disasters are not one-dimensional: there is no 'typical' disaster any more than there is a typical crime. There are no simple defining criteria or parameters. Academics themselves have particular 'frames' within which they recognize 'disaster'. These reflect professional interests and are inevitably varied. There is a danger, however, that a specific focus may neglect both the similarities and the differences between different disaster 'types', or even to deny one type or another as disaster. A critical approach to disaster should ultimately rest upon the recognition, by victims or survivors, that an event or process has had *disastrous consequences* – major loss, hardship or disruption. Events may be disastrous for *those involved*, even if not for official agencies and responders. Berren *et al.* (1989: 44, emphasis added) define disaster as 'any event that stresses a society, a portion of that society, or even *an individual family* beyond the normal limits of daily living'.[2] This may involve loss of life, physical or mental injury, or severe social or economic harm. Official definitions, in their emphasis upon acute impact, mass harm and the overwhelming of services, exclude from view the extent to which disaster happens every day. This leaves endemic harms and injustices understated and their continuities with officially recognized mass-fatality disaster under-analysed. Widespread loss and injury are no less 'disastrous' for being commonplace.

It is not possible to do justice to such an inclusive definition of disaster in this limited space. This chapter, of necessity, restricts itself to cases where disastrous consequences are borne by at least several people linked closely in time and/or space. That is to say that it concerns itself generally, with key aspects of disaster as officially defined. This is not to minimize individual, familial or small group harms, or to suggest that these are not 'real' disasters. Such events frequently involve similar issues – variations in exposure to risk, inequalities in mitigation and struggles over truth, justice and accountability – as those with more dramatic effects. Nor is it to ignore the fact that there may be large numbers of individual disasters that can advantageously be considered in the aggregate. A misleading dichotomy between the 'extreme' and the 'normal' understates the links between the two, indeed the location and origin of one within the other. Hewitt (1995: 332) notes critically, that hazards that are dispersed, if widespread are not considered by the disaster field as requiring special attention:

> That is so, even though the chronic dangers and damages involve by far the largest privations, material losses and untimely death, and by far the largest investments in public safety and national security. Normal life in such a context, is not so much ordinary, everyday, or safe, but obedient to large scale goals, regulated and disciplined centrally.

Disasters are frequently framed as 'accidental' or 'unintended'. As discussed below, this can lead to a misplaced assumption that 'blame' is of limited applicability. Moreover, it can place a false limit on the 'disaster territory'. Most civil disasters, and even many 'natural' disasters, involve profound human failure, individual, systemic and structural. Such a framing may also place beyond reach disastrous events such as war, on the basis that they lie within, or indeed constitute, another category. It would be strange to exclude from consideration this, the most disastrous human activity of all. That being said, it is not possible to do justice here to the diversity, complexity and importance of state violence of which war is one, by no means exclusive, example.

In conclusion, a critical approach interrogates 'commonsense' representations of disaster. It recognizes a broad conceptualization of chronic social and economic dislocation as disaster, rejecting the idea that the subjective experience of those disastrously affected is secondary to dominant 'objective' classification. For the critical researcher the question *behind* the question of definition must also be 'who is doing the defining' (Hewitt 1995)? While 'experts' debate the finer points of definition, the broader social construction of disaster involves a combination of proximity, visibility and acute impact. These factors, taken together, can combine to propel relatively small-scale tragedies into national and international awareness. Conversely, their absence may obscure the disastrous consequences of long-term, hidden or distant events and processes, even where they entail very large loss of life.

Disaster 'experts': research management and practice

The problems of disaster management, and their solutions, have been framed as primarily technical. Constructed in this way, the events and processes of disaster management are depoliticized. The views of professional 'experts' – the holders of the requisite technocratic knowledges – dominate the production of knowledge about the causes of, and appropriate responses to, disasters. In common with other areas of criminological interest, the predictions and prescriptions of the experts frequently aspire to 'scientific' status in which problematic, incomplete or distorted data are often presented as if precise (Smithson 1990; Wynne 1992). The specialized conclusions of the experts are assumed to be superior to the local knowledges of the disaster-vulnerable or disaster-affected. 'Risk' assessment attempts to quantify the dangerousness of a wide range of hazards, from the factory floor to the flood plain.[3] In the aftermath of radioactive rainfall following the Chernobyl disaster, for example, English hill farmers' scepticism of scientists' reassurances and recommendations proved to be well founded (Wynne 1992). Their own potentially crucial contributions about the interaction between climate, terrain and farming practices were ignored. Similarly, in the immediate aftermath of the *Exxon Valdez* supertanker disaster 'it was action by the state of Alaska and a home-grown guerrilla navy of fishermen that got the most done ... the creativity, knowledge, energy, and organization of local communities is a resource that is not adequately tapped under the current contingency planning processes' (Kelso cited in Browning and Shetler 1992: 487–8).

At the social level, official concerns tend to range from breakdown of group norms and behaviour, to the dislocation of services and public authority. From the tasks of risk assessment and emergency planning, to the practice of post-trauma therapy, experts define and process the 'material' of disasters – people. Geographer Ken Hewitt (1995: 321) complains that:

> The vocabulary is not merely one of geophysical and technological processes; of magnitudes, temporal or spatial frequency, polygons and zones. Persons, communities and their concerns are also – and in this paradigm perhaps, must be reduced to mass, collective units, statistically described data points, and functions of abstract dimensions. Society is redescribed as ... boxes ... linked by arrows in models that are, apparently, demonstration or organizational flow charts.

Significantly, Dynes (1994, 2003) notes the persistent preoccupation of disaster planners with the (re)establishment of 'command and control' in the face of exaggerated fears of social breakdown and disorder. Hewitt (1995: 330) insists upon the need to focus on the accounts of those directly involved in catastrophe:

> To pay close attention to what they say, their story and concerns, gives them direct entry into the concepts and discussions of social and disaster research. This is an essential step towards giving those who do not get published, some participation in and control over the impersonal processes and citadels of expertise, that tend to dominate the disaster community.

Victimization and response

As some disasters are less recognized than others, so victimization may be hidden, denied or minimized. Victimization in disasters, as with conventional crime, is contextualized by class, race, gender and age. Those most marginalized and with least access to resources in non-emergency situations are most likely to be disadvantaged when disaster strikes. Financial losses impact differentially according to structural factors such as vulnerability, insurance, employment conditions and benefit status. Not only are the poor routinely more vulnerable to hazards (living on the worst land, in the poorest housing, employed in the most dangerous jobs, for example) but their interests can also be factored out of disaster planning and relief (Wisner 1998; Fothergill and Peek 2004). At a global level, some people are far more likely to be disaster victims than others. The proportion of GNP lost in natural disasters decreases with increasing economic rank (Alexander 1997). The economic dominance of the North over the South (Alexander 1997: 293) has resulted in 'the concentration of mitigation investment in countries which can easily afford it. Hence at the world scale there is only a weak correlation between the need for disaster mitigation and the level of investment in it.'

Although Fordham (1998: 127) observes that 'an acknowledged gender perspective [in disasters] has not advanced beyond the earliest phases of feminist studies', it is clear that disaster affects women and men differently. Women are disproportionately likely to be victims in natural disasters (Butterbaugh 2005). Where employment in industries is demarcated by gender, so will be the likelihood of victimization within such settings. Less obviously, response to the threat and the impact of disaster may be gendered. Official responses to disaster are male dominated. Warning information, for example, may be disseminated via media to which women have little easy access. Instead, warnings may be passed from men to other men (Fordham 2001). This in turn may make it impossible for women to prepare themselves or their families for impending disaster. Should the need to evacuate arise, women may be less mobile than men. This may be due to caring responsibilities, reluctance to leave homes, lack of the means of doing so or for cultural reasons. The impact of disaster on women can exacerbate their pre-existing subordination. They may suffer direct losses and lose further income when they are obliged to provide unpaid reproductive/caring work (Yonder *et al.* 2005). Moreover (Yonder *et al.* 2005: 4), material entitlements in disaster relief 'favour men over women, giving priority to property owners, tenants of record, bank account holders and perceived heads of household. Where employment assistance concentrates on workers in the formal economy and business aid is awarded to formal enterprises, women's economic position is eroded further.'

In the developed world this is reflected in a preoccupation with the public sphere of post-disaster work, a 'male' conception of 'home', a lack of comprehension of the different disaster worlds inhabited by men and women and a failure to involve women in disaster planning or response (Fordham 1998). What we know, or suspect, about disaster reality is often a male reality.

The impact of disaster is also mediated by class, race and age. The poor, the old and the marginalized find themselves in the worst housing on the worst land with the least resources to cope with the unexpected. Moreover, they also find themselves least able to access and shape the policies, practices and resources of public agencies. From a critical perspective, the experiences of victims and survivors at the hands of insensitive, inadequate or oppressive responses to disaster are not comprehensible without reference to the structured oppression of the 'everyday'. At one extreme, the refusal of the authorities to respond humanely to the plight of New Orleans after Hurricane Katrina is comprehensible only within the context of prevailing racism (see, for example, 'The hurricane that shamed America', *Dispatches*, Channel 4, 31 October 2005; Butterbaugh 2005; Enarson 2005; Street 2005). At another, less visible extreme, the deaths of over 700 elderly Chicago residents in the heatwave of 1995 and of 13,000 French elderly in the European heatwave of 2003 scarcely even registered as 'disasters'. As in the case of New Orleans, natural hazards cannot explain the full horror of what occurred. As Langer (2004: 275) puts it:

> Both the Chicago and French disasters made visible a series of social/community conditions that are always present for which the social organization of the cities were responsible, not nature. Evolution of urban society has made it possible for so many elderly to die ... as well as the circumstances that make their deaths so easy to dismiss and forget.

The impacts even of 'natural' disasters such as these are no longer unforeseeable. Hazards can be assessed, and preventive or mitigating policies put in place. It is not difficult to anticipate who will most likely be affected. Yet success in reducing vulnerability to natural disasters has been limited (Alexander 1997: 291). Key factors responsible for this are rooted in structural relations. Tackling the conditions that underpin vulnerability requires political commitment on the part of the state. Neoliberal economic ideology can undermine progress and ultimately lead to the failure to implement necessary measures. Wisner (2001) concludes, for example, that the failure of El Salvador to implement lessons from Hurricane Mitch in 1998 and earthquakes in 2001 is directly traceable to such policies. Here, the root cause of vulnerability to natural hazard lies in:

> the long history of elite control of the land and the wars that have resulted from it. These two fundamental historical factors have shaped the country's population distribution and settlement pattern, one which exposes two groups to very high risk: the urban poor, especially those living in and near the ravines ... and the rural poor who live on steep slopes or near rivers ... [or in] ... drought-prone areas (Wisner 2001: 254).

Vulnerability to 'natural' disaster, in this example, is clearly rooted in social arrangements. Measures to tackle such arrangements, or offset their effects, are resisted by political and economic elites. El Salvador, escaping relatively unscathed from Hurricane Mitch, was well placed to learn the lessons of that disaster as it affected neighbouring states. However, health care (and capacity to respond to crisis) was cut, the rural crisis for small landowners continued and the problem of poor-quality 'temporary' housing persisted with little effort to resettle poorer people on less dangerous land (Wisner 2001). Rather, the government placed its faith in a neoliberalism that promotes business interests, unfettered by regulation and aimed to minimize government involvement and capacity. At national and local levels government proved unable or unwilling to plan, resource and operationalize preventive programmes. Before the onset of the rainy season in 2001 (Wisner 2001: 261, emphasis added) 'drainage works needed to be cleaned, rubble and debris removed, basic sanitary provisions supplied to the many people still in shelters or temporary housing. This [was] the minimum required to avoid additional public health, flood and landslide disasters. *The central government itself new this.'*

Instead of completing this work, the Ministry of Public Works' entire fleet of machinery lay idle as arrangements were made to pass it to the army pending sale to the private sector. The impact of even 'natural' disasters, as this example illustrates, is socially rooted.[4] That such political acts or omissions are not normally considered as 'criminal' diminishes neither their harmful consequences nor the culpability of those who take the decisions.

Reflecting developments in broader victimology, recent years have seen an intensifying concern about the psychological impact of disaster upon the bereaved and survivors. This sits, paradoxically, alongside various forms of denial of what experiencing disaster is 'really' like. Within the complex shaping of public knowledges, tastes and sensitivities, 'normal' society has not wanted to *hear* what disaster and trauma are really like (Dasberg 1992). In Western society 'our primary myths emphasise justice and control, optimism and a positive outlook ... There is little place for losers' (Janoff-Bulman 1992: 154). This sets a context within which victims are not necessarily met with sympathy and still less with empathy. Moreover, the experience of disaster victims suggests that this lack of understanding and its demand that the victim return promptly to normality are institutionally expressed. 'Secondary victimization' is evident at several levels. In the first place, the immediate response of the state and its professional agencies may be overtly hostile, repressive and even brutal. Second, formal 'processing' may be insensitive and dismissive of victims' rights and needs. Third, the longer-term struggles around truth and justice discussed in more detail below may add considerably to the burden of victims and survivors.

At its starkest the heavy hand of state response was evidenced in the 'zero tolerance' of 'looters' in New Orleans. In other instances the brutality of the state can *be* the disaster. The response to threats of 'disorder', for example, may involve extreme repression (Barbato 2003; Dawson 2005; Rolston and Scraton 2005). While it may be relatively rare in disasters within liberal democratic states for response to be so brazenly oppressive as in the case of Katrina, this does not mean that state responses usually meet the needs and expectations of those affected. Official responses to disaster claim to 'balance' psychosocial needs, on the one hand, with the requirements of emergency management and medico-crimino-legal investigations on the other (Home Office/Cabinet Office 2004). This neat 'dualism', however, is difficult to sustain. It has become clear that, at the very least, the processes of the latter, experienced as obstructive, partial and sometimes even oppressive, have had profound impacts on the former (Coleman *et al.* 1990; Scraton *et al.* 1995; Davis and Scraton 1997, 1999; Scraton 1999). While official recognition of the traumatic potential of disaster has grown, less progress has been made in recognizing the harm that can be caused by social and official responses themselves. Official and media processes and demands tend to take priority over the needs of victims. For those bereaved by sudden disasters, death may become part of a national, even international, 'event'. The media circus, and disaster responses themselves, form a bewildering, unfamiliar and public context for personal tragedy (Coleman *et al.* 1990; Scraton *et al.* 1995; Jemphrey and Berrington 2000). Within the media maelstrom, the bereaved seek answers to deeply personal questions. They often want to know *exactly* what happened to their loved ones (Coleman *et al.* 1990; Davis and Scraton 1997, 1999; Scraton 1999). One father who lost his daughter in the Lockerbie disaster explained:

> you are thinking, 'did she cry out?' Was there a time ... did she feel the pain, all these sorts of things? Did she want her mum and dad? Was she scared? Was there time to be scared? And somehow you feel you want to get into that, to experience as much of what she experienced as possible (personal interview).

Information, provided quickly and accurately, is vital, even if it is just that at the time there *is* little or no information. Time and space with the deceased within which to touch and hold them are important. Less obviously, visits to the disaster site and the return of possessions may provide the bereaved with links to the death experience.

In terms of each of these needs, official agendas may conflict with those of survivors and the bereaved. The authorities may face seemingly insuperable logistical and practical problems. When resources are completely overwhelmed, the dead become a hindrance. Behind the practical problems, however, lies a forensic imperative. There is a danger that bodies may become puzzles to be solved, rather than people. In terms of identification, establishing the causes of death and of the disaster itself, bodies are evidence. They are items to be controlled and examined, described and dissected. Scanlon (1998: 289) distinguishes between widespread disasters and site-specific incidents. In the former, bodies are often recovered, moved and even buried not by officials but by relatives and friends. Uncertainty may remain even as to the total numbers of deaths. At 'site-specific' acute disasters, the site is quickly controlled by law enforcement agencies and bodies are marked before they are moved. 'Securing' the site of disaster while necessary from a professional point of view can exclude the bereaved both from speedy access to the deceased, and from a site which itself is of considerable significance.[5]

Mitchell (1993) describes how, after the Lockerbie disaster, officials were taken by surprise at the reaction of bereaved people to the sanitization of places where bodies had hit the ground. Bereaved parent John Mosey (personal interview) obtained the map reference where his daughter's body had been found. It was high up on a mountainside. He searched on the ground for signs of an indentation, where she might have hit the ground, but 'the soil was too thin'. He acknowledges that the significance of finding such an indentation would have been 'irrational', but explains that it was to do with making his daughter's experience tangible to himself.

Even where logistical issues do not preclude early visual identification, official agencies have restricted access to the dead, denied it completely or given it in the most insensitive manner (Coleman *et al.* 1990; Davis and Scraton 1997, 1999). For one family, denied permission to view the dead after a major UK disaster, 'the undertaker stopped half-way down the motorway [and let them see] which was a crazy, crazy thing to do really' (personal interview, bereaved relative). The denial of access to the deceased, in the case of the *Marchioness* disaster, was found by relatives to be as sinister as it was incompetent or insensitive. The sealed coffins hid the fact that the hands of half of the dead had secretly been severed in post-mortem examinations. The testimony of the bereaved demonstrates that, within the organizational politics that characterize the immediate aftermath, their needs are regularly subordinated to organizational interests (Coleman *et al.* 1990; Davis and Scraton 1997, 1999). It is a major achievement of the bereaved and survivors of the *Marchioness* disaster that access to the deceased is finally addressed within the Clarke Inquiry (2001a) as a matter of rights rather than professionally calibrated 'needs'.[6] On the other hand there is growing concern that, in the aftermath of recent terrorist attacks, models of response and the frameworks within which they operate are shifting back to a post-cold war 'civil defence' orientation which may involve 'more authoritarian, less participatory, forms of crisis management' (Alexander 2002a: 209). In the UK the Civil Contingencies Act 2004 confers drastic powers upon the executive. These include the power to enforce or ban movement, ban assemblies, confiscate and/or destroy property, ban other activities that are specified as necessary for preventing or delaying the recovery of services, business or public affairs or that might increase the risk of matters deteriorating. This might include the censoring or restriction of the media. Emergency regulations do not require parliamentary approval and are able to create new criminal offences of non-compliance, which may be adjudicated through new tribunals.

Repeated official failure to meet the needs of victims in a wealthy, developed state such as the UK raises the question: why do agencies continue to fail in such circumstances? There are clearly specific problems for organizations dealing with unpredicted and overwhelming events. However, there are also clear connections between disaster behaviour and pre-existing values, policies and practices. The principle of 'continuity' suggests that 'the best predictor of behaviour in emergencies is behaviour prior to the emergency. Emergencies do not make sinners out of saints, nor Jekylls out of Hydes' (Dynes 1994: 150).

Substantial evidence of official insensitivity and of the dominance of official agendas in the disaster aftermath cannot, according to 'continuity', be divorced from 'everyday' policy and practice. The unnecessary and secret mutilation of bodies of those killed in the *Marchioness* disaster was not, it later turned out, an isolated incident derived in the intense stresses of disaster aftermath. It was, rather, only one manifestation of a pervasive, institutionalized and 'normal' disregard for the ethics and law surrounding treatment of the dead. Statutory provisions had been ignored for decades, in 'normal' as well as in disaster settings (see, for example, Redfern 2001). Disaster, critically examined, offers a window on practices and dominant assumptions that usually remain hidden.

Compounding the experience of official insensitivity in the immediate aftermath, there is the likelihood that neither will a truthful account of events be easily forthcoming nor will justice readily be done. In the case of the *Marchioness* disaster, police failed to seal the *Bowbelle,* the vessel that collided with and sank the pleasure craft, as a scene of crime (Hartley and Davis 1999). Senior managers of the company were not interviewed. Charges against the company were not pursued and on the eve of private prosecutions the state released the findings of its private inquiry, unsubstantiated by listed evidence or transcripts and begging even the most obvious questions. It disclaimed the role of inquiry itself beyond the narrowest technical questions. The role of the regulatory authorities and their failure to enforce even the limited regulatory requirements of the day, it placed beyond itself. To compound the anguish of the bereaved their dead were placed in sealed coffins after (in many cases) their hands had been severed. It was only through the efforts of survivors and bereaved, over the course of a decade, that new inquiries, held in public, were able to provide answers to most, if not all, of the controversial questions (Clarke 2001b). The *Marchioness* was one of a series of disasters that in the UK at least, significantly eroded public confidence in some of the basic assumptions of disaster: disaster as accident, the state as benevolent, rigorous and neutral.

In the longer term, for many, there can be no 'resolution' of grief and trauma without justice. One father, bereaved in the *Marchioness* disaster, explained:

It puts a hell of a lot of strain on, but you get strength from seeking the truth, when there is a total injustice put on your family ... I could never look my son's photograph in the eye and say I did not do everything possible to find out why they did this to you, and all the others (personal interview).

Contesting truth, seeking justice

Two parents bereaved in the Lockerbie disaster expressed their differing conceptions of what they wanted in the aftermath:

I am often asked if I am looking for justice? People assume that I am, and they are wrong ... justice implies retribution, an 'eye for an eye', my 'pound of flesh'. My daughter along with 269 others is dead because, almost certainly, because of retribution ... I think many of us would rather say we are looking for the truth. Justice we leave to a higher court (Reverend John Mosey, 10th Anniversary Remembrance Service, Westminster Abbey, *BBC News 24*, 21 December 1998).

I want them dead. I want them dead (Daniel Cohen, *After Lockerbie*, ITV, 21 December 1998).

While some who are bereaved, or otherwise harmed, by disaster see justice in terms of criminalized retribution, a minimum demand is for 'truth'. However, there are fundamental difficulties with current judicial and quasi-judicial responses to large-scale tragedy. Disaster does not necessarily imply that 'lessons will be learnt', let alone that those responsible will be punished (Gephart 1984; Toft 1992; Toft and Reynolds 1994). Rather: 'Processes of organizational and cultural learning may often become disrupted or blocked as just collateral damage to political infighting and organized cover-up' (Turner and Pidgeon 1997: 176).

Following the work of Turner (1978), unintended disaster has come to be understood as originating in longstanding pre-existing assumptions and practices. What Turner failed, initially, to appreciate was how these assumptions and practices, rather than being 'exposed' and overthrown by the occurrence of disaster, often persist. Attempts are made to impose particular 'truths' on the disaster event. This process is 'linked to culturally and organizationally based interests and motives. It is basic to the process of domination in contemporary society' (Gephart 1984: 213). In cases of environmental disaster, for example, 'corporations and government minimize the dangers of events across all stages of the disaster' (Gephart 1984: 214).

Sipika and Smith (1992: 7) concur that 'crisis events bring in their wake, a legitimation process wherein the organization has to regain the confidence of the public, government, shareholders or other stakeholder groups'. Strategies to achieve this 'turnaround' may be defensive or offensive, and during the first period, when an organization may be under intense threat, can include 'scapegoating' (Sipika and Smith 1992: 10). Thus, responsibility for an event may be projected upon actors outside the responsible organization. Injustice is a central and recurring feature of disaster. This may involve the inappropriate or unfair attribution of blame to individuals. Where inquiries themselves are tainted by vested interest, this 'naming and shaming' has official weight. McLean and Johnes (2000a) for example, examine the conduct and findings of the inquiry into the loss of the *Titanic*. They conclude (2000a: 729) that:

the disaster was an early example of the kind of injustice and regulatory failure that has often been central in more recent catastrophes. A regulatory body had, in effect, to inquire into its own shortcomings; therefore too little blame was laid in high places, and too much in low places.

Worse, in some cases, victims themselves are blamed. Where disastrous consequences follow the actions of military, police or security agencies, demonstrators, or those with whom they are 'associated', can be portrayed relatively easily as bringing harm upon themselves: official representations that are fiercely resisted (Ardoyne Commemoration Project 2002; Barbato 2003; Dawson 2005; Rolston and Scraton 2005). It may therefore suit official agencies to play the 'disorder' card at the earliest opportunity, painting the victims of official failure as responsible for their own fates. The Hillsborough disaster, perhaps the clearest recent UK example, was represented as the product of drunken 'hooliganism'. News media, habitually pliant to official techniques of public relations management, have been all too eager to accept uncritically the official construction of demonstrators as rioters, hurricane survivors as looters and football supporters as hooligans. Stories after Hillsborough went so far as to suggest that Liverpool supporters had, in the immediate aftermath, urinated on their own dead (Coleman *et al.* 1990; Scraton *et al.* 1995; Scraton 1999; Jemphrey and Berrington 2000).

The state is generally motivated to protect and promote the corporate interests upon which it is dependent while reassuring its citizens that its priority remains their health and safety. While its material and ideological investment in the dangers presented by individual crime and anti-social behaviour is enormous, the prevention, mitigation, policing and punishment of harms perpetrated by its powerful corporate allies are minimal. Mainstream academic research, meanwhile, abdicates its responsibility to take such crime seriously (Snider 2000). The appearance of 'justice', in the event of such crimes, is preserved through the application of judicial and quasi-judicial forms. The public is reassured that the root of 'the problem' will be discovered and remedied. 't Hart (1993: 43) notes that government emphasizes 'evocative terms such as "full scale inquiry", "objective" and "evaluation"'. Inquiries, although charged in the mind of the public with establishing truth, approach disasters with limited 'frames of reference'. They are a key feature of the aftermath not because they find and remedy the disaster's causes but because they 'de-politicize the crisis events and … counteract the attendant de-legitimation processes by employing a "non-partisan" channel for defining the situation and assessing success and failure' (t Hart 1993: 42). 'Objectivity' is a myth. Inquiries are responses to 'crises of legitimacy' and are key parts of the process of 're-affirming political and ideological hegemony' (Burton and Carlen cited in Rolston and Scraton 2005: 552). Knowles (2003: 11) notes that 'in any number of disasters over the past two centuries, the "disaster investigation", far from proving itself the dispassionate, scientific verdict on causality and blame, actually emerges as a hard-fought contest to define the moment in politics and society, in technology and culture'.

The struggle for truth is not restricted to the setting of official inquiries. Rather, it is fought out in a confusing variety of formal and informal settings. The criminal court may be one setting. Another may be the contestation of compensation claims. The 1989 'settlement' of the Bhopal disaster, for example, saw mass claims represented (without the possibility of opt-out) by the government of India in the capacity of *parens patriae* (Fortun 2000). Here, the interests of the government clearly conflicted with those of the victims it represented. Government institutions owned 22 per cent of Union Carbide India Ltd. Moreover:

In the view of government officials, the future of India and its people depended on foreign investment … the Government of

India needed the Bhopal case to demonstrate that India is an amiable site for foreign investment. The particularities of gas victims themselves had to fit within this general frame (Fortun 2000: 192).

By implication, challenging the responses of the state here became an act within broader resistance:

Contesting the settlement of the Bhopal case became a way to contest the way globalisation was 'justified' through accounting processes that foreclosed certain lines of inquiry, disabled certain forms of knowledge and legitimated discriminatory social categorization – through rhetorics that highlighted the harmonization of world order and effaced globalization's manifestation on the ground (Fortun 2000: 189).

The legal politics of the aftermath are invariably complex. Both 'truth' and 'justice' are determined within an array of countervailing interests. The state, of course, is neither monolithic nor necessarily vindictive. Various investigations feed into criminal, civil, inquest and inquiry proceedings. Outcomes, unsurprisingly, are unpredictable. Victims find themselves negotiating procedures and interpreting judgements, verdicts and findings that seem incomprehensibly contradictory. The official tribunal into the 1966 Aberfan disaster, for example, roundly condemned the National Coal Board (NCB) (McLean and Johnes 2000b). It seemed an unequivocal victory. Yet nobody was prosecuted, nobody lost their jobs, only £500 in damages was paid to the family of each dead child and the publicly donated disaster fund was 'raided' of £150,000 to pay towards the cost of removal of remaining coal tips (McLean and Johnes 2000b: 18). Such outcomes cannot be understood without reference to specific political-economic contexts. In this case, government, the ruling Labour Party, trade unions and the coal-mining community as a whole shared an interest with the NCB. In South Wales in 1966, coal was an industry whose decline had to be managed. Specifically (McLean and Johnes 2000b: 44):

If the Aberfan compensation claims had been debited to Merthyr Vale, and still more if the cost of removing the tips had been, it would have shown a very heavy operating loss. This could have had consequences for jobs that were so obvious that they shimmered below the surface of the inquiry, breaking out acrimoniously, once or twice.

While there is insufficient space here to do justice to the variety of harms and losses encompassed within a critically inclusive concept of disaster, it would be remiss to make no comment upon the state's most disastrous act of all – war. Here, the state is even less the objective arbiter among competing interests than it is in civilian disaster. It is, rather, the author of disaster. Disaster literatures increasingly recognize war as disaster and military violence has been drawn belatedly into the criminological focus. The label of 'war' itself covers a wide range of conflicts, international and internal, declared and undeclared. 'Responsibility' may be very difficult to specify. It is frequently dispersed across a range of social, economic and political systems. Pinpointing 'criminality' in such circumstances may be impossible and where proceedings are brought there are obvious dangers of 'victor's justice'. Deepening our understanding of the roots of such manifest social harm, however, remains an urgent necessity. Excluding it from definitions of either crime or disaster clearly limits the criminological imagination. It also risks losing sight of the relevance of critical work in other academic disciplines (see, for example, Hewitt 1987, 1994).

This urgency is compounded by the relish with which the state itself has seized the opportunities presented to it by 'terrorist' disaster to launch and legitimize disasters of its own. Surges in public sympathy and a carefully orchestrated escalation of fear have been used to justify repressive and criminal responses. The attacks of 11 September 2001, for example, have allowed the USA and UK to introduce draconian domestic policies and to legitimate catastrophic wars in both Afghanistan and Iraq (Alexander 2002b; Chomsky 2004; Conlon 2004; Curtis 2004). In the UK the Prime Minister (press conference, 5 August 2005) made it clear when announcing a raft of measures aimed at asylum seekers, Muslims and others, that 'the rules of the game are changing'. For criminology the links between the national and international behaviour of states have never been clearer. Nor has the potential of the disaster to 'change the world' been more evident.

Yet the 'changed world' of post-9/11 is itself a particular framing of those and subsequent attacks, a framing that de-historicizes them and asserts the 'truths' of the powerful. The state is able to deploy powerful and extensive resources in reconstructing its own violence. Expert opinion elaborates information from 'security' and 'defence' sources to justify or explain 'our' actions. An unreflective media, with honourable exceptions, reproduce, in their selection of information, images and even in their use of grammar, the 'common sense' that, while it may be many things – heroic or tragic, justified or questionable, straightforward or risky – the violence of 'our' state (and that of its allies) is not criminal (Curtis 2003, 2004; Davis 2004; Gordon 2004; Lukin *et al.* 2004; Stanyer 2004; Chouliaraki 2005; Guterman 2005; Phythian 2005). Any expectation of 'truth' that might have attended official sense-making would have been misplaced. The two key inquiries into the Iraq war did not examine the political decision to attack a sovereign state in defiance of international law. Rather they examined, respectively, the death of a government adviser and the state of intelligence upon which the war was officially based. The decision to attack Iraq led to the deaths of an estimated 100,000 Iraqis (Roberts *et al.* 2004). Yet the disaster around which the inquiries circled was not in any sense an 'accident'. It was the direct and deliberate consequence of public policy. 'Sceptical commentators', Doig (2005: 122) suggests:

> may argue that both Hutton and Butler knew only too well the primacy of public policy imperatives ... Indeed the findings of both have followed the tradition of other such inquiries in recognizing that, while mistakes are made and over-enthusiasm occurs, both occur in pursuit of the interests of the state ... No-one, therefore, is to blame, or to be blamed.

The Butler Inquiry, of the two, the more 'critical', 'was a balance of intransigence and compliance' (Danchev 2004: 460). The evidence it uncovered was in some ways unprecedented. It 'exposed the shameful frailty of the edifice constructed by the [Joint Intelligence Committee]' (Danchev 2004: 460–1). Yet, 'by deliberate intent, it drew no blood' (2004: 460).

One could take the view that the Hutton and Butler Inquiries were not disaster inquiries at all. This depends upon definition. If we take the view that war and disaster are different categories, however, we must still note the continuities between inquiries as official responses in both settings. Regardless of their specific forensic thoroughness, in neither case do they tend to extend themselves to issues beyond narrowly circumscribed remits. In the case of Hutton and Butler they inevitably failed to address an outrage that can only be made sense of within the historical context of Western states' involvement in and support for foreign intervention, including 'pre-emptive' attack and state terrorism (McSherry 2002; Robertson 2002; Chomsky 2003, 2004; Curtis 2003, 2004; Leffler 2003; Turner 2003; MacMaster 2004). The terrorist disasters of the early millennium have been matched and exceeded by the terrorism and aggression of the liberal democratic states that proclaim as their evangelic mission the extension of peace and freedom. 'Our' own emergency plans, meanwhile, are radically reshaped in order to cope with the perhaps inevitable, if overdue, disastrous consequences.

'Disaster crime'

Intimately related to the contestation of truth are questions of blame and punishment. The extent to which actors are, or should be, held to be responsible, blameworthy and/or criminal for disastrous events is related to the way such events are labelled. Whether an event is termed a disaster, and whether it is labelled in addition, or instead, as something else (an act of 'terrorism', a 'riot', an 'accident', a 'war', a 'crime') imposes a version of how it has been 'caused'. The notion of cause that is generally applied here is narrow, individualized and linear. It emphasizes specific actions over policy and context. Implicit within such accounts lie deeply rooted conceptions of legitimacy and authority.

Although individually harmful acts are commonly considered to be 'criminal' where they involve intention or culpable negligence, corporate or state behaviour of this sort is frequently treated very differently. Nevertheless, recent years have seen escalating demands that those 'at fault' should be held accountable. The aftermath of tragedy is riven by a politics of blame and, where losses are profound, the question of responsibility becomes explosive. Whether or not this is framed in terms of criminality (and it usually is not), governments, their agents or allies may find themselves exposed to blame.

Where states or corporations are accused of responsibility or even criminality, crisis management involves the minimization of the severity of events, and/or the deflection of responsibility on to others. Even where harm is recognized, official narrative 'acknowledges that something has happened, but refuses to accept the category of acts to which it is assigned' (Cohen 2001: 77). Civil catastrophe may be an 'accident', or indeed a 'disaster', but seldom is it successfully prosecuted as a serious 'crime', at least against the corporation or state (individuals are usually more expendable).[7] Criminal accountability for deaths resulting from disasters remains compromised by individualized assumptive frameworks. Bergman (2000: 31) notes that, while 'disasters … are the worst form of corporate harm …

they are, however, not common'. In terms of more common or 'less extreme' examples involving death and injury:

> criminal accountability is almost non-existent. The likelihood of police investigating these incidents is almost non-existent ... When investigations do take place, they are in most cases conducted by regulatory inspectors concerned only with regulatory offences. Criminal charges – in the few instances when they are laid – relate to companies and not directors and are heard in the Magistrates rather than the Crown Court, where the fines imposed bear no relation to the wealth of the company (Bergman 2000: 31).

Even when disasters are recognized as such, powerful interests and domain assumptions often coincide, seeking to ensure that, as truth remains partial, blame remains localized. Justifications are prepared and motives are obscured. Positivist legal methodologies are applied. In civil disaster, where companies are small, there is some possibility that corporate manslaughter charges may be successfully brought. Where culpable organizations are larger, disasters may be attributable in part to individual errors made at relatively junior levels. However, although there is increasing official and public recognition that inadequate and dysfunctional organizational systems play a major part in the genesis of tragedy, what is strongly resisted by authorities, and what is extremely difficult to establish in law, is that responsibility extends upwards to the most senior levels of the corporation and the state. Difficulty in identifying individual managers who are the 'directing mind' of companies has been the key stumbling block in cases such as the *Herald of Free Enterprise* and the Southall rail crash (Bergman 1993, 2000; Rice 2003). Furthermore, by divesting themselves of the operational, elites are able to distance themselves from the consequences of policy failure.

Even at the level of basic investigation, state responses can be wholly inadequate. From the beginning, the response of police to the *Marchioness* disaster[8] lacked the urgency and focus that might have been expected in an investigation into mass homicide (Hartley and Davis 1999). Information gathering was dilatory and evidence placed before the subsequent private inquiry was incomplete. After the Hillsborough disaster police officers were instructed not to record events in their notebooks (Scraton 1999). Successful prosecutions for corporate manslaughter have been made where the smaller size of companies made it easier to demonstrate the personal responsibility of named individuals (Slapper and Tombs 1999; Bergman 2000; Rice 2003). Where investigations have been robust, the framing of corporate manslaughter usually poses an insuperable hurdle to the achievement of justice. More broadly, the political and ideological contexts that frame practices and policies are seldom identified as underpinning disastrous consequences.

Civilian disaster, as noted above, is often 'unintentional'. This may seem to make it less worthy of punishment. What is constructed as 'real' crime is commonly equated with intent. The criminal justice system, however, does treat some offences of criminal negligence as seriously as those involving greater fault (Bergman 1993, 2000; Slapper and Tombs 1999). Moreover, it does seem that the tide is moving towards a less forgiving conception of (some) disasters (Helsloot and Ruitenberg 2004). The potential risks arising from the negligent operation of an organization are often higher than those of a negligent individual. Moreover, as with some economic crimes, the health and safety violations that lead to disasters are often 'more calculative than conventional crime' (Alvesalo and Tombs 2002: 33) and as the paradigm of rational choice theory is more applicable than with conventional crime, 'both specific and general deterrence are key informing concepts' (2002: 34). Not only are disastrous consequences reasonably foreseeable – the test for cases of 'gross negligence' – they are *so* foreseeable that it must be reasonable to conclude that, in many cases, they must have *been* foreseen – the test for recklessness. In this sense a company management may not have known *whom* they would kill, but they can have been fairly sure *somebody* would die or suffer injury. Lack of intent does not, therefore, reduce the importance of responsibility, morally, legally or politically.

In war, too, the defensive application of law has become a significant and worthwhile investment for liberal democratic states. It is important to have both god and law on one's side. As *jus ad bellum* has 'withered', the intricacies of *jus in bello* offer opportunities for the criminal wood to be hidden behind the legal trees. Criminality is denied, with fatality becoming 'collateral damage', and destruction a state-defined 'necessity' (Calhoun 2002; Smith 2002; Curtis 2003, 2004; Chomsky 2004; Rockmore 2004). In the cases of both civil and military disaster, political strategy is to minimize or neutralize the extent of disaster while denying wherever possible the suggestion of serious criminality.

In the aftermath of a series of civilian disasters in the UK during the 1980s and 1990s, the criminal justice system was spectacularly unsuccessful in bringing those responsible to serious account (Bergman 2000). Survivors and bereaved usually had to be content with, at most, a public inquiry. Campaigns by those affected by disaster made significant progress in terms of specific state responses to individual disasters. They also raised the profile of the issue of corporate manslaughter law. Nonetheless, there remains a glaring lack of justice in such cases, rooted in a combination of poor law, inadequate investigation, skilful public relations and political rearguard actions within dominant ideological frameworks that elevate corporate production above safety. The double standard at the heart of representations of crime and harm condemns and excoriates the stereotypical individual criminal while it excuses, glamourizes and even fetishizes the powerful corporations and states that wreak havoc on a global scale.

Conclusion: 'disasters', 'crime' and power

Much criminological and criminal justice endeavour is expended upon relatively small crimes committed by individuals. Extensive resources are committed to their detection, and prosecution. Punishment is the basis for entire industries. It is not to minimize the harm inflicted by such acts, whether intentional, reckless or grossly negligent, to emphasize the extraordinary contrast that is evident when considering crimes and harms of the powerful.

It is clear that even 'natural' disasters are only disasters to the extent that 'natural' hazards impact upon human social systems. When they do so, the structured inequalities within such systems ensure that the marginalized suffer the consequences disproportionately. Despite the intensity and scale of disaster harm, those affected cannot rely upon the authorities to respond sensitively and efficiently, to search energetically and diligently for 'truth' or to deliver 'justice'. This is no accidental state of affairs. Disaster responses are often insensitive, partial and ineffective precisely because they are grounded in insensitive, impartial and ineffective responses to *non*-disaster situations. For official systems to respond vigorously and rigorously to major tragedy would require approaches that challenge the practices, policies and ideologies of the 'everyday'.

The 'system failures' that are held responsible for today's disasters take place within their own determining contexts. That states and corporations might ultimately pay a commensurate price for the devastation they cause is currently such a low 'risk' that 'system

159

failure', in a broader sense, is not a 'failure' at all. Military and civilian systems *succeed* in meeting their strategic, political and economic objectives, secure in the knowledge that the inevitable collateral damage is highly unlikely to lead chief executives, presidents or prime ministers to the courtroom or the prison. Leaders sanction human and ecological devastation through actions that are lawful and in pursuit of objectives that are reified.

The failure to take such crime seriously represents a stark double standard that understandably leaves victims' belief in 'justice' all but crushed. It also provides minimal deterrence to organizations faced with daily trade-offs between their own overriding objectives, on the one hand, and safety on the other.

The powerful do not always succeed in quashing alternative accounts. Nor do the priorities of official processing of disaster go uncontested. Successes may be rare and the result of tireless struggle. But survivors and the bereaved are not without power. Domestically, campaigners after the *Marchioness* disaster, with the assistance of a range of allies over many years, have achieved notable successes. Internationally, struggles are evident across the globe with individuals and groups pitted against the state and its allies. Some approximation to a 'truthful' account, however, often seems to be the best that can be hoped for – 'justice' is often beyond reach.

There is room for debate regarding questions of definition. This chapter has suggested a broad reading of disaster that does not highlight the acute and the visible at the expense of the chronic and the obscured. The consequences that follow the intentional actions of the state, in war for example, may also be considered, in the truest sense, 'disastrous'. Whether they should be included *as* disaster within a critical and inclusive approach is a matter for further discussion. What criminology cannot continue to do is to ignore the destruction of life and property – always harmful, often unambiguously criminal – on a vast scale. That they may result from deliberate policy does not, in itself, make them less harmful or less criminal.

Notes

1 See, for example, the Civil Contingencies Act 2004.
2 The notion of 'normal limits of daily living' of course presupposes some shared consensus as to what 'normal' might be. In a related point the construction of the category of 'post-traumatic stress disorder' as reaction to 'abnormal' events has been criticized. Simpson (1993) and Godsi

(1995), for example, have noted that, for many, life itself is a trauma. There is a danger that disaster, when defined in terms of events beyond normality, will apply to events in the privileged West but not to similar events where such losses are 'normal'.

3   The management and 'treatment' of disaster-affected individuals and communities are also predicated upon positivist methodologies that identify 'dysfunction', symptomatology and treatment (Davis 1999).

4   Examples of the structural mediation of 'natural' hazard are plentiful. Green (2005), for example, considers the historic context of the 1999 Marmara earthquake in terms of the politics of planning and building policies in Turkey. She concludes that in this light the earthquake could be considered a state crime.

5   Access may not be denied, by contrast, to VIPs – a fact that caused anger among relatives after the 1988 Lockerbie diasaster (bereaved relative, personal interview).

6   It took 12 years for Lord Justice Clarke (2001a: 140–1) finally to conclude that: 'if what I regard as the correct question had been asked in each case, namely whether it was necessary to remove the hands as a last resort, it is more probable that none of the hands would have been removed.'

7   There is a distinction to be made here between 'serious crime', such as homicide, and the breach of health and safety regulations. In the latter case, major disasters do increasingly lead to prosecutions. Victims, understandably, see convictions of this sort to be very much 'second best' and in stark contrast to the 'justice' administered in cases of individual homicide. It is also necessary to note the points made above that neither is the state monolithic, nor are its responses simply determined. Competing approaches may be evident between branches of government reflecting different responsibilities, functions and political agendas. See, for example, the political struggles between regional and national government and between states themselves after the Bhopal disaster (Shrivastava 1992; Fortun 2000).

8   When the *Marchioness*, a small pleasure craft, was sunk on the Thames in 1989 by collision with the much larger dredger, *Bowbelle*, visibility from the bridge of the latter was almost completely impaired by the machinery on its deck. It was sailed by crew who had not slept, who had been drinking heavily and who were not required to post a lookout forward. Walkie-talkie radio communication between bow and bridge was inoperable. Unsurprisingly, the vessel had accrued a spectacular record of collisions and this had been a long-term concern among river-boat owners. See Clarke (2001b) for an account of the disaster.

References

Alexander, D. (1997) 'The study of natural disasters, 1977–97: some reflections on a changing field of knowledge', *Disasters*, 21: 284–304.

Alexander, D. (2002a) 'From civil defence to civil protection – and back again', *Disaster Prevention and Management*, 11: 209–13.

Alexander, D. (2002b) 'Nature's impartiality, man's inhumanity: reflections on terrorism and world crisis in a context of historical disaster', *Disasters*, 26: 1–9.

Alvesalo, A. and Tombs, S. (2002) 'Working for criminalization of economic offending: contradictions for critical criminology', *Critical Criminology*, 11: 1–40.

Ardoyne Commemoration Project (2002) *Ardoyne: The Untold Truth.* Belfast: Beyond the Pale.

Barbato, C.A. (2003) '"Embracing their memories": accounts of loss and May 4, 1970', *Journal of Loss and Trauma*, 8: 73–98.

Bergman, D. (1993) *Disasters: Where the Law Fails: A New Agenda for Dealing with Corporate Violence.* London: Herald Charitable Trust.

Bergman, D. (2000) *The Case for Corporate Responsibility.* London: Disaster Action.

Berren, M.R., Santiago, J.M., Beigel, A. and Timmons, S. (1989) 'A classification scheme for disasters' in R. Gist and B. Lubin (eds) *Psychosocial Aspects of Disaster.* Chichester: Wiley.

Browning, L.D. and Shetler, J.C. (1992) 'Communication in crisis, communication in recovery: a postmodern commentary on the Exxon Valdez disaster', *International Journal of Mass Emergencies and Disasters*, 10: 477–98.

Butterbaugh, L. (2005) 'Why did Hurricane Katrina hit women so hard?', *Off Our Backs*, 35: 17–19.

Calhoun, L. (2002) 'Legitimate authority and "just war" in the modern world', *Peace and Change*, 27: 37–58.

Chomsky, N. (2003) *Hegemony or Survival: America's Quest for Global Dominance.* London: Penguin Books.

Chomsky, N. (2004) 'On law and war', *Peace Review*, 16: 251–6.

Chouliaraki, L. (2005) 'Spectacular ethics: on the television footage of the Iraq war', *Journal of Language and Politics*, 4: 143–59.

Clarke, L.J. (2000) *Thames Safety Inquiry: Final Report by Lord Justice Clarke.* London: HMSO.

Clarke, L.J. (2001a) *Public Inquiry into the Identification of Victims following Major Transport Accidents. Vol. 1.* London: HMSO.

Clarke, L.J. (2001b) *Marchioness/Bowbelle: Formal Investigation under the Merchant Shipping Act 1995. Vol. 1.* London: HMSO.

Cohen, S. (2001) *States of Denial: Knowing about Atrocities and Suffering.* Cambridge: Polity Press.

Coleman, S., Jemphrey, A., Scraton, P. and Skidmore, P. (1990) *Hillsborough and After: The Liverpool Experience First Report.* Liverpool: Liverpool City Council.

Conlon, J. (2004) 'Sovereignty vs. human rights or sovereignty and human rights', *Race and Class,* 46: 75–100.

Curtis, M. (2003) *Web of Deceit: Britain's Real Role in the World.* London: Vintage.

Curtis, M. (2004) *Unpeople: Britain's Secret Human Rights Abuses.* London: Vintage.

Danchev, A. (2004) 'The reckoning: official inquiries and the Iraq war', *Intelligence and National Security,* 19: 436–66.

Dasberg, H. (1992) 'The unfinished story of trauma as a paradigm for psychotherapists', *Israeli Journal of Psychiatry and Related Science,* 29: 44–60.

Davis, C. (2004) 'Ban on photos of war dead prompts important history lesson', *Quill Magazine,* September: 18–19.

Davis, H.W. (1999) 'The psychiatrization of post–traumatic distress: issues for social workers', *British Journal of Social Work,* 29: 755–77.

Davis, H.W. and Scraton, P. (1997) *Beyond Disaster: Identifying and Resolving Inter-agency Conflict in the Immediate Aftermath of Disasters.* Ormskirk: Centre for Studies in Crime and Social Justice, Edge Hill College.

Davis, H.W. and Scraton, P. (1999) 'Institutionalised conflict and the subordination of "loss" in the immediate aftermath of UK mass fatality disasters', *Journal of Contingencies and Crisis Management,* 7: 86–97.

Dawson, G. (2005) 'Trauma, place and the politics of memory: Bloody Sunday, Derry, 1972–2004', *History Workshop Journal,* 59: 151–78.

Doig, A. (2005) '45 minutes of infamy? Hutton, Blair and the invasion of Iraq', *Parliamentary Affairs,* 58: 109–23.

Dynes, R. (1994) 'Community emergency planning: false assumptions and inappropriate analogies', *International Journal of Mass Emergencies and Disasters,* 12: 141–58.

Dynes, R. (2003) 'Noah and disaster planning: the cultural significance of the flood story', *Journal of Contingencies and Crisis Management,* 11: 170–7.

Enarson, E. (2005) 'Women and girls last? Averting the second post-Katrina disaster', *Understanding Katrina: Perspectives from the Social Sciences* (www. understandingkatrina.ssrc.org/Enarson).

Fordham, M.H. (1998) 'Making women visible in disasters: problematising the private domain', *Disasters,* 22: 126–43.

Fordham, M.H. (2001) 'Challenging boundaries: a gender perspective on early warning in disaster and environmental management.' Paper presented at the United Nations Division for the Advancement for Women International Strategy for Disaster Reduction Expert Group Meeting on 'Environmental management and the mitigation of natural disasters: a gender perspective', 6–9 November, Ankara, Turkey.

Fortun, K. (2000) 'Remembering Bhopal, refiguring liability', *Interventions: The International Journal of Postcolonial Studies*, 2: 187–98.

Fothergill, A. and Peek, L.A. (2004) 'Poverty and disasters in the United States: a review of recent sociological findings', *Natural Hazards*, 32: 89–110.

Gephart, R.P. (1984) 'Making sense of organizationally based environmental disasters', *Journal of Management*, 10: 205–25.

Godsi, E. (1995) 'Life as trauma', *Changes*, 13: 261–9.

Gordon, N. (2004) 'Rationalising extra-judicial executions: the Israeli press and the legitimation of abuse', *International Journal of Human Rights*, 8: 305–24.

Green, P. (2005) 'Disaster by design: corruption, construction and catastrophe', *British Journal of Criminology*, 45: 528–46.

Guterman, L. (2005) 'Dead Iraqis: why an estimate was ignored', *Columbia Journalism Review*, March/April: 11.

Hartley, H. and Davis, H. (1999) *Thames Safety Inquiry Written Submission, 2nd November*. Ormskirk Centre for Studies in Crime and Social Justice, Edge Hill College.

Helsloot, I. and Ruitenberg, A. (2004) 'Citizen response to disasters: a survey of literature and some practical implications', *Journal of Contingencies and Crisis Management*, 12: 98–111.

Hewitt, K. (1987) 'The social space of terror: towards a civil interpretation of total war', *Society and Space*, 5: 455–74.

Hewitt, K. (1994) '"When the great planes came and made ashes of our city ...": towards an oral geography of the disasters of war', *Antipode*, 26: 1–34.

Hewitt, K. (1995) 'Excluded perspectives in the social construction of disaster', *International Journal of Mass Emergencies and Disasters*, 13: 317–39.

Home Office/Cabinet Office, (2004) *Guidance on Dealing with Fatalities in Emergencies*. London: Home Office Communication Directorate.

Horlick-Jones, T. (1996) 'The problem of blame', in C. Hood and D. Jones (eds) *Accident and Design*. London: London University College Press.

Janoff-Bulman, R. (1992) *Shattered Assumptions: Towards a New Psychology of Trauma*. New York, NY: Free Press.

Jemphrey, A. and Berrington, E. (2000) 'Surviving the media: Hillsborough, Dunblane and the press', *Journalism Studies*, 1: 469–83.

Knowles, S.G. (2003) 'Lessons in the rubble: the World Trade Center and the history of disaster investigations in the United States', *History and Technology*, 19: 9–28.

Langer, N. (2004) 'Natural disasters that reveal cracks in our social foundation', *Educational Gerontology*, 30: 275–85.

Leffler, M. (2003) '9/11 and the past and future of American foreign policy', *International Affairs*, 79:5 1045–1063.

Lukin, A., Butt, D. and Matthiessen, C. (2004) 'Reporting war: grammar as "covert operation"', *Pacific Journalism Review*, 10: 58–74.

MacMaster, N. (2004) 'Torture: from Algiers to Abu Ghraib', *Race and Class*, 46: 1–21.

McLean, I. and Johnes, M. (2000a) '"Regulation run mad": the Board of Trade and the loss of the *Titanic*', *Public Administration*, 78: 729–49.

McLean, I. and Johnes, M. (2000b) *Aberfan: Government and Disasters*. Cardiff: Welsh Academic Press.

McSherry, J.P. (2002) 'Tracking the origins of a state terror network', *Latin American Perspectives*, 29: 38–60.

Mitchell, M. (1993) 'The eye of the storm: police control of the Lockerbie disaster', in T. Newburn (ed.) *Working with Disasters: Social Welfare Intervention during and after Tragedy*. Harlow: Longman.

Peto, J., Decarli, A., La Vecchia, C., Levi, F. and Negri, E. (1999) 'The European mesothelioma epidemic', *British Journal of Cancer*, 79: 666–72.

Phythian, M. (2005) 'Hutton and Scott: a tale of two inquiries', *Parliamentary Affairs*, 58: 124–37.

Quarantelli, E.L. (2001) 'Statistical and conceptual problems in the study of disasters', *Disaster Prevention and Management*, 10: 325–38.

Redfern, M. (2001) *The Royal Liverpool Children's Hospital Inquiry Report*. London: HMSO.

Rice, P. (2003) 'Companies making a killing – new UK proposals for corporate killing', *Environmental Claims Journal*, 15: 501–7.

Roberts, L., Lafta, R., Garfield, R., Khudhairi, J. and Burnham, G. (2004) 'Mortality before and after the 2003 invasion of Iraq: cluster sample survey', *The Lancet*, 364: 1857–64.

Robertson, G. (2002) *Crimes against Humanity: The Struggle for Global Justice*. London: Penguin Books.

Rockmore, T. (2004) 'On pre-emptive war and democracy', *Peace Review*, 16: 305–10.

Rolston, B. and Scraton, P. (2005) 'In the full glare of English politics: Ireland, inquiries and the British state', *British Journal of Criminology*, 45: 547–64.

Scanlon, J. (1998) 'Dealing with a mass death after a community catastrophe: handling bodies after the 1917 Halifax explosion', *Disaster Prevention and Management*, 7: 288–304.

Scraton, P. (1999) *Hillsborough the Truth*. Edinburgh: Mainstream.

Scraton, P., Jemphrey, A. and Coleman, S. (1995) *No Last Rights: The Denial of Justice and the Promotion of Myth in the Aftermath of the Hillsborough Disaster*. Liverpool: Liverpool City Council.

Shaluf, I.M., Ahmadun, F. and Said, A.M. (2003) 'A review of disaster and crisis', *Disaster Prevention and Management*, 12: 24–32.

Shrivastava, P. (1992) *Bhopal: Anatomy of a Crisis*. London: Paul Chapman.

Simpson, M. (1993) 'Bitter waters: effects on children of the stresses of unrest and oppression', in J.P. Wilson and B. Raphael (eds) *International Handbook of Traumatic Stress Syndromes*. New York, NY: Plenum Press.

Sipika, C. and Smith, D. (1992) 'The failed turnaround of Pan American Airlines', *Crisis Management Working Papers 1*. Liverpool: Home Office Emergency Planning College and Liverpool John Moores University.

Slapper, G. and Tombs, S. (1999) *Corporate Crime*. London: Longman.

Slim, H. (1995) 'The continuing metamorphosis of the humanitarian practitioner: some new colours for an endangered chameleon', *Disasters*, 19: 110–26.

Smith, T.W. (2002) 'The new law of war: legitimising hi-tech and infrastructural violence', *International Studies Quarterly*, 46: 355–74.

Smithson, M. (1990) 'Ignorance and disasters', *International Journal of Mass Emergencies and Disasters*, 8: 207–35.

Snider, L. (2000) 'The sociology of corporate crime: an obituary', *Theoretical Criminology*, 4: 169–206.

Stanyer, J. (2004) 'Politics and the media: a Crisis of trust?', *Parliamentary Affairs*, 57: 420–34.

Street, P. (2005) 'Framing Katrina: dominant media and damage control in the wake of a not-so natural disaster', *Dissident Voice* (www.dissidentvoive. org/Sept05/Street0918).

Taylor, A.J. (1987) 'A taxonomy of disasters and their victims', *Journal of Psychosomatic Research*, 31: 535–44.

't Hart, P. (1993) 'Symbols, rituals and power: the lost dimensions of crisis management', *Journal of Contingencies and Crisis Management*, 1: 36–50.

Tierney, K.J. (1989) 'The social and community contexts of disaster', in R. Gist and B. Lubin (eds) *Psychosocial Aspects of Disaster*. Chichester: Wiley.

Toft, B.A. (1992) 'Limits to the mathematical modelling of disasters', in C. Hood and D. Jones (eds) *Accident and Design*. London: London University College Press.

Toft, B.A. and Reynolds, S. (1994) *Learning from Disasters: A Management Approach*. Oxford: Butterworth-Heinemann.

Tombs, S. (1999) 'Death and work in Britain', *Sociological Review*, 47: 345–67.

Tombs, S. (2002) 'Understanding regulation', *Social and Legal Studies*, 11: 113–33.

Turner, B.A. (1978) *Man-made Disasters*. London: Wykeham.

Turner, B.A. and Pidgeon, N.F. (1997) *Man-made Disasters* (2nd edn). Oxford: Butterworth-Heinemann.

Turner, S. (2003) 'The dilemma of double standards in US human rights policy', *Peace and Change*, 28: 524–54.

Wisner, B. (1998) 'Marginality and vulnerability: why the homeless of Tokyo don't count in disaster preparations', *Applied Geography*, 18: 25–33.

Wisner, B. (2001) 'Risk and the neoliberal state: why post-Mitch lessons didn't reduce El Salvador's earthquake losses', *Disasters*, 25: 251–68.

Wright, K.M., Ursano, R.J., Bartone, P.T. and Ingraham, L.H. (1990) 'The shared experience of catastrophe: an expanded classification of the disaster community', *American Journal of Orthopsychiatry*, 60: 35–42.

Wynne, B. (1992) 'Misunderstood misunderstanding: social identities and public uptake of science', *Public Understanding of Science*, 1: 281–304.

Yonder, A., Akcar, S. and Gopalan, P. (2005) *Women's Participation in Disaster Relief and Recovery*. New York, NY: The Population Council.

Chapter 8

Towards a criminology for human rights

Elizabeth Stanley

Building on radical work that exposed the skewed way in which criminologists approached their studies, a number of critical criminologists have begun to turn their attention to the ways in which 'crime' is constructed, undertaken, regulated and punished by states, corporations, paramilitaries and transnational financial institutions, among other previously unchallenged actors. The author's own writing on Chile, South Africa and Timor-Leste (East Timor) has reflected this criminological shift (see Stanley 2001, 2002, 2004, 2005a, 2005b).

Drawing on research undertaken in Timor-Leste, this chapter directs the criminological imagination towards the norms of human rights. It will consider how criminologists might begin to analyse multiple violations that cause death and severe suffering. In the focus on Timor-Leste, this chapter exposes how victims of gross human rights violations receive little 'truth' or 'justice' in the wake of their experiences. It also shows that survivors of physical human rights violations (such as genocide, torture, rape and 'disappearances') continue to face life-threatening and painful realities – they live in extreme poverty and they struggle to access basic services such as shelter, food, water, health care and education. While the extensive direct violence may have stopped, victims have been faced with the trauma of ongoing violations of economic, social and cultural rights. Finally, this chapter identifies that the responsibility of human rights violations cannot be directed solely to any one group. While the state continues to dominate, the realities of globalization have ensured that a multitude of organizations and individuals are involved in perpetrating, supporting and resisting human rights violations.

State crime and human rights

Much of the recent criminological literature on state crime has detailed the lack of recognition given by the discipline to acts that are undeniably violent, destructive or harmful, undertaken by state officials and their operatives. The arguments on why this situation has evolved and been sustained are relatively well versed, including: 1) the difficulties of establishing a consensual definition of state crime; 2) the criminological reticence to study acts that are not deemed criminal through law or that extend beyond the sovereign borders of nation-states; 3) the resistance by academic and other institutions to develop, fund, support, teach and publish academic research on the topic; 4) the problems of researching an issue in which the data are often hidden or where the acts hold legitimacy through political and public acceptance; and 5) the reluctance to raise social problems which are not easily solvable through 'quick fix' reformist measures (see Schwendinger and Schwendinger 1975; Chambliss 1989; Barak 1991; Cohen 1993; Kauzlarich and Kramer 1998; Ross *et al.* 1999; Kauzlarich *et al.* 2001; Kramer *et al.* 2002; Tombs and Whyte 2003; Green and Ward 2000, 2004; Morrison 2004).

These matters, relating to the lack of recognition of state crime, have featured heavily in critical criminological writings and, this academic hand-wringing has sometimes acted as an 'obstacle to substantive work on the issues' (Tombs and Whyte 2003: 9).[1] As a result, despite the extensive misery and harm caused by state officials, the criminological imagination has not readily extended beyond those crimes committed by individuals against nation-states. The development of criminological study in the UK, for instance has resulted in a situation where, in a snapshot 1991–2000 study of five dominant criminological journals, only 17 (2 per cent) out of 1,058 articles took state crime as their central theme (Tombs and Whyte 2003). In addition, with singular exceptions like Penny Green and Tony Ward's (2004) excellent contribution, there is a dearth of textbook literature on the topic.

Without doubt, state crime research does require something of a leap of imagination for many criminologists. The central tenets of mainstream criminology – such as the legal basis of 'crime', the individualistic nature of criminal activity, the domestic focus of study, the structural and historical decontextualization of crime acts – are called seriously into question by human rights-based research. After all, we cannot develop understanding without an assessment of the ways in which states are joined by other third parties such as paramilitary groups, militias, private contractors, corporations and transnational financial bodies in the committal of human rights violations. Nor can we expect to progress analyses if we remain parochially fixed on sovereign states; even the most preliminary historical overview tells us that violations regularly occur across state boundaries and with the ideological encouragement, technological assistance or economic support of global parties. Moreover, the imperatives of advanced global capitalism, built upon the 'historical' experiences of slavery, colonization and imperialism, cannot be disconnected from the equation; these structural relations of class, intersecting with those of 'race', patriarchy and age, underpin the everyday social injustices faced by those hit hardest by state criminality.

In short, state criminality raises deep questions about the limits of criminological attention. The silencing or neutralization of these issues from mainstream disciplinary attention may even add credence to the discourses and practices that provide legitimacy for state criminality. The challenge, as Morrison (2004: 163) puts it, is that 'criminology must change its boundaries and imaginative domain, for a global criminology ... must be a critical and reflective one, otherwise it may just become the servant of a new and duplicitous complex of global power networks.'

Invoking this spirit, yet with an awareness of space limitations, this chapter will now turn to a brief examination of three issues that are particularly pertinent to the East Timorese situation: first, the framework of human rights; second, the role of states and other actors in criminal activity; and, third, the possibilities of accountability and redress.

The human rights frame

Human rights have framed many of the discussions regarding state crime. This literature is not assessed here;[2] rather, some of the problems that emerge from a mainstream human rights approach are exposed.

While the debates on human rights are wide-ranging – encompassing whether rights are culturally relative, whether they can be applied to groups of people, whether the rights of certain groups should override those of others and so on – rights-based policies and practices have generally confined themselves to direct, violent acts. For instance, organizations like Amnesty and Human Rights Watch generally contain their campaigns to violations such as torture, 'disappearances', illegal detention and genocide, while the loans from international monetary organizations (such as the World Bank or the International Monetary Fund (IMF)) to 'third world' states are based on demands of adherence to such human rights standards (Green and Ward 2004).

The dominant version of human rights that is presented at an international level gives a biased emphasis to civil and political rights (Chomsky 1996; Evans 2001; Green and Ward 2004). This concentration may be derived from a belief that there are certain things that are so atrocious that they should not be repeated. However, as Chandler (2002: 227) argues, this concern for particular kinds of victims 'is not only fickle but also highly superficial' as it undermines attempts to understand the long-term economic, social, cultural and developmental violations in 'trouble-torn societies.'

As a case in point, consider the experiences of Maria in Timor-Leste. During the Indonesian occupation of Timor, further details of which are given below, Maria was subjected to a number of human rights violations at the hands of military and policing officials as well as militia members – she was illegally detained on numerous occasions; her family had considered her to be 'disappeared' as they could not retrieve information about her arrest or detention from state officials; and over years, she was subjected to numerous tortures, including sexual assaults, electro-shock, beatings, cuttings, withdrawal of food, and she had had her fingernails pulled out. Such experiences can, certainly, be classified as human rights violations. However, Maria's personal realities of violation went further still. Speaking from her one-room home, in her only clothes, she explained that her violations went beyond the visible signs of torture, and she argued:[3]

> These scars are from years ago … there must be justice in a country which has law and order … but look at my situation now [here, she gestured to her surroundings and dress], this is about violence and rights. The economic situation of this country is important too. We have nothing, not even a monument for those who died. My family needs support.

For Maria, the violence against her has progressed on a continuum. There have been instances of severe physical pain and suffering, inflicted by Indonesian military and security officials, yet her principal concern is how she is going to survive the seemingly endless, everyday violations and human insecurities that pervade her life. Over decades, her victimization – multiple detentions without trial, torture, poor housing, unemployment, lack of health care – has been deeply connected to diverse violations of human rights and linked to structural inequalities that frame, direct and manage life in Timor-Leste. However, from a mainstream human rights approach, most of these violations do not count; as Herman (2002: viii) points out:

> human rights are confined to political and personal rights ('that prohibit cruel and arbitrary punishments, protect freedom of expression and entitle each person to matter equally regardless of race, ethnicity, religion or gender'); they do not include economic rights to subsistence, education, health care, housing and employment. Thus, if immiseration follows from the normal workings of the market system ... no human rights violations are involved.

Economic and social violations are defined out by conventional human rights discourses; they do not appear as a problem because they are rendered invisible and are the results of 'normal' working practices rather than the 'evil' endeavours of identifiable individuals (Mathiesen 2004). Correspondingly, in many instances it may be difficult to determine immediately who might be responsible for violations, or what might be done to provide redress or accountability. For some individuals (such as the former US Ambassador to the UN, Jeane Kirkpatrick), the documentation regarding economic, social and cultural rights presents nothing more than 'a letter to Santa Claus', driven by unfeasible demands (Chomsky 1998: 32). In mainstream political and legal terms, then, the UN Covenant of Economic, Social and Cultural Rights carries less weight than its civil and political counterpart. Yet, economic, social and cultural rights do bear the same legal status as civil and political rights, each giving rise to binding obligations to preserve the inherent dignity of individuals,[4] and it can be strongly argued that violations of the former cause far more death and suffering than the latter. With this in mind, how might attention be directed to activities that are not criminalized or that result from seemingly unspecific sources? How might criminology begin to respond? To begin to answer these questions, it is useful to consider who might be responsible for violations in the current global order.

Tracing responsibility for violations

Human rights have been inextricably linked to the state. Human rights thinking consolidated in line with the the rise of the modern state and the idea and practice of rights has functioned as 'part of the state's package of compensations for its assumption of power' (Woodiwiss 2005: 11). In more recent times, however, this basis of human rights has been regarded as outdated. The state-centric understandings on which rights have been based have been overtaken by the 'deepening', 'stretching' and 'speeding up' of state interactions, not just with other states but with a whole gamut of global actors (McGrew 1998). State activities are finally viewed as being 'enmeshed' within divergent networks of actors that are not 'confined to the boundaries and dictates of the nation-state' (Hayden and el-Ojeili 2005: 5).[5] In turn, national governments regularly throw their hands in the air and plead: 'What can we do? These violations are a result of corporate/militia/international financial institution activity over which we have no control.' Thus, the acknowledgement of how power is wielded across international boundaries has undermined the principle of the state as the sole guardian of human rights and it is often viewed that states are reacting to rather than dictating policies or events (Evans 1998). As a result, much debate has rested on questioning how rights might be protected when the violation of rights is perpetrated by non-state actors (McGrew 1998).

The activities of corporations, paramilitary groups, mercenaries and international institutions such as the World Trade Organization, the World Bank and the International Monetary Fund (IMF), among others, may each lead to human rights violations (Green and Ward 2004). Furthermore, such organized bodies are operationalized within a context of global structural inequalities which means that sometimes their everyday operations create 'devastating financial and human consequences for large numbers of especially vulnerable people' (Friedrichs 2004: 147). Consequently, the imposition of 'austerity packages' by the IMF, in which states with weak economies have to 'tighten their belts' to repay debts, leads to violations of economic and social rights[6] – and, undoubtedly, the cuts in health, housing, education and food will be felt more deeply by those already at the bottom of socio-economic hierarchies (women, children, the elderly, minority populations and other devalued groups) – but it also leads to violations of civil and political rights, such as 'increasingly repressive policing measures' (Green and Ward 2004: 188). Within a globalized world, then, criminologists can demonstrate that responsibility for harms does lie with various non-democratically accountable bodies and they may analyse the conditions and relations that give rise to violations.

Given this globalization context, it is sometimes tempting to argue that states are tending to irrelevance. In response, it is fruitful to consider how, historically, states have been built along diverse boundaries and organized in relation to other powerful actors. As Coleman and Sim (2005: 104) detail, states are crafted:

> the state exists and is constituted through alliances and partnerships that – however momentarily and with contradictory tendencies – define its boundaries and scope of action. Neither 'sovereignty' nor state power is on the decline, but these categories are *both* processual *and* dialectical and are subject to rescaling, and relegitimation … The state is not a 'thing' reducible to fixed, static boundaries but an active and creative process of institution-building and intervention.

In other words, states are continually in the process of being made. The difficulties in determining exactly who is responsible for violations, as responsibility is filtered through ever more complex networks, and the argument that states no longer have the capacity to engage in or effectively deal with violations, must therefore be reflected upon with reference to such *statecraft*. State sovereignty and control are in a constant process of realignment and, at any one time, states remain central actors 'in building collaborative power arrangements' to respond to economic, ideological and political challenges (Coleman 2003: 95).

Of course, states have to circumnavigate contradictory demands and how they respond to these pressures will depend on their particular power and positioning at that point in time.[7] What is evident, however, is that states regularly prioritize ideological and economic interests over the rights of populations (George 1995; McCorquodale and Fairbrother 1999). While the South African apartheid system represents this *in extremis*, it is clear that other countries like Nigeria (Green and Ward 2004), China (Evans and Hancock 1998) and India (Roy 1999) have forcibly displaced, violated and impoverished communities in the interests of industry. Similarly, human rights violations in East Timor 'were entirely subordinated to trade and other self-interested considerations' (Herman 2002: xi); powerful Western states (such as the USA, the UK, Australia and New Zealand) all chose to support the Indonesian ruling elite as they offered favourable climates for trade and investment as well as a challenge to the perceived threats of communism and socialism. It is also instructive to consider that Indonesian President Suharto lost favour with his sponsors as a result of economic mismanagement and corruption, not as a consequence of his involvement in gross violations. Suharto's immediate family enjoyed major economic and political gains through their allocated control of 'major banks, real estate, shipping, oil and gas exploration, petrochemicals, auto production, hotels, and transportation systems, among other enterprises'; during his 32 years in power, his family is thought to have 'acquired' approximately '\$73 billion' (Friedrichs 2004: 126). His fall from power, therefore, rested on economic misdemeanours. Until this point, the relationship of Western powers to this persistent, serious violator was based on ensuring a stable trade relationship (Evans 1998) and 'on helping to maintain a favourable, pro-Western, configuration of power' in a strategic area 'of the developing world' (Phythian 2000: 148). In thinking about responsibility for human rights violations, the dynamic global political economy is key (Kauzlarich *et al.* 2003).

It is also clear that states are active in concealing their responsibility in violations. Cohen (2001) and Mathiesen (2004) illustrate how crimes come to be denied and silenced through complex techniques that cut across state, institutional and personal relations. Similarly, Jamieson and McEvoy (2005) show that states attempt to avoid legal accountability by hiding their affiliations in combat; normalizing abusive practices within respectable organizational cultures; colluding with third-party actors such as death squads, militias or other violation-friendly states; hiring mercenaries or private security firms; exploiting or changing the rules of jurisdiction; and engaging in juridical othering, where victims are deemed not to exist or not worthy of judicial protection. Thus, even the most 'blatant violations of human rights can be made nearly invisible' by the fact that there are no easily identifiable perpetrators (George 1995: 276).

The task for criminologists is to unpack the involvement of various powerful actors in violations. With reference to violations in East Timor, state responsibility for genocide, torture, rape and other crimes of violence is relatively visible. However, state actors are also clearly linked to other violations through the training of militia groups, the sales of military equipment and training, the lack of humanitarian intervention, the silencing of the East Timorese situation in the UN and, in the mainstream media, the acquisition of East Timor's oil, the lack of prosecutions for serious violators and so on. While violations in East Timor have involved a variety of actors, state responsibility has rested on a continuum (Kauzlarich *et al.* 2003). State officials have directly engaged in violations but they have also funded or directly supported other states or bodies that undertook violations, they have failed to regulate the activities of parties where they have held a clear mandate to do so and they have shown distinct indifference to violations.

Allocating responsibility for violations is therefore a difficult exercise. Criminologists must move away from a strict individualistic model of criminal responsibility to consider the collaborative power arrangements that exist at local, national and global levels. This involves getting to grips with complex economic, ideological, legal and political relations that are operationalized across national borders.

Accountability and redress

While an analysis of direct and indirect perpetration of rights must encompass different groups, attention must also be paid to how diverse groups and individuals experience or suffer violations. Criminology needs to understand and interpret 'the structure of a globalizing world; the direction(s) in which this world is heading; and how diverse groups' experiences are shaped by wider social, political and economic processes' (White 2003: 484). It is evident that individuals and groups will face separate rights, concerns and victimization in different ways on account of their identity, politics, social standing, gender, 'race' and so on (Stanley 2005a). Further, while a response to victimization may depend on the consciousness of the people involved (that is, whether they view their situation as a rights problem)[8] it is also reliant on the resources and standing of those victimized. It is, after all, relatively easy to dismiss claims for 'truth' or 'justice' from those who have little economic, social or cultural capital (Stanley 2005a). In terms of accountability and redress, there is a need to be attentive to the capabilities of groups to make rights claims.

The wider political context in which rights operate in law cannot therefore be disregarded. The law can be quite overt in its distribution of power and privileges to particular groups of people and taking criminal proceedings may not be the most appropriate way to achieve social transformation (Smart 1989). Indeed, pursuing legal rights may actually inhibit opportunities to resolve inequalities for certain groups. For example, despite its apparently neutral and objective language, human rights law and practice tend to be male focused and women continually struggle to get their specific sufferings heard within courtrooms (Chinkin 1998). Similarly, minority populations may find that they do not have the finances or knowledge to access criminal proceedings (Ewing 2001). For such groups, law may just reinforce existing social inequalities.

Related to this is the issue that the law responds to an individualistic language of rights (McColgan 2000). International tribunals and courts focus on those individuals responsible for directing or committing acts of violence. In this context, international human rights law concentrates attention on civil and political violations, and ultimately a narrow version of justice is addressed. Yet, as detailed above, human rights injustices are wide in scope. Many acts of redress or justice might need a focus on groups, institutions and structures, not an individualized response. Issues of social justice cannot be neatly separated from those of criminal justice.

Of central importance is the reality that victims of human rights violations are not a homogeneous group and the forms of justice they seek are diverse. For example, a family of a 'disappeared' person may demand the retrieved body of their loved one while a torture survivor may require medical or psychological assistance to deal with his or her trauma (Stanley 2004). Many survivors of physical violations have 'relatively realistic expectations' such as to have their experiences officially acknowledged, to 'get medical attention, a tombstone, exhumations, further investigations' and so on (Hamber *et al.* 2000: 34). Others want to see perpetrators ousted from their employment, or publicly shamed. And many want to entrench new values into the institutions that have allowed violations to occur unhindered (Hayner 2001). Finally, others will want further action regarding their experiences of inequality. Thus, women who have been subject to rape may seek a challenge to the institutionalization of patriarchy within state or civil society practices and those who experience poverty may be strongly supportive of strategies for economic justice (Stanley 2005a).

Human rights discourse is useful in terms of couching claims as agreed 'social wrongs' (Smart 1989: 143); however, if we want to challenge the wider harms that cause death and suffering, we also sometimes need to look beyond the current hierarchy of human rights that elevates individualism and legal responses. Research has to understand local and personal 'troubles' in terms of histories, ideologies, relations and structures at a global level. The following case study pursues these aims in an examination of repression and justice in Timor-Leste. In working through the issues, this overview reveals the fundamental inadequacy of mainstream human rights discourse to respond to criminal and social injustices.

Repression and terror in East Timor

Timor-Leste (East Timor)[9] is a small country situated just off the north coast of Australia. The island of Timor had been used by the Portuguese as a strategic trading post since the early sixteenth century and it was designated an official colony in 1702. The separation of the island into East and West Timor came in 1913 as, following years of dispute, Portugal eventually ceded the western part of the island to the Dutch (this subsequently became part of Indonesia in 1949) while retaining control over the eastern half, the enclave of Oecussi in the West, as well as the islands of Atauro and Jaco (Jardine 1999; Taylor 2003).

Portugal sustained a role of 'benign neglect' in East Timor, doing little to build the colony during most of its rule. While the Portuguese language and state structures were reflected in Timorese life, the vast majority of East Timorese lived in self-sufficient mountain villages that were governed by traditional rulers (Simons 2000). This situation irredeemably changed on 25 April 1974, when a coup [10] in Portugal resulted in a decision to engage with the self-determination struggles of Portuguese colonies through Africa and Asia (Taylor 2003). Portugal commenced a 'strategy' of decolonization, leaving a power vacuum in East Timor. Three principal parties, 'Freitilin'[11] (the Front for an Independent East Timor), 'UDT'[12] (Timorese Democratic Union) and 'APODETI'[13] (Timorese Popular Democratic Association), emerged and, following a short civil war, Freitilin garnered widespread support from the population. The ensuing period of peace was short lived. For economic, political and ideological reasons, the Indonesian government proposed that an independent Timor could not exist.[14]

Following Portugal's decision to leave, Indonesia commenced a campaign of destabilization in the region. This subversion strategy took many forms – Indonesian forces undertook military attacks on towns near the border with West Timor, solicited international support for integration, gathered intelligence and undermined Freitilin members, strengthened oppositional political parties and encouraged UDT leaders in an attempted coup (Taylor 1991). Portuguese officials removed themselves from the region and refused to participate in a 'decolonization process' and so, sensing they were on their own, Freitilin leaders declared the independence of East Timor at the United Nations on 28 November 1975. Nine days later, with the full support of Western powers, the Indonesian government launched an attack by air, sea and land. The subsequent occupation lasted almost a quarter of a century.

The violence inflicted on the East Timorese population by Indonesian powers was, without doubt, extremely brutal. It is estimated that up to 183,000 people (approximately, a third of the population) were killed during occupation. Many people died in *ad hoc* killing sprees, planned massacres and bombing raids; others were killed in military actions, such as the 'fence of legs' operations that used Timorese civilians as human shields when Indonesian troops went to search for Freitilin-armed resisters. Tens of thousands were slowly starved to death in the 'resettlement camps' established by the Indonesian military to move people from the mountains to closely surveilled and controlled villages in low-lying, unfertile and malaria-infested areas.[15] While these camps were set up to control the population, they also marked the 'beginning of the military campaign to systematically restructure the territory economically and to "resocialize" its people' (Taylor 2003: 175). The Indonesians forced villagers into work, and Timorese self-sufficiency and the ability to work directly with the land were reappropriated, over decades, into cash crops and labour for Indonesian infrastructure (Nairn 1997).

As detailed in the Indonesian Army's 'Established Procedures' manual, the force's main role was to control all aspects of community life (Nairn 1997). In particular, those directly involved or supporting the independence movement were to be crushed by all means possible. Subsequently, Timorese people were routinely killed, forcibly removed from their homes and land, 'disappeared', raped and detained without trial. Torture became an integral feature of the occupation, and was commonplace in prisons and detention facilities across the region (HRW Asia 1994). Among other things, such techniques were used to spread terror, to coerce compliance, to punish, to gather information, to humiliate, to create informers or regime 'supporters', to demonstrate the power of the state and to make political opposition ineffective (Pinto 1997; Stanley 2004). Civilians were violated because of their differing political views or because they refused to become pro-Indonesian militia members or because they listened to foreign short wave radio or because they were suspected of 'thinking prohibited thoughts' or other such reasons (Nairn 1997: xv; see also HRW Asia 1994). In sum, human rights violations formed a central plank of Indonesian control (Amnesty 1985).

The independence movement in Timor was not, however, crushed and a complex network of fighters and supporters was established to counter this repression (Jardine 1999). While this fight ran throughout the 1970s and 1980s, it was not until the 1990s that the situation in East Timor received significant international attention. The 'Santa Cruz' massacre of 12 November 1991, in particular, presented a landmark shift. The unprovoked brutality of this event, in which approximately 270 people were shot or beaten to death by Indonesian soldiers in a Dili cemetery, was broadcast around the world. From this time, the campaign for self-determination in East Timor gained a momentum that eventually could not be stopped by the Indonesian government and on 27 January 1999, the government announced that the Timorese people could choose between autonomy and independence in a referendum. Despite increased violence against the population, to 'encourage' votes in support of Indonesia, 78.5 per cent voted against the autonomy proposal on 30 August 1999.

The Indonesian retribution was swift. It is estimated that over 1,400 individuals were killed, supporters of independence were raped and beaten, over 75 per cent of all buildings and infrastructure was destroyed and burnt, approximately three quarters of the population fled their homes to hide in the mountains or to make their way across the border to West Timor and UN staff were evacuated after being held under siege (Robinson 2002). A UN multinational military force eventually landed on 20 September 1999 and, over the following months, peace was established. In May 2002, the country finally gained full independence.

In the midst of such struggles, where might criminology see the networks of responsibility? The Indonesian state is, of course, responsible for violations; however, its actions cannot be addressed without also looking at the role of Western powers, the global media, militia members and transnational organizations. Timor's brutal history cannot be ascertained without a historical assessment of the multiple actors involved in the committal, support and denial of human rights violations. It is this to which this chapter now turns.

Tracking criminal actors

It is evident that the violence inflicted by Indonesian officials in East Timor cannot be viewed as aberrational acts; rather, these human rights violations must be viewed within the wider context of violence across Indonesia. The techniques applied by the Suharto-led Indonesian government in East Timor reiterate and are built on the methods undertaken by the same government against the Communist Party of Indonesia (PKI) in 1965–6 (Nairn 1997). During this time, President Suharto led a policy in which those identified as Communist Party members or supporters were persecuted and murdered –

Amnesty (1977) estimates that more than one million people were killed in less than two years. Even the head of the Indonesia's state security system assessed the toll at half a million people, with another 750,000 jailed or sent to concentration camps (Jardine 1997). While such activities represent a clear historical example, one only has to examine the recent Indonesian repression in places like Aceh and Papua (Martinkus 2004) to understand that the violence in East Timor illustrates a continuity of Indonesian state repression across different time periods. Further, this connected state violence has been both organized and institutionalized. This can be identified by the training manuals, constructed 'in-house' for serving officers, that instructed soldiers how to avoid public antipathy by not photographing prisoners stripped naked or being tortured by electric shocks, not circulating photographs and by ensuring that witnesses were not present during interrogations (Amnesty 1983).

Of course, the Indonesian government found ready support from other powerful allies. General Suharto's seizure of power in Indonesia was noted, by *Time* magazine, to be the 'West's best news for years in Asia' (Pilger 1998) as, unlike his predecessor, President Sukarno, Suharto was viewed as being pro-USA and anti-communist. Consequently, the US Embassy were 'generally sympathetic with and admiring of what the army was doing' in the region (Jardine 1997: 22). The initial invasion of East Timor was given the green light by US, UK and Australian politicians on the basis that an independent East Timor would be both unviable and a potential communist threat (Taylor 2003). Accordingly, despite numerous UN Security Council resolutions that called for Indonesia's immediate withdrawal from East Timor, violations were denied and no action was taken (Kiernan 2002) and, during ongoing UN debates on East Timor, powerful states would convince others to fall in line. For example, in 1982, the Vanuatu representative to the UN was 'quietly informed by the Australian delegate that his government might curtail its aid to Vanuatu unless its prime minister took a less supportive stance on self-determination for East Timor' (Taylor 2003: 180).

Indonesia held, then, geographic, ideological and political interests for the 'West'; however, it also presented an economic opportunity for strategic resources. USA-based multinational companies such as Goodyear and Caltex had strong interest in Indonesia's rubber plantations and oil industry (Jardine 1997) and major investors in Indonesia, such as General Electric and AT&T, lobbied to support Suharto following the Dili massacre that attracted international condemnation (Nairn 1997). Similarly, Australia ultimately gave full recognition to Indonesia's claim over East Timor in a bid to access oil and mineral reserves in the Timor Sea. In 1989, Australia signed the Timor Gap Treaty with Indonesia, which gave 'possession' of an estimated seven billion barrels of oil belonging to Timor (Pilger 1998); as detailed below, this is a central economic issue for the Timorese people today.

The Indonesian invasion of East Timor in 1975 was also assisted by external military training. As Gareth Evans, Australian Foreign Minister from 1988 to 1996, admitted, while politicians tried to downplay human rights violations, 'much of Australia's military training "helped only to produce more professional human rights abusers"' (cited in Robinson 2002: 164). Moreover, supporting states also supplied arms and arsenal throughout the occupation – the USA and UK, for instance, covered 'ground attack aircraft, helicopters, missiles, frigates, battlefield communication systems, [and] armoured vehicles' for Indonesia (Taylor 2003: 178). During the initial invasion of East Timor, some 90 per cent of Indonesian weaponry was supplied by US companies (Jardine 1997) and, throughout the occupation, the US administration approved over US$1 billion of weapons sales (Chomsky 2000). Following grassroots pressure, the US Congress voted to block weapons delivery[16] and Britain eventually became Indonesia's largest arms provider (Phythian 2000). Notwithstanding growing international pressure for Indonesia to withdraw from East Timor, British arms sales to Indonesia consolidated throughout the 1990s. In 1996, when New Labour came to power, sales were valued at 438 million pounds (Phythian 2000). Throughout this period, British politicians accepted Indonesian government guarantees that equipment would not be used for internal suppression (Chomsky 2000).

This supportive stance was assisted by weak media coverage of events. The experiences of the East Timorese were generally not of interest to Western newspaper editors or TV programmers and those few journalists who attempted to subvert Indonesian attempts to stop any reporting in the region were regularly frustrated by the lack of media interest in gross human rights violations (Nairn 1997; Martinkus 2001). For example, between August 1975 and the invasion, the *Los Angeles Times* ran 16 articles on East Timor. After the invasion, this situation dramatically changed: 'In fact, there was not a single mention of East Timor in the *Los Angeles Times* from March 1976 until November 1979' – precisely the time that killings were occurring indiscriminately (Jardine 1997: 23). This position was not unique, and when the situation in Timor was reported, it relied heavily on Indonesian misrepresentations and sustained the agendas of supporting states (Chomsky 1996; Klaehn 2002).

Of course, there was a great deal of alternative reporting that illuminated the East Timorese situation – this is precisely why José Ramos Horta and Bishop Belo were awarded the Nobel Peace Prize in 1996 and it is why human rights activists hammered British Aerospace Hawk Jets in the same year (Pilger 1998)[17] – yet powerful states and transnational bodies continued to ignore the plight of the East Timorese people and, in many cases, directly assisted the Indonesian government to implement repressive policies. The World Bank, for instance, provided significant money to the Indonesian government to instigate a 'birth control' programme throughout East Timor and subsequently awarded a 'population prize' to President Suharto for his efforts (Anderson 2001). With even the smallest amount of research, World Bank officials would have discovered that, in fact, Indonesian officials were pursuing a forced sterilization programme against East Timorese women.

Responsibility for the Timorese situation can, then, be ascertained at international levels. Many states, corporations and transnational bodies ignored human rights standards in pursuit of their own strategic, economic and ideological goals. While the Indonesian state was central to repression in East Timor, it could not act on its own. Indeed, as shown through the eventual withdrawal of Indonesia from East Timor in 1999,[18] these crimes could have been halted at any moment by the withdrawal of support to Indonesia on the issue (Chomsky 1996).

Yet, it can also be noted that Indonesian officials also built internal support for its operations through the use of militia groups. Militias had been operationalized from the start of the Indonesian invasion; however, their role became increasingly significant in 1998 and 1999 as groups developed throughout East Timor and engaged in widespread attacks against the population (Robinson 2001). Militia commanders, providing extensive support for Indonesian military officials, were paid a salary for the recruitment, training, co-ordination and retention of local members and, as a result, they attracted and coerced many Timorese peasants into their ranks (Dunn 2003).

Responsibility for violent repression in East Timor can therefore be attributed to complex networks of responsibility that encompass individual states, the global media, corporations, transnational organizations and militia members. Each of these groups may be found to be responsible for human rights violations in the region. Yet, who is made accountable for violations? And is justice being secured for the range of violations that have occurred since 1975? This chapter will now assess the criminal justice mechanisms established in the transition to an independent Timor-Leste.

Bringing human rights violators to account?

At the start of the transition from Indonesian occupation in Timor-Leste, the UN made a commitment to participate in bringing those responsible for 'grave violations of international humanitarian and human rights law' to account (UN 2000a). In 1999, the work of the UN's International Commission of Inquiry culminated in a recommendation that an international human rights tribunal should be established to try to sentence those guilty of violations (UN 2000b). The Indonesian government, however, persuaded the UN to allow them to prosecute their own high-ranking officials and so, in 2002, the Indonesian government established an 'Ad Hoc Human Rights Court' in Jakarta. This court brought 18 defendants to trial. Ultimately, only one man (a Timorese defendant) was convicted and punished; all others were acquitted at trial or on appeal. As Cohen (2003) argues, the court was 'intended to fail' from the outset as, among other issues, prosecution teams failed to press their cases with professional commitment and government officials demonstrated a distinct lack of political will to support the court.

In Dili, the UN set up a criminal justice process, and the 'Special Panels for Serious Crimes' (SPSC) and the 'Serious Crimes Unit' (SCU) were both established in June 2000 through UN Transitional Authority in East Timor (UNTAET) regulations.[19] The SPSC, a judicial tribunal that brings together international and national judges, was formed to try serious criminal offences. It has universal jurisdiction over charges of genocide, war crimes and crimes against humanity and can adjudicate over murder and sexual offence cases if they occurred between 1 January 1999 and 25 October 1999. The SCU was formed to conduct investigations and prosecute cases in the SPSC.

At first glance, the criminal justice process in Dili looks to have been relatively successful – the SCU has charged 392 individuals in 95 indictments, and 74 defendants have been convicted of serious crimes and crimes against humanity in the SPSC (ODGP 2005). Compared with the international tribunals for the Former Yugoslavia and Rwanda, these are healthy figures indeed. Further, the serious crimes process in Timor has operated with just a fraction of the cost – examining the annual budget for 2001, for instance, Timorese courts procured just over $6 million while the international tribunals spent over $100 million each and the Sierra Leone tribunal had a budget of over $20 million (Cohen 2002). Notwithstanding such quantitative achievements, there are a number of issues that raise serious concern about the nature of justice for Timor-Leste.

First, despite a remit to consider serious crimes from the start of Indonesian occupation, the SCU has failed to bring any charges for events that occurred before 1999.[20] While this 1999 focus can be understood – the violations received international attention; the UN felt that its authority had been attacked; and the evidence would be more readily remembered and collected (Open Society and CIJ 2004) – this practical narrowing of the UNTAET mandate is at odds with the wishes of the general public in Timor-Leste. Consultations undertaken by the Judicial System Monitoring Programme (JSMP) and the Commission for Reception, Truth and Reconciliation (the East Timorese Truth Commission) have repeatedly shown that there is a widespread desire to hold trials for serious human rights abuses committed from 1975 onwards (Stanley 2005b). The events in 1999, while serious, do not illustrate the decades of repression suffered by the population and represent under 1 per cent of all occupation killings.[21]

Second, the transitional justice system in Timor-Leste has failed to prosecute Indonesian officials for their implementation of and involvement in human rights violations. Most of those indicted by the SCU are Timorese and the vast majority of defendants brought to the SPSC have been Timorese – for example, all 26 men prosecuted on torture charges have been Timorese (Stanley 2005b). These individuals tend to be illiterate farmers who became involved in low-level militia activity, often through coercion. While this may provide some sense of justice for those who have suffered, it cannot hide the issue that those who bear most responsibility remain free, and seemingly untouchable. At present, 303 suspects are presumed to be in Indonesia (ODGP 2005) and many remain in active service within the military and criminal justice institutions. Little has been done by the SCU, the Timor-Leste government, the UN or the international community to find and detain them.

Third, serious concerns have been raised about the nature of due process in the special panels. For instance, the defence counsel have lacked adequate staff and resources. Most defence counsel have no previous experience in international law and have struggled to access resources to assist them (Open Society and CIJ 2004). In the first 14 trials at the SPSC, no defence witnesses were called (Cohen 2002). The panels have also suffered from a lack of translators. The courts operated in four main languages – Tetum, Bahasa Indonesia, Portuguese and English; however, there are over 20 indigenous languages in Timor. The author has observed a panel hearing in which one defence counsel was by no means fluent in the operational language (English) and defendants could not understand any of the proceedings. Given the charges of crimes against humanity, as well as the UN grounding of the SPSC, such operations seem distinctly inappropriate. Further, defendants, who sometimes appear to be convicted on the briefest of evidence (Stanley 2005b), are disadvantaged in their opportunities for appeal by the complete lack of court transcripts. While panel hearings are recorded, there is no systematic transcription of hearings and they are not accessible to defence counsel or the public.

For such reasons, the serious crimes process in Dili must be brought under considerable scrutiny. It has failed to provide an adequate judicial response to the crimes against humanity committed since 1975 in East Timor and has concentrated attentions on low-level Timorese militia members. It has not established a judicial truth about the role of diverse powerful actors in sustaining and perpetrating human rights violations and has failed to bring those violators to account.

The SCU has just ended all investigations and trials. It remains unclear what will happen now to judicial attempts to deal with serious crimes. Most survivors in Timor-Leste have a profound sense that the 'international community' has an obligation to pursue criminal justice options for crimes against humanity. As Antonio[22] explained:

> There must be justice … how can we make reconciliation without justice? … there will only be good relations among the people if there is justice … the peace can only be maintained if there is justice … There must be an international tribunal, set up by the United Nations. It is their responsibility.

Evidently, trials and punishment are an important part of 'dealing with the past.' Yet, it is currently difficult to ascertain whether these options will be pursued further. At the time of writing, the East Timorese government has established a 'Friendship Commission' with the Indonesian government. The reasoning behind this is that the former cannot economically afford to pursue negative relations with the latter; in effect, the new government of Timor-Leste does not have the power to demand prosecutions of high-ranking violators.[23] Opportunities for criminal justice are thus entwined with the economy, trade and social justice.

Opportunities for social justice?

The people of Timor-Leste continue to wait for an appropriate international judicial response to the civil and political violations inflicted against them. Yet, the connection between such violations with others based on economic, social and cultural rights should not be readily lost. As detailed above, survivors tend to experience diverse violations over time and those who suffered political violations of rights will regularly face other economic and social violations. As Isabel,[24] an ex-political prisoner, explained: 'Now, we continue to suffer. Ex-prisoners cannot afford to send their children to school, some are now handicapped and cannot find work ... some only have broken corrugated iron roofing for shelter, their life conditions are worse than before ... we sacrificed our life for the independence.'

Without doubt, almost everyone in Timor is affected by grinding poverty. Timor-Leste is one of the poorest countries in the world and the poorest country in the Asia Pacific region. Its economy is propped up by donations from international sponsors. Almost half the population live on less than 55 US cents a day, which means that the reality for many is that even basic food, clothing and education needs are not met. Life expectancy is 57 years and people struggle to receive even basic health care. An estimated 43 per cent of the population is illiterate, many adults do not possess work skills and there is over 50 per cent unemployment (UNDP 2002).

The tasks imposed on the Timorese government, donor states, the UN, the World Bank and non-governmental organizations have undoubtedly been difficult. When Indonesian powers left, they ensured that Timor was stripped of its resources. Thus, for the most part, development has been directed towards building basic infrastructure. However, the UN, which has taken the major role in nation-building, has been criticized for its lack of capacity building. Few Timorese were placed in important roles in the planning and running of the reconstruction effort. As Jose Ramos Horta complained: 'We saw time going by and no Timorese administration, no civil servants being recruited, no jobs being created' (Chandler 2002: 204). A similar pattern has emerged in the court system, as the internationally led serious crimes process has failed to train local Timorese in legal and court skills. While the UN has undoubtedly spent time and resources in Timor, it has not ensured that Timorese people sense ownership over the new systems and, importantly, have the skills to 'stand on their own feet.'

The development that has been imposed on Timor is also reliant on a Western model of imported capital and technology, rather than on building local skills and resources. George (1995: 273) regards this as a 'mal-development model' as it does 'little or nothing to improve living standards of the poor, since most economic development money' is 'devoted to the export sector, not towards the satisfaction of basic needs.' One of the fundamental problems with this model is that there are so many countries placed into this situation that poor countries are pitted against each other. For example, coffee represents 80 per cent of all Timorese exports and is a key focus for economic growth (Amaral 2003). Of course, this crop is grown around the world and, as recent events show, its price can fluctuate drastically; while Timor must obviously develop what it can, concerns must be raised about the viability of directing such dominant attentions to such an export crop.

Further problems of Western modes of development can be gleaned from the World Bank's implementation of its $18 million Community Empowerment and Local Governance Project. While most Timorese wanted schools and medical centres to be established in their areas (UNDP 2002), the World Bank focused opportunities on micro-credit loans for individuals wishing to establish businesses. The idea behind such loans is that local, rural economies can be invigorated. In reality, as Moxham (2004) details, villagers end up obtaining loans to set up their only business option – kiosks to sell small household items. The problems arise as there will be several kiosk owners in the village who can only source the same goods, and village customers do not have the money to purchase goods. Some World Bank researchers have concluded that, in 70 per cent of cases, those taking out loans will not even make enough money to pay back the original loan (Moxham 2004).

However, the principal economic issue that affects independent Timor is related to the oil reserves in the Timor Sea. The opportunities for economic reconstruction of Timorese society, at present, rest heavily on current negotiations regarding oil reserves between Timor-Leste, the Australian government and oil companies[25] (Scheiner 2004). Following the Timor Gap Treaty, the Australian government has refused to release its control of the major oil fields that lie within Timorese maritime waters. While this situation is currently subject to international negotiations, Australian success would ensure that Timor-Leste would not have the economic resources to maintain even basic services over forthcoming years (La'o Hamutuk 2004).

Overall, it is evident that, while Timor-Leste has undoubtedly faced severe economic challenges in the transition to democracy, the

Timorese people continue to suffer human rights violations (Stanley 2005a). Further, these violations are regularly made worse as a result of those policies and practices of external states and transnational organizations that are underpinned by an advanced global capitalist agenda. The realities of Timorese people's lives, therefore, appear uncertain for the foreseeable future and a question could still be raised: is Timor-Leste yet free?

Conclusion

While the extensive gross violations inflicted by Indonesian officials and their supporters may have ended in Timor-Leste, this case study highlights the importance of economic social and cultural rights in the day-to-day existence of ordinary people. Moreover, Timorese people are still vulnerable to new and different violations inflicted by those who, at first glance, appear to help. For instance, while the Australian state played a crucial role during 1999, ensuring that Indonesian military forces left the region and participating in the immediate reconstruction of the country, a question needs to be raised about the current Australian approach to Timor Sea reserves which could only serve to intensify human rights violations in Timor-Leste. Criminology, therefore, needs to be attentive to the ways in which civil and political human rights approaches, by powerful nations and bodies, can be used as a cover to pursue individual geographic, political, social or economic interests (Morrison 2004).

The principal challenges facing the people of Timor-Leste, victims of a horrific catalogue of civil and political right violations, are compounded by their current experience of grinding poverty. It is the right to food, water, health, education and shelter that structures suffering in the country. The case example of Timor-Leste presented here raises two key issues for criminologists to consider. First, it cautions against the tendency for notions of state crime and state harm to be linked too closely to civil and political human rights discourses. Criminology must begin to account for the relationship between violations that are unambiguously described as 'state crime' and economic, social and cultural human rights violations. Moreover, it is imperative that criminologists become more adept in tracking the ways in which structural contexts – such as advanced capitalism, patriarchy, neocolonialism and age – underpin violations in a globalizing world. Second, criminologists must become minded of the ways in which victims suffer a continuum of violations, across time, at the hands of diverse actors who support, organize and inflict them. It is, as we have seen here, relatively easy to dismiss claims for 'truth' or 'justice' from those who have little economic, social or cultural capital. There is a need for criminology to expose violations when they occur and critique dismissals for rights claims. The global power networks that underpin violations in all their forms are ripe for analysis and challenge.

Notes

1 Indeed, my partner, Acky, loves to tell me that criminologists sit around their offices, drinking tea, going 'eeeh, in't it terrible?' without actually doing anything else.

2 See Schwendinger and Schwendinger (1975), Cohen (1993), Green and Ward (2004) for further details.

3 In interview with the author, Dili, Timor-Leste, 23 November 2004.

4 There are, however, textual differences in international human rights law. Under Article 2.1 of the Covenant of Economic, Social and Cultural Rights, rights may be progressively realized according to the maximum available resources. This tempering of obligations is not evident in the Covenant of Civil and Political Rights.

5 Taking a critical analysis, Coleman and Sim (2005) detail that these state relations are not new, or the product of globalization, as the state has always worked through a range of actors. From this perspective, dominant human rights discourses (that have directed a focus on nation-states) have always been inadequate.

6 Chossudovsky (1997: 37) argues that the seemingly neutral interplay of market forces is even a form of 'economic genocide.' As he proposes, the 'restructuring of the world economy under the guidance of the Washington-based financial institutions' means that countries face becoming just cheap reserves of labour and natural resources. Structural adjustment programmes, imposed to 'guide' states to repay international financial loans, have led to critical unemployment, high food prices and cuts to welfare, all of which worsen and shorten the lives of affected populations.

7 For instance, the demands of the IMF, which impose conditionalities on loans which make human rights practices virtually impossible to attain, will often take precedence over UN human rights agencies or NGOs that attempt to hold states responsible for violations (Freeman 2002). Similarly, economically powerful states have not shied away from using their status, and offers of financial support, to gain compliance from economically weak states on a range of issues, from the environment to the 'war on terror.' And transnational corporations, which have

trade levels which surpass the GDP of most states, regularly base their investment decisions on nation-state adherence to their demanding conditions on environmental conditions, employment rules and labour laws that do violate rights (Evans and Hancock 1998). We cannot lose sight, however, of the integral role that states play in sustaining and orchestrating these conditions of globalization (Evans and Hancock 1998). Powerful governments will appoint their 'finest minds' and political allies to the boards of transnational organizations and corporations, they will promote firms and ease trade conditions for corporations, they will engage in violent force to quell dissent and they will regulate national economies. Further, as shown in Argentina, where the government initially refused to pay back IMF loans because of national economic instability, states may also have the ability not to act upon international financial demands. In short, 'globalization is what States have made of it. States themselves have established the rules and institutions to maintain order amid the diversity of their cultures' (Dunne 1999: 28). Without doubt, however, this an uneven process of globalization that is 'propelled by hegemonic centers of power', so while G8 states may be 'key agents in shaping the agenda of the major financial institutions', less powerful countries have limited ability to resist these neoliberal economic and social policies (Dunne 1999: 29). The characteristics and nature of power, through political and economic circuits, cannot be underplayed (Coleman 2003).

8   White (2003) makes this point with regard to environmental harms. Given this focus, he also proposes that ,in some instances, a 'basic "equality" of victims' can be identified, as some environmental problems like ozone depletion or global warming 'will threaten everyone in the same way' (2003: 493). Of course, victims of such global problems are placed in distinct situations with regards to response. New technologies and strategies to deal with such environmental harms are not implemented with a notion of equivalence and it is evident that environmental 'disasters' have far more damaging consequences for those who are already disadvantaged at social and structural levels.

9   East Timor was officially renamed 'Timor-Leste' with the move to full independent status, in May 2002. The name 'East Timor' will be used in this chapter for events before this date.

10   This coup, the 'Carnation Revolution', was forced by the Armed Forces Movement, 'a group of left-leaning military officials dedicated to democracy within Portugal and the decolonization of all its overseas territories' (Jardine 1997: 13). They overthrew the fascist government of Marcelo Caetano.

11   Initially named the Association of Timorese Social Democrats, Fretilin based their programme on socialism, democracy and a rejection of colonialism. They also focused on the need for educational and agricultural reform.

12 UDT represented Timor's wealthiest citizens, having conservative and pro-Portugal policies.

13 This group favoured integration with Indonesia. The party was 'largely a product of Indonesian intelligence' (Jardine 1997: 14).

14 There are a number of reasons why Indonesia took this decision: 1) it was viewed that an independent East Timor might set a 'negative example' for other economically beneficial areas of Indonesia that sought independence (Nairn 1997; Taylor 2003); 2) East Timor had its own financial potential in its oil reserves in the Timor Sea (Taylor 2003); 3) the Indonesian government wanted to demonstrate, particularly to the USA, a commitment to fighting communism in the region (Amnesty International 1977); and 4) Indonesia wanted to retain control over the full archipelago (Taylor 2003).

15 Details given by members of the Timorese truth commission, in interview with the author, February and November 2004.

16 Although it is clear that the USA did continue to support Indonesia and increased Indonesia's military aid (Nairn 1997).

17 These Ploughshares activists subsequently successfully argued in court that their actions were in fulfilment of the UN Genocide Convention as the Hawk Jets were being used by Indonesia to bomb the East Timorese population.

18 The eventual withdrawal of Indonesia from East Timor was the result of diverse factors: as a result of changing popular the opinion and reporting on the issue, there was an ideological shift to self-determination from supporting countries such as the USA, UK and Australia; the replacement of President Suharto with President Habibie in May 1998 also brought a new reformist attitude to Indonesian politics; and the World Bank and the IMF also began to support self-determination and based their further economic support to Indonesia, which desperately needed their assistance, on a commitment to honour the Timorese referendum (Taylor 2003).

19 UNTAET Regulation 2000/15 and UNTAET Regulation 2000/16.

20 The previous Deputy General Prosecutor, Nicholas Koumjian, argued that this SCU policy was based on the fact that no bodies or individuals – including the UN Security Council, the UN Secretary General, the General Prosecutor and the Timorese government – instructed the SCU to do otherwise. He also stated that the Timorese Constitution (which has taken precedence since independence in May 2002) actually bars the SCU from considering cases that fall outside 1999.(iIn interview with the author, Dili, 23 November 2004).

21 From October 2003, the SCU also narrowed its focus to crimes of murder and rape. This has meant that those who suffered other crimes, such as torture, will not find clear representation in court. See Stanley (2005b) for further details.

22 In interview with author, Dili, 24 November 2004.

23 A UN 'Commission of Experts' has also evaluated both the Human Rights Court in Jakarta and the serious crimes process in Dili. The Friendship Commission is widely viewed to be an attempt by the Indonesian and Timorese governments to redirect attention away from a potential international court.

24 In interview with the author, Dili, 18 November 2004.

25 Principally Woodside Petroleum, ConocoPhillips, Royal Dutch Shell and Osaka Gas.

References

Amaral, F. (2003) *Prospects for Coffee Development in East Timor.* Dili: Timor-Leste Ministry of Agriculture, Forestry and Fisheries (http: //www.gov. east-timor.org/MAFF/English/Coffe.htm).

Amnesty International (1977) *Indonesia.* London: Amnesty International.

Amnesty International (1983) *Troops in East Timor Given Secret Manual Permitting Torture.* News Release 10/83, AI Index ASA 21/06/83.

Amnesty International (1985) *East Timor Violations of Human Rights: Extrajudicial Executions, 'Disappearances', Torture and Political Imprisonment 1975–1984.* London: Amnesty International.

Anderson, T. (2001) *Aidwatch June Briefing Note: The World Bank in East Timor* (www.aidwatch.org.au).

Barak, G. (1991) *Crimes by the Capitalist State: An Introduction to State Criminality.* New York, NY: State University of New York Press.

Chambliss, W. J. (1989) 'State organized crime – the American Society of Criminology 1988 Presidential Address', *Criminology*, 27: 183–208.

Chandler, D. (2002) *From Kosovo to Kabul: Human Rights and International Intervention.* London: Pluto Press.

Chinkin, C. (1998) 'International law and human rights', in T. Evans (ed.) *Human Rights Fifty Years on: A Reappraisal.* Manchester: Manchester University Press.

Chomsky, N. (1996) *Powers and Prospects: Reflections on Human Nature and the Social Order.* London: Pluto Press.

Chomsky, N. (1998) 'The United States and the challenge of relativity', in T. Evans (ed) *Human Rights Fifty Years on: A Reappraisal.* Manchester: Manchester University Press.

Chomsky, N. (2000) *A New Generation Draws the Line: Kosovo, East Timor and the Standards of the West.* London: Verso.

Chossudovsky, M. (1997) *The Globalisation of Poverty.* London: Zed Books.

Cohen, D. (2002) 'Seeking justice on the cheap: is the East Timor tribunal really a Model for the future?', *Asia Pacific Issues: Analysis from the East-West Center,* 61 (August). Honolulu, HI: East-West Center.

Cohen, D. (2003) *Intended to Fail: The Trials before the Ad Hoc Human Rights Court in Jakarta.* New York, NY: International Center for Transitional Justice.

Cohen, S. (1993) 'Human rights and crimes of the state: the culture of denial', *Australian and New Zealand Journal of Criminology*, 26: 97–115.

Cohen, S. (2001) *States of Denial: Knowing about Atrocities and Suffering*. Cambridge: Polity Press.

Coleman, R. (2003) 'CCTV surveillance, power, and social order: the state of contemporary social control', in S. Tombs and D. Whyte (eds) *Unmasking the Crimes of the Powerful: Scrutinizing States and Corporations*. New York, NY: Peter Lang.

Coleman, R. and Sim, J. (2005) 'Contemporary statecraft and the "Punitive Obsession": a critique of the new penology thesis', in J. Pratt *et al.* (eds) *The New Punitiveness: Trends, Theories, Perspectives*. Cullompton: Willan Publishing.

Dunn, J. (2003) *East Timor: A Rough Passage to Independence* (3rd edn). Double Bay, NSW: Longueville Books.

Dunne, T. (1999) 'The spectre of globalization', *Indiana Journal of Global Legal Studies*, 7: 17–33.

Evans, T. (1998) 'Introduction: power, hegemony and the universalization of human rights', in T. Evans (ed) *Human Rights Fifty Years on: A Reappraisal*. Manchester: Manchester University Press.

Evans, T. (2001) *The Politics of Human Rights: A Global Perspective*. London: Pluto Press.

Evans, T. and Hancock, J. (1998) 'Doing something without doing anything: international human rights law and the challenge of globalisation', *International Journal of Human Rights*, 2: 1–21.

Ewing, K.D. (2001) 'The unbalanced constitution', in T. Campbell *et al.* (eds) *Sceptical Essays on Human Rights*. Oxford: Oxford University Press.

Freeman, M. (2002) *Human Rights: An Interdisciplinary Approach*. Cambridge: Polity Press.

Friedrichs, D.O. (2004) *Trusted Criminals: White Collar Crime in Contemporary Society* (2nd edn). Belmont, CA: Wadsworth/Thomson.

George, S. (1995) 'The structure of dominance in the international geo-economic system and the prospects for human rights realization', in A. Eide and B. Hagtvet (eds) *Conditions for Civilized Politics: Political Regimes and Compliance with Human Rights*. Oslo: Scandinavian University Press.

Green, P. and Ward, T. (2000) 'State crime, human rights, and the limits of criminology', *Social Justice*, 27: 101–15.

Green, P. and Ward, T. (2004) *State Crime: Governments, Violence and Corruption*. London: Pluto Press.

Hamber, B., Nageng, D. and O'Malley, G. (2000) '"Telling it like it is ...": understanding the truth and reconciliation commission from the perspective of survivors', *Psychology in Society*, 26: 18–42.

Hayden, P. and el-Ojeili, C. (2005) 'Confronting globalization in the twenty-first century: an introduction', in P. Hayden and C. el-Ojeili (eds) *Confronting Globalization: Humanity, Justice and the Renewal of Politics*. Basingstoke: Palgrave Macmillan.

Hayner, P. (2001) *Unspeakable Truths: Confronting State Terror and Atrocity.* London: Routledge.

Herman, E. (2002) 'Foreword', in D. Chandler, *From Kosovo to Kabul: Human Rights and International Intervention.* London: Pluto Press.

Human Rights Watch Asia (1994) *The Limits of Openness: Human Rights in Indonesia and East Timor.* New York, NY: HRW.

Jamieson, R. and McEvoy, K. (2005) 'State crime by proxy and juridical othering', *British Journal of Criminology*, 45: 504–27.

Jardine, M. (1997) 'Introduction', in C. Pinto and M. Jardine (eds) *East Timor's Unfinished Struggle: Inside the Timorese Resistance.* Boston, MA: South End Press.

Jardine, M. (1999) *East Timor: Genocide in Paradise* (2nd edn). Cambridge, MA: Odonian Press.

Kauzlarich, D. and Kramer, R. C. (1998) *Crimes of the American Nuclear State at Home and Abroad.* Boston, MA: Northeastern University Press.

Kauzlarich, D., Matthews, R. and Miller, W. (2001) 'Towards a victimology of state crime', *Critical Criminology*, 10: 173–94.

Kauzlarich, D., Mullins, C.W. and Matthews, R.A. (2003) 'A complicity continuum of state crime', *Contemporary Justice Review*, 6: 241–54.

Kiernan, B. (2002) 'Cover-up and denial of genocide: Australia, the USA, East Timor and the Aborigines', *Critical Asian Studies*, 34: 163–92.

Klaehn, J. (2002) 'Corporate hegemony: a critical assessment of the globe and Mail's news coverage of near-genocide in occupied East Timor 1975–1980', *Gazette: The International Journal for Communication Studies*, 64: 301–21.

Kramer, R.C., Michalowski, R.J. and Kauzlarich, D. (2002) 'The origins and development of the concept and theory of state-corporate crime', *Crime and Delinquency*, 48: 263–82.

La'o Hamutuk (2004) *The La'o Hamutuk Bulletin*, 5(2), March.

Martinkus, J. (2001) *A Dirty Little War.* Milsons Point: Random House Australia.

Martinkus, J. (2004) *Indonesia's Secret War in Aceh.* Milsons Point: Random House Australia.

Mathiesen, T. (2004) *Silently Silenced: Essays on the Creation of Acquiesence in Modern Society.* Winchester: Waterside Press.

McColgan, A. (2000) *Women under the Law: The False Promise of Human Rights.* Harlow: Longman.

McCorquodale, R. and Fairbrother, R. (1999) 'Globalization and human rights', *Human Rights Quarterly*, 21: 735–66.

McGrew, A.G. (1998) 'Human rights in a global age: coming to terms with globalization', in T. Evans (ed) *Human Rights Fifty Years on: A Reappraisal.* Manchester: Manchester University Press.

Morrison, W. (2004) 'Globalisation, human rights and international criminal courts', in J. Muncie and D. Wilson (eds) *Student Handbook of Criminal Justice and Criminology.* London: Cavendish Publishing.

Moxham, B. (2004) *The World Bank's Land of Kiosks*: 'Community Driven Development' in East Timor (http: //www.globalpolicy.org/socecon/bwi-wto/wbank/2004/1012easttimor.htm).

Nairn, A. (1997) 'Foreword', in C. Pinto and M. Jardine (eds) *East Timor's Unfinished Struggle: Inside the Timorese Resistance*. Boston, MA: South End Press.

ODGP (Office of the Deputy General Prosecutor for Serious Crimes Timor-Leste) (2005) *Serious Crimes Unit Update*, 4 February. Dili: SCU.

Open Society and Coalition for International Justice (2004) *Unfulfilled Promises: Achieving Justice for Crimes against Humanity in East Timor*. New York, NY: Open Society and CIJ.

Phythian, M. (2000) *The Politics of British Arms Sales since 1964*. Manchester: Manchester University Press.

Pilger, J. (1998) *Hidden Agendas*. London: Vintage.

Pinto, C. (1997) 'Arrest and torture', in C. Pinto and M. Jardine (eds) *East Timor's Unfinished Struggle: Inside the Timorese Resistance*. Boston, MA: South End Press.

Robinson, G. (2001) 'People's war: militias in East Timor and Indonesia', *South East Asia Research*, 9: 271–318.

Robinson, G. (2002) 'If you leave us here we will die', in N. Mills and K. Brunner (eds) *The New Killing Fields: Massacre and the Politics of Intervention*. New York, NY: Basic Books.

Ross, J.I., Barak, G., Ferrell, J., Kauzlarich, D., Hamm, M., Friedrichs, D., Matthews, R., Pickering, S., Presdee, M., Kraska, P. and Kappeler, V. (1999) 'The state of state crime research: a commentary', *Humanity and Society*, 23: 273–81.

Roy, A. (1999) *The Cost of Living*. New York, NY: Modern Library.

Scheiner, C. (2004) *The Case for Saving Sunrise: A Submission to the Government of Timor-Leste*. Dili: La'o Hamutuk.

Schwendinger, H. and Schwendinger, J. (1975) 'Defenders of order or guardians of human rights?', in I. Taylor *et al.* (eds) *Critical Criminology*. London: Routledge & Kegan Paul.

Simons, G. (2000) *Indonesia: The Long Oppression*. London: Macmillan Press.

Smart, C. (1989) *Feminism and the Power of the Law*. London: Routledge.

Stanley, E. (2001) 'Evaluating the truth and reconciliation commission', *Journal of Modern African Studies*, 39: 525–46.

Stanley, E. (2002) 'What next? The aftermath of organized truth telling', *Race and Class*, 44: 1–15.

Stanley, E. (2004) 'Torture, silence and recognition', *Current Issues in Criminal Justice*, 16: 5–25.

Stanley, E. (2005a) 'Truth commissions and the recognition of state crime', *British Journal of Criminology*, 45: 582–97.

Stanley, E. (2005b) *Torture and Transitional Justice in Timor-Leste: A Report for the Judicial System Monitoring Programme*. Dili: JSMP.

Taylor, J. (1991) *Indonesia's Forgotten War: The Hidden History of East Timor*. London: Zed Books.

Taylor, J.G. (2003) '"Encirclement and annihilation": the Indonesian occupation of East Timor', in R. Gellately and B. Kiernan (eds) *The Specter of Genocide: Mass Murder in Historical Perspective.* Cambridge: Cambridge University Press.

Tombs, S. and Whyte, D. (2003) 'Scrutinizing the powerful: crime, contemporary political economy, and critical social research', in S. Tombs and D. Whyte (eds) *Unmasking the Crimes of the Powerful: Scrutinizing States and Corporations.* New York, NY: Peter Lang.

UN (United Nations) (2000a) *Security Council Resolution 1319,* 20 September UN doc.S/RES/1319.

UN (United Nations) (2000b) *Report of the International Commission of Inquiry on East Timor,* 31 January 2000 UN doc.A/54/726.

UNDP (United Nations Development Programme) (2002) *Ukun Rasik A'an: The Way Ahead – East Timor Human Development Report.* Dili: UNDP.

White, R. (2003) 'Environmental issues and the criminological imagination', *Theoretical Criminology,* 7: 483–506.

Woodiwiss, A. (2005) *Human Rights.* London: Routledge.

Chapter 9

Conclusion: expanding the criminological imagination

Alana Barton, Karen Corteen,
David Scott and David Whyte

Introduction

We began this book by outlining the problematic political context within which criminology as a discipline is operating. In so doing, we highlighted the punitive and exclusionary climate currently impacting on criminal justice policies and practices and, drawing on Mills (1959), we revisited the emergence and consolidation of a critical criminological imagination. The subsequent chapters constitute a series of case studies which demonstrate that the current state of affairs within the discipline can be challenged by the utilization of a critical approach drawing on Mills' key concepts – namely, history, biography and structure. While these chapters comprise individual case studies, what unites them is the way in which they attempt to expand the criminological imagination. Consequently, there are shared principles as to how further to develop the imagination. However there are also tensions. This chapter will identify those shared principles together with the points of conflict. It is not the intention here to construct a rigid or definitive agenda for future critical research or to attempt to resolve any tensions or disagreements but rather to acknowledge the themes of continuity and discontinuity that thread through the work of the contributors and hopefully inspire an imaginative discourse within the discipline which may move the debates forward. But before moving on to these issues, it is important to remind ourselves of the contemporary obstacles facing academics engaging in critical research.

The parasitic discipline: criminology, research and the capitalist state

Criminology's current failure is connected to its history and present relationship with the capitalist state. Criminology has a structural relation to the capitalist state that can only be described as parasitical. By that, we mean that the various juridical apparatuses of crime control constitute the justification for the discipline's existence and provide the very lifeblood upon which it thrives. This parasitical relationship has profound implications for developing a reflexive imagination; for the creative processes that enable us to imagine alternative ways of acting and new responses to the problem of crime. Two aspects of the enterprise of criminological research are worth exploring here. The first is the changing relationship between research and policy, and the second, the liberal conceptual framework that criminology finds so difficult to escape.

The impact upon British criminology of the immediate rise in state funding for criminological research, shortly after the election of 1997, should not be underestimated. New Labour's increase in Home Office external research spend between 1998–9 and 2000–1 amounted to a rise of more than 500 per cent. If this was the most obvious indicator of the direction that criminology was to take, it was by no means the only pressure on the discipline. A series of trends that we can call the marketization of the universities had the combined effect of pushing criminology and, indeed, all the social sciences, closer to a policy-driven or utility agenda (Tombs and Whyte 2003a). Those trends include: the structural underfunding of universities during a period of rapid teaching expansion; the tightening of priorities established by research funding councils; and the restructuring of the labour market in higher education and research (which created a new army of researchers on temporary, casualized contracts).

The effect of research has been a disciplinary one. The marketization process has a disciplinary function encouraging researchers to stick closely to a policy agenda in order to maximize the chance of contract renewal or of winning new contracts that might extend tenure for a short period. As researchers are pulled deeper into a relationship with their funders, the capacity (in terms of time, resources and experience) for producing independent research is fatally reduced. For some, the incentive for research funding is greater than it is for others. As the academic binary divide in the UK has been reinstated after its very brief hiatus, the incentive for researchers in the institutions that are not insulated by their 'ancient' or 'traditional' status has been a strong one. Research time is increasingly difficult to secure unless external funding is obtained that enables lecturers some 'buy out'. For the growing army of full-time researchers, which David Harvie (2000) refers to as a research proletariat, external funding is their livelihood. By the end of the 1990s, less than half of all academics in Britain were on permanent contracts (Chitnis and Williams 1999). For research staff, the corresponding figure is likely now to be as low as 5 per cent (Tombs and Whyte 2003a).

This is not to say that the stifling of critical imagination is a necessary effect. For the more enterprising, of course, there are always ways to resist. Many researchers manage to escape the shackles of the policy world and rewrite and publish their data in forms that are different from those required by policymakers, and as such are able to reach out to wider audiences. But this does not change the fact that the overwhelming tendency in social science in general, and criminology in particular, in this era of 'utility' or policy driven research, has been a corrosion of the autonomy and the critical potential of research (van Swaaningen 1997; Walters, Chapter 2, this volume). The prospects for a criminological agenda that is completely severed from the influence of funders, if it ever was possible, now seem remote. Academic researchers, if they fail to break out of the state and policy-funded trap, are expected to spend their entire careers working to research specifications and answering research questions designed by bureaucrats. The disciplinary aspects of this process are obvious, as are the less remarked-upon effects of alienation experienced by this growing army of contract researchers in universities. The important trend here is not simply about the encouragement or stifling of imagination *per se*, but the development of a criminological imagination which stands outside the boundaries imposed by utility research and is therefore capable of contributing to progressive social change.

The difficulty of using state-funded research to imagine alternatives or to present a challenging agenda is palpably difficult. Research findings are used selectively by the state, so that the government mantra of 'evidence-based policy' can be easily translated into 'policy-based evidence' (Tombs and Whyte 2003b). Indeed, one comprehensive study of the impact of government research has concluded that doing criminological research for government makes absolutely no difference to policy whatsoever (Walters 2003). Governments tend only to respond to the research results that suit a preordained agenda. And yet for all the cost and effort of evaluation, the impact of crime science, whether in CCTV or burglary initiatives, has been wholly inconclusive. Indeed, in some cases the new strategies and technologies of control have exacerbated social conflict and crime. Take, for example, the use of Anti-Social Behaviour Orders (ASBOs) against young people. Rather than enabling communities to resolve conflicts, the use of ASBOs has had the effect of heightening tensions and has precipitated a sharp rise in the incarceration of young people. One thing that the discipline must face up to – and is less likely to in the current climate – is that criminology itself has become an entirely counterproductive enterprise, creating more and more knowledge that is destined to be manipulated for a political purpose or simply ignored. The more we know about 'crime', it seems, the less we understand. John Major's famous turn of phrase following the James Bulger case has been realized in contemporary criminological agendas.

Unfortunately, this is not how some senior criminologists are reading the discipline at the moment. In the main, the prominent voices in criminology are ambivalent about the pressure to work within the defined agendas of the capitalist state. A view commonly heard among colleagues is that if we don't do the work for the government, then some objectionable positivist or administrative criminologist will. This, of course, may well be the case, but it does not help us think about the wider issue of the apparent ease with which the state 'captures' criminologists in order to do its work. The lack of any sustained concern about the embeddedness of criminology's enterprise in policy-driven research agendas is remarkable. As Hillyard and Tombs (2004) have noted, while Foucault is one of the most frequently quoted intellectuals in criminology, and perhaps its most influential thinker, his disdain for criminology as a state-defined discipline is rarely acknowledged by criminologists. There are, of course, moments when the criminological community does raise objection to the closing down of autonomy and imagination. At the June 2003 conference of the British Society of Criminology (BSC), four papers were pulled by Home Office paymasters because of their content. None was particularly critical of the government; they simply reported mixed success in government crime initiatives. Among the authors of this censored research were some well respected establishment names. The move outraged the traditionally conservative BSC and prompted a summit meeting between the society and senior civil servants.

Despite those infrequent periods of resistance, the general disciplinary trajectory of marketization remains uninterrupted; indeed it has become hegemonic (Clarke and Newman 1997). In the sense that officially funded research is increasingly seen as the most legitimate and influential form of research, universities and external assessment place a premium value on contract research (Hillyard *et al.* 2004a). Government research is thus now more likely to be worn as a status symbol, a badge of honour and prestige, rather than something which raises questions about the independence or analytical potential of the research.

The conceptual straitjacket of crime and the criminal law

If the previous section outlines a trend in the funding structure and the governance of universities that is relatively recent, the principle of policy utility in criminology has been an ever-present one. The most fundamental fact to grasp about the academic 'discipline' of criminology is that its object of study is bound closely to a state-produced account of crime. The problem is that even when criminology has placed the social conditions that produce criminality at the centre of its analysis, the net effect of its enterprise has been to obscure the production of social harms and violence (poverty; injury and death at work; violence against women; homophobic violence; see Hillyard *et al.* 2004b). Indeed, the net effect of criminology has been to encourage a highly unequal hierarchy of harms that does little to ameliorate the violence suffered by the most vulnerable.

It is commonplace in criminological literature to find acknowledgement that the discipline has historically been unable to escape the straitjacket of officially defined 'crime'. What remains relatively unexplored are the conceptual and epistemological problems associated with being guided by the form that the criminal law takes (for an important overview, see Hall and Scraton 1981). It is uncontroversial in legal history that the rapid evolution of criminal law following the industrial revolution was related to the need to maintain a particular social order, one that ensured that the property rights of the new class of owners were to be protected. The form of criminal law that developed apace in the eighteenth and nineteenth centuries has several features that are worth noting. First, it was based upon a rigid methodological individualism. In other words, the criminal law developed methods of punishing harms committed by individuals and suffered by individuals rather than harms produced collectively and experienced collectively. Second and closely related, the criminal law became closely linked to the notion of intent. Harms caused by negligence or caused by omissions – harms produced as a result of non-decisions – were largely exempt from the system of criminal punishment. This is important, because systems of power generally relied not upon violence committed directly by members of the dominant group, but on indirect forms of violence that result from indifference or refusal to make basic health provisions or limit working hours, even when the deadly effects of those were entirely predictable. Third, the distinction between 'public' and 'private' domains ensured that a whole series of harms (violence suffered in the home, in the factory, in the prison and asylum) remained essentially outside the reach of the criminal law. Wherever attempts were made to break this distinction, they were met with a solid resistance from the judiciary, anxious not to destabilize a fragile industrial social order (Carson 1979).

Of course, this is not to say that the criminal law was not at all equipped to deal with harms that fell outside its normal ambit. For, as Norrie (2001) argues, it is impossible to understand the criminal law unless we accept that it is fundamentally contradictory. Anatole France's famous aphorism ('The law in all its majesty equality forbids rich and poor alike to sleep under bridges, to beg in the streets and to steal bread') captures well the point that the contradiction lies in the *structure* of the criminal law rather than simply the bias inherent in its application (see also Sim *et al.* 1987). Recognizing the criminal law as fundamentally contradictory has perhaps been most clearly captured in debates on the criminalization of sexual violence (Gregory and Lees 1999), domestic violence (Dobash and Dobash 2000), violence against children (Scraton 1997) and white-collar and corporate crime (Slapper and Tombs 1999).

The point that we cannot lose sight of here is that, although criminal law may be biased in the sense that its structure penalizes those that threaten the (capitalist/patriarchal/neocolonial/heterosexual) order of things, even when penalties can be applied to the powerful, they rarely are. The key historical example here perhaps is the emergence of a new set of health and safety offences as defined in the first Factory Acts of the mid-nineteenth century. They were originally designed unambiguously as crimes, with tough penalties for factory owners. It became obvious that those laws would be difficult to implement after factory inspectors found that magistrates and sheriffs refused to convict respectable members of their own social class. In order to justify its misapplication, a new criminal category of 'strict liability' offence was applied to deaths and injuries at work. Thus, the contradictory structure of the criminal law itself created new contradictions when the Factory Acts were applied.

Criminology has had very little to say about the most significant social fact about the criminal law: its evolution was neither a natural one aimed at controlling harmful human activities, nor did it advance in a particularly rational manner. At the same time, as the preceding comments indicate, a historical understanding of the development of the criminal law means little unless we understand its significance as a social-ordering process; as a process which guaranteed the protection of particular interests, and at the same time ensured the maintenance of the social order. To understand crime and criminal justice, then, we must understand power. This brings us to a more fundamental issue at stake for criminology. Imprisoned as it is within the Western liberal conception of crime, the organizing objects of the discipline's concern draw it towards a liberal conception of power. As Steven Lukes' classic sociological study has noted, power does not operate only at the level of observable conflict. Lukes argues that, according to a one-dimensional or 'liberal' view, power operates in its most visible manifestation through concrete, individually chosen decisions in situations where there is an obvious conflict of preferences. He states:

> the supreme and most insidious exercise of power [is] to prevent people to whatever degree, from having grievances by shaping their perceptions, cognitions and preferences in such a way that they accept their role in the existing order of things, either because they see or imagine no alternative to it, or because they see it as natural or unchangeable, or because they value it as divinely ordained and beneficial (1974/2005: 24).

Lukes was concerned with the problem of 'seeing' structural power; in particular how to see the structurally determined 'exercise' of power. This dilemma – essentially one that must resolve the individual autonomy of decision-makers – was famously summed up by Marx when he pointed out that people make their own history but not under the conditions of their own choosing. Utilizing Gramsci's (1971) conception of hegemony, Lukes (1974/2005) argued that the aim of the critical social scientist is to challenge the taken-for-granted state of social relations of power and uncover the forms of mystification supporting existing inequitable social structures. The key task of critical criminology remains: to escape the criminological straitjacket and 'see power'. The chapters in this book represent a renewed effort on this front and, although different chapters may be informed by contradictory theories or traditions, there are a number of themes and principles which unite the work of the authors. It is to a consideration of these themes that the chapter now turns.

Adopting a 'social harm' perspective

It is not enough merely to move beyond current definitions and understandings of the criminal law. Critical analysis must also offer an alternative formulation of social problems. This has entailed, in recent years, an analysis of social harms and the rearticulation of the concept of 'crime' as conflicts, troubles and problematic behaviours (Hulsman 1986; de Haan 1990; Hillyard and Tombs 2004; Hillyard *et al.* 2004a). In an important contribution to the debate, Hillyard *et al.* (2004a) have argued that there should be a focus upon all the different types of social harm that humans experience. Rather than simply considering criminal events, the social harm approach calls for an analysis of the different factors which impact upon a person's health, wealth and well-being during his or her life cycle (Hillyard and Tombs 2004). Hillyard *et al.* (2004a) argue that it is counterproductive to separate out criminal harms from other kinds of social harms that are also socially, economically or psychologically damaging. Their intention is not to downplay the harm caused by criminal acts, but rather to expand our focus to encapsulate these and *other* harms.

Hillyard and Tombs (2004) provide a detailed definition of the social harm perspective. First, a social harm perspective encompasses *physical* harms. This would include considering the suffering and hardships created through a range of actions and events such as war; state terror, state torture and state killings; government corruption; exposure to pollutants; health and safety crimes; white-collar crimes; racial violence; sexual violence; and the physical and sexual abuse or neglect of children. What unites this diverse and far from comprehensive list of 'crimes' is their relationships to the systematic abuse of the wrongdoer's position of power or privilege and the subsequent invisibility or marginalization of this problem in contemporary debates on 'crime' and crime control. Second a social harm perspective would consider *financial* and *economic* harms, including both the theft of property and the needs of the property-less. Importantly, it would also take 'cognisance of the personal and social effects' (Hillyard and Tombs 2004: 20) of the social exclusion created through unemployment and low wages. Third, the social harm perspective encompasses *emotional* and *psychological* harms, including the trauma, stresses and suffering created by the harm. Finally, this perspective advocates *cultural safety*, which includes commitments to personal development through access to cultural and intellectual resources and the protection of individual autonomy.

Both Davis and Stanley (Chapters 7 and 8, this volume) contend that the criminological imagination cannot just focus on the *immediate* impact of such harms. Instead, it must incorporate a conceptualization of the implications of long-term harms. For example, Davis discusses the way that 'disasters' are often conceptualized as immediate and short-term events with little consideration given to the lasting and long-term impacts of such incidents, in terms of injustice for victims and in terms of the consequences of secondary effects such as famine, homelessness, disease and poverty. Similarly, Stanley highlights the enduring effects of human rights violations, including 'the trauma of ongoing violations of economic, social and cultural rights', such as poor housing, unemployment and lack of health care. Of course it is not only large-scale events or abuses that can lead to long-term social harm effects. The harsh and reactionary processes and practices of criminal justice, applied to a range of relatively mundane, petty offences (see both Coleman and Malloch, Chapters 3 and 6, this volume), can have lasting consequences. Measures such as Anti-Social Behaviour Orders or increasingly punitive anti-drugs policies can lead to the escalation of (already marginalized) individuals or groups through the criminal justice system. Further, and more worryingly, such measures promote and perpetuate a culture of intolerance, within the criminal justice system and at the societal level, of any form of (what is officially defined as) 'deviant' or problematic behaviour.

An expanded criminological imagination must therefore be informed by a vision that can be reflexive and accommodate the impact of both short-term and long-term harms at the individual and structural levels. Thus, while individual physical, emotional and psychological harm cannot and should not be ignored, structurally embedded harm, such as unemployment, poor housing, inadequate health care, lack of education and other forms of social and cultural exclusion, has to become part of the consciousness of the criminological imagination.

Problematizing dominant definitions around 'crime' and prioritizing the responsibility and accountability of the powerful

There is no clear structure connecting the wide range of situations brought together under the term 'crime'. 'Crime' is a social and historical construction and its definition has no temporal or spatial stability (Christie 1986). In short this means that there is 'no *ontological reality* of crime' (Hulsman 1986: 28). What is important is the manner in which certain actions and social categories have, or have not, been labelled as crimes and who has the *power* to determine the application of this label. The criminalized 'suitable enemies' (Christie 1986: 42) do not in reality form a special category of person, though they may be stigmatized as outsiders in this way (Becker 1963). Historically the use of the criminal law has been one of the main strategies in the control and regulation of the illegalities of those who have been described variously as the sub-proletariat, the relative surplus population, the non-productive labour or the under- or un-employed (Hall *et al.* 1978; Rusche and Kirchheimer 2003; Mathiesen 2006).

Critical criminologists have a long tradition of promoting the ethics of care, shared humanity and the promotion of the social responsibilities of the powerful for the vulnerable and excluded (Campbell 1983; Christie 1986; de Haan 1991). The intention is to stretch the individualistic notion of criminal responsibility so as to allow for a much wider investigation and *allocation of responsibility* for the creation and perpetration of 'crimes' and harms. In this way it allows for a much clearer focus on political and legal accountability of the powerful for the harms they have created or neglected (Cohen 2001; Hillyard and Tombs 2004).

To expand the criminological imagination we need to reinvigorate scrutiny of the range of powerful players, organizations and institutions involved in the commission of 'crime' and harm. Therefore, as several contributors to this volume have highlighted, businesses and corporations and the key locations of power should be subjected to the same level of state investigation and intervention currently experienced by the relatively powerless. For example, Stanley (Chapter 8, this volume) argues that human rights violations cannot be understood without an exploration of the ways in which 'states are joined by ... third parties such as paramilitary groups, militias, private contractors, corporations and transnational financial bodies'. She points to the activities of supranational bodies such as the World Trade Organization, the World Bank or the International Monetary Fund and contends that such activities lead inevitably to human rights violations. Moreover, contributions to this volume have clearly demonstrated the significance of global contexts and transnational issues to concerns around 'crime' and social justice at the local level (Coleman, Malloch, Davis and Stanley).

The questionable practices of the locally powerful (Coleman, Chapter 3, this volume) or local agencies responsible for disaster management (Davis, Chapter 7, this volume) are excluded from narrow definitions of 'crime' and criminality and, as such, these agencies are frequently overlooked in criminological inquiry. In the narrow construction of 'what is crime' and 'who is criminal', the harm and victimization caused by the criminal justice system itself are largely discounted or denied. Yet, as the contributions of Malloch, Corcoran and Ballinger to this volume articulately illustrate, keeping sight of criminal justice agencies and practitioners when exploring what constitutes 'crime', criminal behaviour and harm is imperative to the critical agenda.

Placing the capitalist state at the centre of analysis of neo-liberal societies

Much recent literature around governance in neo-liberal societies has downplayed the centrality of the capitalist state in its analysis (Rose 1996). Though recognition should be given to new decentralized forms of disciplinary regulation and 'responsibilization', this does not necessarily involve either a 'roll-back' or a decentralization of state power. Though the capitalist state, since the Thatcherite era of the 1980s, has been in the process of changing from provider to purchaser of public services, it continues to maintain a coercive core and central role in the shaping and defining of social problems and the social and legal response to such problems (Clarke and Newman 1997). The delivery of some aspects of state power may have changed but its orchestration remains relatively unchanged. One of the most important contributions of critical analysis since the 1970s has been the identification and theorization of the anti-democratic and authoritarian aspects of the capitalist state's coercive apparatus (Hall *et al.* 1978; Poulantzas 1978; Hall and Scraton 1981; Scraton 1987; Hillyard and Percy-Smith 1989; Clarke and Newman 1997; Sim 2000).

In order to maintain and expand their imagination, criminologists need to ensure analyses of the state remain at the core of critical research. Coleman (Chapter 3, this volume), draws our attention to the role of the state in the spatial organization of urban areas and the production of socio-spatial injustices. In addition, Walters (Chapter 2, this volume) develops and applies this analysis to the production of knowledge. He discusses the stifling effect that the state agenda and state funding has had on critical academic autonomy and research. However, both Walters and Corcoran (Chapters 2 and 5, this volume) remind us in different contexts of the necessity of resistance to coercive state practices. Walters, for example, calls for academics to resist through the production and dissemination of 'deviant knowledge' which exposes and challenges state discourses that maintain and reproduce unequal and oppressive relations.

Critical criminologists have, for many years, utilized the 'view from below' in order to challenge and respond to the narrowly focused criminological gaze and in so doing have raised consciousness around a series of marginalized issues, such as male violence, deaths at the hand of the state or the harms created by corporations and states. In keeping with this tradition the contributors to this book have promoted the subjugated voices of a range of marginalized individuals, groups or communities, such as drug users (Malloch), political prisoners (Corcoran), victims/survivors of human rights abuses (Stanley), victims/survivors of 'disasters' (Davis) and those who are unable to speak for themselves; in this instance, women who were subjected to the ultimate manifestation of judicial power and put to death by the state (Ballinger).

Nonetheless, while resistance to state power is imperative, a tension arises regarding the extent to which resistance requires disengagement with the capitalist state and state agents. So, while some critical academics advocate complete detachment from the state (for example, Walters' call for a boycott of state-funded academic research in Chapter 2, this volume) others contend that conducting research with state agencies need not compromise research findings as long as the relationship is underpinned by an ethical and critical imagination (Malloch, Chapter 6, this volume).

Escaping the criminological straitjacket

In short, then, any expansion of the criminological imagination must be a modernist critical project that can locate social harms, personal troubles and problematic behaviours within their socio-economic and political contexts. It must have both a deconstructive and reconstructive impulse, critiquing the infamies of the present and calling for social reconstruction based upon inclusive and tolerant policies responding to human need. Such a vision must call for the radical restructuring of the social, in order to foster positive and anti-authoritarian human relationships and new and morally acceptable means of resolving human conflicts.

The criminological imagination must act as a replacement counter-hegemonic discourse, providing an alternative way of thinking about the problem of crime and promoting an alternative vision of morality and justice. But the analysis of, and response to, social harms, individual and collective conflicts, and problematic behaviours, will require a much broader focus than merely the criminal law or the traditional parameters of criminology. An expanded criminological imagination must provide a holistic account of social harms, troubles and problematic behaviours that facilitates a joined-up and multidisciplinary analysis of social problems and wrongdoing. It must challenge the way they are investigated and the way in which policy solutions and penal sanctions are determined in their political economy, social policy, legal and social contexts. Criminology on its own is not up to this task. As the contributors to this volume have demonstrated, critical research frequently demands an engagement with a range of diverse theories drawn from, for example, geography (Coleman and Davis), history (Ballinger), politics (Corcoran), economics (Stanley), feminisms (Ballinger), social policy (Malloch and Walters) and human rights (Stanley). In other words, for critical criminology to continue to present an effective challenge to the orthodoxies of the discipline, it must roll back the boundaries of 'criminology' and engage with other disciplines that are not restrained in the same straitjacket.

Critical criminologists have consistently placed the principle of social justice at the centre of their analysis. Social justice has two key components: the equitable distribution of the social product, and the recognition of human suffering and shared humanity (Cohen 2001; Fraser and Honneth 2003). Social justice as equitable distribution has traditionally been a very strong theme in critical analysis (Hall and Scraton 1981) and calls to transform the distribution of wealth can be found in Marxist-inspired criminologies (Taylor *et al.* 1973). This necessarily entails a commitment, not only to highlighting structural contexts, but also to changing them and providing greater support and help for the vulnerable. These calls have been echoed in recent critical criminological literature. Neo-abolitionists, for example, have advocated the development of positive welfare rights for citizens (van Swaaningen 1997). For such writers a critical criminological imagination has been characterized as a political commitment to the recognition of the suffering of both victims and offenders and often this has been underpinned by a human rights perspective (Scraton 1997; Scott 2006).

It is ethically and politically essential that wrongdoers are treated with tolerance and respect; that they are responded to as human beings; that their needs and suffering do not go unheeded (Hudson 2003). This leads to responsibility for the recognition of human dignity and respect for those dealt with by the criminal justice system, and the promotion of more appropriate means of resolving disputes and responding to problematic behaviours. If the development of a critical criminological imagination is to play a part in escaping the straitjacket that criminology has created, then we have once again to think in terms of *social* justice rather than *criminal* justice, to enhance, rather than undermine, democratic and legal accountability, and to develop research agendas that provide the potential to challenge, rather than consolidate, the interests of the powerful.

References

Becker, H. (1963) *Outsiders*. New York, NY: Free Press.

Campbell, T. (1983) *The Left and Rights*. London: Routledge & Kegan Paul.

Carson, W. (1979) 'The conventionalisation of early factory crime', *International Journal of the Sociology of Law*, 7: 37–60.

Chitnis, A. and Williams, G. (1999) 'Casualization and quality' (mimeo). London: NATFHE.

Christie, N. (1986) 'Suitable enemies' in H. Bianchi and R. van Swaaningen (eds) *Abolitionism: Towards a Non-repressive Approach to Crime*. Amsterdam: Free University Press.

Clarke, J. and Newman, J. (1997) *The Managerial State*. London: Sage.

Cohen, S. (2001) *States of Denial: Knowing about Atrocities and Suffering*. Cambridge: Polity Press.

de Haan, W. (1990) *The Politics of Redress*. London: Sage.

de Haan, W. (1991) 'Abolitionism and crime control: a contradiction in terms' in K. Stenson and D. Cowell (eds) *The Politics of Crime Control*. London: Sage.

Dobash, R. and Dobash, R. (2000) 'The politics and policies of responding to violence against women', in J. Hanmer and K. Itzen (eds) *Home Truths about Domestic Violence*. London: Routledge.

211

Fraser, N. and Honneth, A. (2003) *Redistribution or Recognition? A Political-philosophical Exchange.* London: Verso.

Gramsci, A. (1971) *Selections from the Prison Notebooks* (ed. and trans. Q. Hoare and G. Novell-Smith). London: Lawrence and Wishart.

Gregory, J. and Lees, S. (1999) *Policing Sexual Assault.* London: Routledge.

Hall, S., Critcher, C., Jefferson, T., Clarke, J. and Roberts, B. (1978) *Policing the Crisis: Mugging, the State and Law and Order.* London: Macmillan.

Hall, S. and Scraton, P. (1981) 'Law, class and control', in M. Fitzgerald *et al.* (eds) *Crime and Society: Readings in History and Theory.* London: Routledge/Open University Press.

Harvie, D. (2000) 'Alienation, class and enclosure in UK universities', *Capital and Class*, 71: 103–32.

Hillyard, P. and Percy-Smith, J. (1989) *The Coercive State.* London: Fontana.

Hillyard, P. and Tombs, S. (2004) 'Beyond criminology?' in P. Hillyard *et al.* (eds) *Beyond Criminology: Taking Harm Seriously.* London: Pluto.

Hillyard, P., Tombs, S., Pantazis, C. and Gordon, D. (2004a) 'Introduction' in P. Hillyard *et al.* (eds) *Beyond Criminology: Taking Harm Seriously.* London: Pluto.

Hillyard, P., Tombs, S., Pantazis, C. and Gordon, D. (2004b) 'Conclusion' in P. Hillyard *et al.* (eds) *Beyond Criminology: Taking Harm Seriously.* London: Pluto.

Hudson, B. (2003) *Justice in the Risk Society.* London: Sage.

Hulsman, L. (1986) 'Critical criminology and the concept of crime', in *Contemporary Crises: Law, Crime and Social Policy. Vol. 10* (reproduced in Bianchi, H. and Swaaningen, R. van (eds) (1986) *Abolitionism: Towards a Non-repressive Approach to Crime.* Amsterdam: Free University Press).

Lukes, S. (1974/2005) *Power: A Radical View* 2nd ed. London: Palgrave.

Mathiesen, T. (2006) *Prison on Trial* 3rd ed. Winchester: Waterside Press.

Mills, C.W. (1959) *The Sociological Imagination.* Oxford: Oxford University Press.

Norrie, A (2001) *Crime, Reason and History: A Critical Introduction to Criminal Law* 2nd ed. London: Butterworths.

Poulantzas, N. (1978) *State, Power, Socialism.* London: Verso.

Rose, N. (1996) 'The death of the social? Refiguring the territory of government', *Economy and Society*, 25: 327–89.

Rusche, G. and Kirchheimer, O. (2003) *Punishment and Social Structure.* London: Transaction Press.

Scott, D.G. (2006) 'Ghosts beyond our realm: a neo-abolitionist analysis of prisoner human rights and prison officer occupational culture.' Unpublished PhD, Lancashire Law School, University of Central Lancashire.

Scraton, P. (ed) (1987) *Law, Order and the Authoritarian State: Readings in Critical Criminology.* Milton Keynes: Open University Press.

Scraton, P. (1997) 'Whose "childhood"? What "crisis"?' in P. Scraton (ed) *'Childhood' in 'Crisis'?* London: UCL Press.

Sim, J. (2000) 'Against the punitive wind: Stuart Hall, the state and the lessons of the Great Moving Right Show', in P. Gilroy *et al.* (eds) *Without Guarantees: In Honour of Stuart Hall*. London: Verso.

Sim, J., Scraton, P. and Gordon, P. (1987) 'Introduction: crime, the state and critical analysis', in P Scraton (ed) *Law, Order and the Authoritarian State: Readings in Critical Criminology*. Milton Keynes: Open University Press.

Slapper, G. and Tombs, S. (1999) *Corporate Crime*. Harlow: Longman.

Taylor, I., Walton, P. and Young, J. (1973) *The New Criminology*. London: Routledge and Kegan Paul.

Tombs, S. and Whyte, D. (2003a) 'Scrutinizing the powerful: crime, contemporary political economy and critical social research', in S. Tombs and D. Whyte (eds) *Unmasking the Crimes of the Powerful: Scrutinising States and Corporations*. New York, NY: Peter Lang.

Tombs, S. and Whyte, D. (2003b) 'Shining a light on power?', *Socio-legal Studies Newsletter*, 41.

van Swaaningen, R. (1997) *Critical Criminology: Visions from Europe*. London: Sage.

Walters, R. (2003) *Deviant Knowledge: Criminology, Politics and Policy*. Cullompton: Willan Publishing.

Index